The Civil War on the Outer Banks

The Civil War on the Outer Banks

A History of the Late Rebellion
Along the Coast of North Carolina
from Carteret to Currituck,
with Comments on Prewar Conditions
and an Account of Postwar Recovery

BY FRED M. MALLISON

McFarland & Company, Inc., Publishers
Jefferson, North Carolina, and London

Cover: Capt. Horatio Williams.
Courtesy North Carolina Maritime Museum

British Library Cataloguing-in-Publication data are available

Library of Congress Cataloguing-in-Publication Data

Mallison, Fred M., 1924–
    The Civil War on the Outer Banks : a history of the late rebellion
along the coast of North Carolina from Carteret to Currituck,
with comments on prewar conditions and an account of postwar
recovery / by Fred M. Mallison.
        p.   cm.
    Includes bibliographical references and index.
    ISBN 0-7864-0417-5 (case binding : 50# alkaline paper) ∞
    1. North Carolina — History — Civil War, 1861–1865.   2. Outer
Banks (N.C.) — History, Military.   I. Title.
E524.M35   1998
975.6'03 — dc21
                                                            97-40304
                                                            CIP

Manufactured in the United States of America

McFarland & Company, Inc., Publishers
  Box 611, Jefferson, North Carolina 28640

Acknowledgments

ANY PEOPLE HELPED ME write this book, beginning with the encouragement of my thesis committee at East Carolina University: Dr. Mary Jo Bratton, director; Professor Donald R. Lennon, reader; Dr. Michael A. Palmer, reader; and Dr. W. Keats Sparrow, consultant. I am grateful to Professor Gordon Watts of the Maritime History Department who generously furnished material and advice, as did Ann Merriman, M.A., who shared with me the results of her research on shipping in the sounds.

All the staff of the Manuscript Section of the Joyner Library at East Carolina were most helpful, particularly Mary Boccaccio, who demonstrated her amazing talent for reading contorted script on faded and tattered documents. The personnel of the Brown Library, the Beaufort-Hyde-Martin Regional Library, the Beaufort County Community College Library in Washington, and the Carteret County Library in Beaufort gave great assistance. Special thanks go to librarians Mary Frances Jones, Penny Sermons, Carolyn Burke, and Pat Guyette who handle inter-library loans, and for bringing hard-to-find books from far away to the researcher in his local library. Wynne Dough, curator of the Outer Banks History Center at Manteo, contributed a great deal of information not found elsewhere.

Ellen Fulcher Cloud of Ocracoke and Stella Jean Day of Newport, historians and writers, have sent me material from their published works and allowed me to use material from their private collections. Historian Connie Mason of the Maritime Museum in Beaufort directed me to additional sources of eastern North Carolina history. Many friends have let me read cherished family letters and diaries of the period.

Much help was given me by my old friend and comrade-in-arms, historian Lee Wallace, who led me through the mazes of the National Archives and the mountains of literature on the Civil War. From the Official Records, he directed me to regimental histories by contemporaries and to more recent unit histories, not the least of which are his own books.

I would never have completed the manuscript without the aid of Phil Mead, the computer wizard.

Last, but foremost, I thank my editor-in-residence, critic, grammarian, and encourager, my dear wife Pattie.

I am much obliged to all of you.

—FRED M. MALLISON

Table of Contents

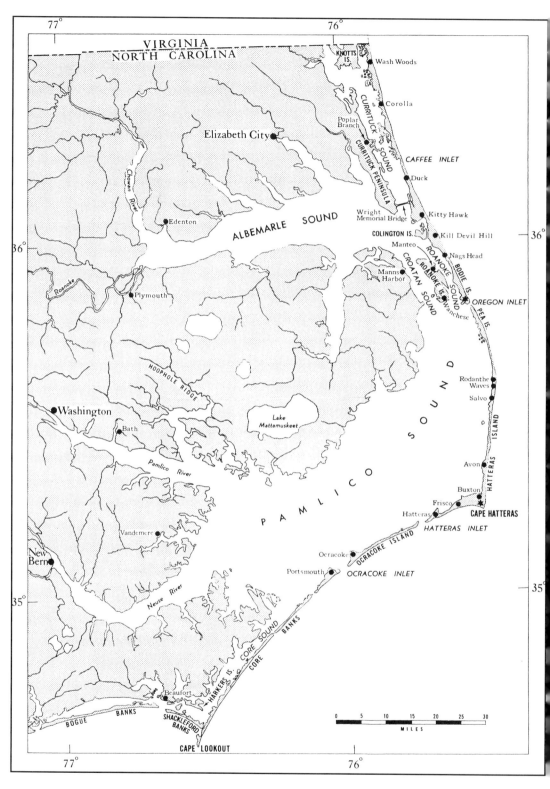

Map of northeastern North Carolina coast, from Gary S. Dunbar, *Historical Geography of the North Carolina Outer Banks* (Baton Rouge: Louisiana State University Press, 1958), 4. Courtesy Gary S. Dunbar.

Preface

God be with thee, gladsome Ocean!
How gladly greet I thee once more!
Ships and waves, and ceaseless motion,
And men rejoicing on thy shore...
—COLERIDGE

THE CIVIL WAR has long been the most popular subject in all of American historical writing. The same claim might be made for the Outer Banks in North Carolina writing. This book is about both. It was born during childhood summers spent exploring some of the islands, afoot and afloat, as the islands became a lifelong love. A half century's reading of Civil War and North Carolina history backed by service as an infantryman in World War II helped me to understand the soldier's viewpoint, and a B.S. degree in engineering gave me a foundation for writing about technical matters. With a more recently earned master's degree in history, I felt I had assembled the qualifications for writing this book.

My intent is to present a complete history of North Carolina's chain of barrier islands in the Civil War from the towns of Beaufort and Morehead City northward to the Virginia line. The western boundary of the geographic scope considered extends to include the river ports on the mainland, inseparable in war and peace from the Sand Banks. Those battles and political events occurring here that had a direct effect on the Banks are described or summarized.

The book contains accounts of military and naval conflict for the short period of active warfare on the Banks. It also delves into the social and economic history of the islands, topics of longer duration than the conflict and more complicated in their cultural impact.

The time span of the book begins some decades before the war in order to describe the economic changes of the mid–nineteenth century that altered the islanders' lives. The Reconstruction period, more changes, and the methods of recovery bring the narrative almost to the end of the Gilded Age.

In a lifetime of reading, certain books in the field began to loom large. John G. Barrett's splendid *The Civil War in North Carolina* was particularly useful. Gary Dunbar's *Historical Geography of the North Carolina Outer Banks* and David Stick's *The*

Outer Banks of North Carolina both contain chapters on the Civil War. Once I identified a book as outstanding, the author's bibliography became my reading list. In this manner I was led to articles in older North Carolina histories, in journals, and in almost innumerable magazines. Above all is the mother lode of information contained in *The War of the Rebellion: A Compilation of the Official Records of the Union and Confederate Armies*, compressed into 130 stout volumes, and the 31 volumes of the sister set, *Official Records of the Union and Confederate Navies in the War of the Rebellion*. When a particular regiment was mentioned, I sought the regimental history for more details. A search for more information about individuals led me to unpublished private papers, letters, and memoirs in the manuscript collections in the libraries of East Carolina University, the University of North Carolina at Chapel Hill, Duke University, and the North Carolina Division of Archives and History. Collections from several local libraries yielded more information.

Much of the economic history was gleaned from shipping records, both state and national, as well as private collections. Old newspapers on microfilm added much information on the war years and the Reconstruction period. The social history was obtained from the oral history of the Bankers and from numerous pamphlets and books of family history and recollections that have been privately printed.

The book, once complete, was embellished with quotations from the eminent of the past, and enriched by incidents both tragic and comic in the lives of the Bankers. What follows is as complete a word picture of the islands' and islanders' Civil War experience as I can draw.

Chapter One

From Settlement to War

*I*T WAS A GOOD LAND. "We smelled the fragrance a hundred leagues away, and even farther when they were burning the cedars and the wind was blowing from the land." Thus, Giovanni de Verrazzano, sailing for the French king in 1524, described the coast of Carolina. He identified the shores with such pleasant names as Forest of Laurels and Field of Cedars.[1]

Sixty years later, Arthur Barlowe smelled it, too. He reported to Sir Walter Raleigh, "We found shoal water which smelt so sweetly and was so strong a smell as if we had been in the midst of some delicate garden..."[2]

It was land, well worth wars and fighting. The Englishmen who settled it first fought to take it from the Indians. They fought raiding pirates and Spanish privateers and they fought the mother country twice for control of their new land. As the years rolled past into the mid–nineteenth century, another war loomed, a war that proved to be far greater and bloodier than any previous American war.

Called simply the Sand Banks by the earliest settlers, the chain of barrier islands sweeps down from the Virginia capes in three graceful arcs. The first arc begins at Old Currituck Inlet and runs, slightly concave toward the sea, southward along Currituck Banks, past Kitty Hawk and Nag's Head to Oregon Inlet. The next link in the chain, Hatteras Island runs southward until it reaches Cape Hatteras. The shore here turns southwesterly and again forms a slightly concave seashore, called Raleigh Bay on some early maps. The chain continues along Portsmouth Banks and Core Banks to Cape Lookout, a spearhead pointing out to sea. The coastline turns to the west here and continues along Shackleford Banks, Beaufort Inlet, and Fort Macon on the tip of Bogue Banks. Behind Bogue Banks, across narrow Bogue Sound, lie the towns of Beaufort and Morehead City.

These coastal arcs describe the north-south extent of this study of the Civil War. The western boundary of the book includes not only the towns of Morehead City and Beaufort, but the river ports such as New Bern, Washington, Plymouth, and Elizabeth City. The coastline is much the same along the entire extent of the Banks.

The sandy beach supports no plant life until the berm rises above the high tide line. Hardy, salt tolerant sea grasses grow increasingly thick along the dune line as it rises farther from the sea. Inland from the berm shrubs and small trees appear, growing larger in the center of the islands and on the sound shores. Live oak trees, red cedars, and scattered groves of pines give shade and protection on the sound side, the first inhabited parts of the islands. For most of their length, the Banks are narrow, varying from a few hundred yards wide to two or three miles.[3] The wooded portions include the villages: Portsmouth, Ocracoke, Hatteras, Chicamacomico, Kinnakeet, Nags Head, and a few others. Roanoke Island, the site of the very first village, is both wider and wooded, but it is not an Outer Bank. This island lies inshore of Bodie Island, separated from it by narrow Roanoke Sound, and from the mainland by Croatan Sound, slightly wider.

Taking ship at Beaufort harbor, an observer could climb to the masthead and in some places view scenes remarkably similar to what an observer in 1860 saw. In other places, nothing is the same. Morehead City, in 1860 a fishing village and the terminus of the new Atlantic and East Carolina Railroad, is changed beyond recognition. The original site on the sound has grown to a small city. The formerly bare ocean front is covered with beach houses, hotels, commercial structures, and a pandemonium of condominiums. The harbor, festooned with cranes, towers, gantries, and tanks, is lined with warehouses, spur tracks, and ocean-going vessels. The port has grown toward its promised potential. There is a stretch of open beach, much like 1860, ending at the inlet. Fort Macon still stands guard, its old rose bricks blending with the cream-colored sand and the green of sea oats and myrtle. The fort and the adjacent public beach are a state park.

Across the Newport River on the other side of the harbor, Beaufort retains much of the 1860s appearance in its old central section. Docks line the waterfront and small craft line the docks. Some are commercial fishermen, but most are pleasure craft. The same houses, well maintained, face the sound. The business district's stores and restaurants keep up appearances. The town's growth has been back from the water-front, and far-flung on the flank.

Along the ocean front, the masthead observer can look across Shackleford Banks and see roads and bridges, houses and stores on the mainland. The Cape Lookout lighthouse, just completed in 1859, marks the turn in the coastline. Scanning north-ward, the observer next sees Core Banks, which, like Shackleford Banks, has no mod-ern development. Both islands are part of Cape Lookout National Seashore Park. Portsmouth Island at the northern tip of Core Banks, and Portsmouth village have been uninhabited since 1971 except for a few Park Service personnel. The village is frozen in the time of the late nineteenth century. Across Ocracoke Inlet lies Ocracoke Island and the village of Ocracoke, busily inhabited. The white lighthouse still points to the heavens, and a few roofs peek through the live oaks and yaupon. If the mind's eye can erase the water tower, a signal mast, one obtrusive high-rise motel, and the four-wheel drive vehicles on parts of the beach, the 1860s look is retained here, too. The miles and miles of beach, glowing white to beige in the sun, have no buildings. Ocracoke's beach is preserved by the National Park Service. The public campgrounds might present a problem to the observer, but if he still has some eraser left he can erase the vans and RVs, or better yet, convert them to wagons and teams. The camp-grounds, with their brightly colored tents and striped tabernacles, then become familiar as gaudy camp meetings. From Ocracoke Inlet northward runs the domain of the Cape Hatteras National Park. Cape Hatteras lighthouse is the most prominent feature on the south end of the island, although it is not the same lighthouse that greeted an 1860 mariner. Long stretches of Hatteras beach are preserved by the Park Service, but there are sections of modern beach development at several of the island's villages. An astonishing sight for an 1860 observer would be the high-rise bridge stretching across Oregon Inlet. The next Bank is Bodie Island, still Park Service and National Wildlife Refuge until the traveler reaches Nag's Head. The beach here is heavily built up, although it is not such an astonishing change, as Nag's Head is the oldest beach resort on this part of the coast. There were hotels and commercial buildings here before the Civil War, though the buildings were on the sound side of the island. A few old post-war beach houses still adorn the Nag's Head ocean front, discernible by their simpler lines when contrasted with the slopes and angles of modern stilt-legged beach houses and condominiums. Kill Devil Hills and Kitty Hawk are also developed and have two small state parks which are surrounded by condominiums. Currituck Banks, continuing to the Virginia line, has several villages and developments, as well as a wildlife refuge and some pristine ocean front. Duck and Corolla still have some open ocean front, though it is rapidly being filled.

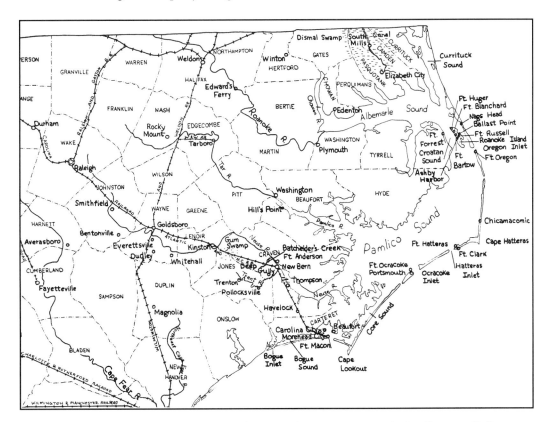

Eastern North Carolina, Carteret to Currituck. From John G. Barrett, *North Carolina as a Civil War Battleground 1861–1865* (Raleigh: N.C. Division of Archives and History).

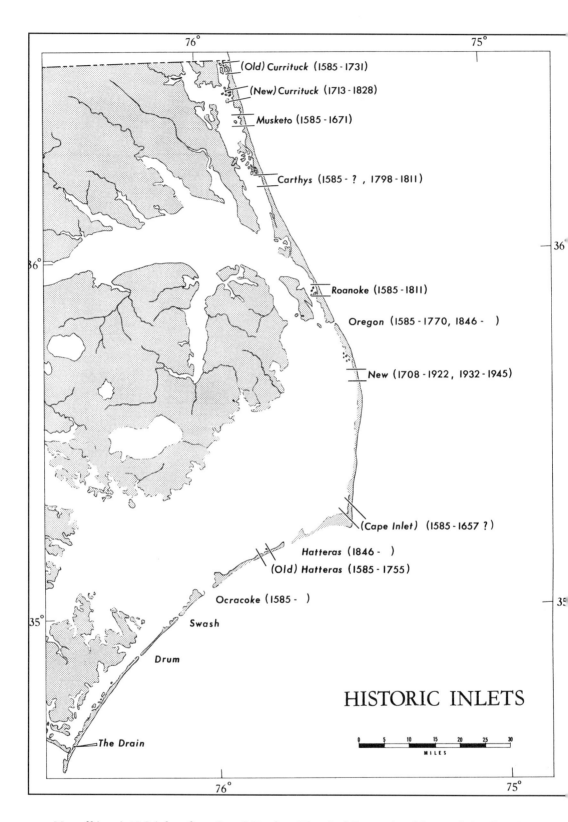

Map of historic N.C. inlets, from Gary S. Dunbar, *Historical Geography of the North Carolina Outer Banks* (Baton Rouge: Louisiana State University Press, 1958), 218. Courtesy Gary S. Dunbar.

The early English settlers used the Indian names for most of the islands, adapting them to European tongues. Currituck passed intact into English. Haterask became Hatteras, Waccocon became Ocracoke, and the island south of Portsmouth was called Core Banks after the Coree Indians. English names were given to other locations later, as we shall see. The string of islands, then as now, is broken by waterways called inlets that are actually outlets for the nearly immensurable volumes of water that flow down the rivers to the sea. These inlet/outlets shift according to nature's unpredictable laws. Modern hydro-geologists can explain much, though not all, of the inlet action, as could an experienced and observant ship's pilot during the Civil War. According to the hydro-geologists:

> Inlets are among the most interesting areas of change on the North Carolina coast. Permanent inlets exist only in the southern half of the coast at the mouths of rivers. Even there, the channels are constantly changing in response to the action of the waves, winds, and tides on the Outer Banks. Inlets are only temporary, formed by the surge of storm waves across the bar. We know from historical records and old maps that more than two dozen inlets have existed at various times on the Outer Banks, although only six are still open. The inlets on the Outer Banks seem to go through a natural cycle of birth, change and death. Whether this takes two hundred years or a few weeks is determined by factors we do not yet fully understand. Inlets may also change position, migrating along a barrier island shoreline if the accretion rate is greater on one side than the other.[4]

On the Outer Banks, only Ocracoke Inlet has remained the same during recorded history. As other inlets closed, shoaled, moved, or new ones opened, Ocracoke Inlet came to be recognized as the best island passage between Cape Fear and Chesapeake Bay. Historian and geographer John Lawson described the position of North Carolina's inlets in his 1714 book. He began with the Bar of Currituck, then in turn, Roanoak, Hatteras, Ocacock, and ended with Topsail. Of this inlet he wrote: "Topsail Inlet is above two Leagues to the Westward of Cape Look-out. You have a fair channel over the Bar, and two Fathom thereon, and a good Harbour..." In Lawson's judgment: "Ocacock is the best Inlet and Harbour yet in this Country: and has thirteen Foot at Low-water upon the Bar." Lawson described the two channels through the inlet with compass courses and the depth of water over the inner bar. He calculated the latitude at 35 degrees 8 minutes N.[5]

The Topsail inlet was known to mariners before John Lawson's time. Artist and governor John White of Raleigh's Roanoke colony included it on his 1585 map of "Virgenia." The map depicted the northern banks accurately, with their Indian names, and the location of the native villages. Southwest of Hatarask the distinctive shape of Cape Lookout is shown, unnamed. West of the cape is an inlet, unlabeled, too.

Some definition of the extent of the Outer Banks or Banks of North Carolina may be useful. One historian wrote in the 1950s:

> The North Carolina Outer Banks constitute the barrier chain between Cape Lookout and the Virginia line. The term "banks" itself is probably

the only topographic term unique to North Carolina. Formerly found, although uncommonly, in other areas, it is now confined to North Carolina. The term "outer banks" is a recent one, and there is no uniformity in definition of its limits. Some take it to mean the barrier islands all the way from the Virginia line to Cape Lookout or even to Beaufort Inlet. Others reserve the term "outer banks" only for the islands of Hatteras and Ocracoke, which lie furthest from the mainland.[6]

As maritime traffic increased in the colony, and settlers moved to the islands, Governor Charles Eden and the colonial General Assembly, in 1715, addressed the problem of pilots for the inlets. Realizing that "the Trade and Commerce of this government is likely to decay very much through want of pilots…," the proprietary government enacted laws appointing pilots and regulating their duties, pay, and fees.[7] Pilots were appointed for Roanoke, Ocracoke, and other of the colony's inlets as increased shipping warranted. Some years later, the colonial government allotted land on Ocracoke Island for pilots to build houses and to have a place on which to haul out their boats. Thus, Ocracoke village was first called Pilot Town by the settlers. The town of Beaufort, however, was founded before the pilot legislation passed. "A map made in 1713 for a 'plan of Beaufort Towne' shows the town fundamentally as it is today with all streets still named as shown on the map." In April 1722 the legislators passed an act "appointing the town of Beaufort a port for unloading and discharging Vessels."[8] Portsmouth, on the south side of the inlet, followed the development of Ocracoke, though it was more officially done. In 1753 the legislature passed an act to appoint commissioners to lay out a town to be named Portsmouth.[9] Other towns and ports followed as maritime trade continued to increase until the outbreak of the American Revolution.

Though Ocracoke Inlet was considered the best of the lot, it was too shallow for large vessels, and the "swash," an inside bar across the channel, was an additional hazard to ships. The whole coast was dangerous, the mid-section particularly so with Diamond Shoals off Cape Hatteras threatening from the north and Frying Pan Shoals clawing up from the south, both traps for shipping, even out to sea.

The Carolinians consoled themselves with the belief that if navigation of their coast was troublesome to them, it would be even more hazardous to invaders and would protect them from seaborne enemies in wartime. This assumption, though often true early on, proved to be fallible.

If the War of Independence brought few enemies to the Banks, it brought vastly more trade. All manner of commerce increased, especially imports of arms and munitions. The geographical formation of the islands invited the transit of friendly ships and repelled those of the enemy, as had been believed. According to one historian:

> Ocracoke was located far from the British supply bases, making it difficult for British vessels to remain on station there. Additionally, the shoals within the inlet kept out the larger vessels of war while allowing smaller smuggling craft a relatively safe haven.[10]

Ocracoke Inlet was an important gateway for supplies for the American Army and even for General George Washington's troops far off at Valley Forge. France shipped arms and munitions on large vessels to be reloaded on lighters from Portsmouth. French ships occasionally tried to sail directly into American deep-water ports, but usually British blockaders prevented this. Most of the trade through North Carolina's ports was carried in schooners and brigs that could sail across the sounds.

Initially, naval stores and timber were the chief exports, but tobacco, still a medium of exchange, soon became the most important cargo. Imports, besides arms and munitions, included large quantities of salt and such valuable goods as rum, molasses, sugar, and coffee. Much of the Carolina trade was with the French and Dutch West Indies. Salt was sometimes imported from the British West Indies in exchange for pork and corn under special license of the state government, and allowed by the British navy. "Ocracoke was the most important outlet for the produce of North Carolina's many small farms: and throughout the war, vessels brought in goods for the consumer market."[11]

If the struggle for independence brought profitable trade, except for a few raids, to the coastal communities, the second conflict with Great Britain, 1812–1815, was more troublesome and less profitable. While ruling the waves elsewhere, Britannia had acquired considerable experience in shoal-water, small-boat operations. The Carolina coast was open to the right sort of expedition.

Instead of harboring smugglers, the North Carolina sounds became havens for privateers, a condition the Royal Navy could not abide. The shipowners in the state's ports who could find cannon outfitted their vessels as private ships of war. The most famous of these, Captain Otway Burns of Beaufort, made several profitable cruises in his ship *Snapdragon*. In May 1813 the British responded with a British schooner flying American colors. It captured four Ocracoke pilots, withdrew, and returned in two days to seize a sloop. Alarm spread to the mainland, which brought out the militia in several river ports.

One month later, the British came in force with the right sort of expedition. Rear Admiral Sir George Cockburn, who had ravaged the shores of Chesapeake Bay, sailed his squadron to Ocracoke Inlet. He brought a large frigate, four small frigates, several schooners, and numerous small boats and rocket craft.[12] The swarm of ships, boats and barges rushed the inlet. Rockets streaked toward the two American ships at anchor, which were boarded and captured.

The privateer brig *Anaconda*, having just returned from a successful cruise, had sent her valuable cargo to Edenton. Consequently, Cockburn captured only the brig and crew along with the schooner *Atlas*. The British ships had been sighted in time for the revenue cutter to secure the customs house records and money and flee to New Bern to spread the alarm.

The British landed on Ocracoke where they wounded one man who tried to escape in his boat. The Royal Navy carried off several hundred cattle and pigs and sixteen hundred chickens, paying for them according to the Britons' estimate of a fair price. Customs Collector Thomas Singleton reported that the British paid only half enough and that they also looted private houses. Admiral Cockburn decided not to attempt crossing the sound with his smaller ships and withdrew from Ocracoke. He was commended by his superiors for his "Zeal and Alacrity."[13]

The people of the Banks profited from the maritime traffic during the wars with England despite the loss of livestock and property to looters. The Bankers looked forward to continuing prosperity after the war, which came with a many-fold increase in shipping. Other great changes came during the succeeding decades, not all of them beneficial to the Bankers.

Chapter Two

Between the Wars

*A*FTER THE PEACE OF GHENT ended the War of 1812, North Carolina began what many chroniclers of North Carolina history have called the "Rip van Winkle" period. Most Tar Heels felt smug and satisfied with themselves and their state. They reasoned that their new country was doing well, that they had whipped the British twice, so they must have done something right. There was no need for change.

All was not well in the state. Prospects were poor for young people who wanted land unless they moved west. The state's rate of population growth slowed, many counties lost population. The state did little for education. Although the University of North Carolina, chartered by the state legislature in 1789, had opened its doors in 1795, by 1810 it was "deserted and frowned upon by the Legislature" and attracted just sixty-five students.[1] Transportation, roads and canals, fared little better. A few men of vision in the state were concerned about the state's backwardness, however, and a great step forward was made in 1835 when the legislature approved a new and more liberal constitution. Many other improvements followed.[2]

Some few improvements were already instituted along the coast long before the state's awakening. Aids to navigation to mark the state's front doors, the inlets, were so essential that even the colonial governments of the royal colonies had made some efforts.

The first coastal project of the new state was a canal designed to avoid the dangerous inlets altogether by routing shipping through Chesapeake Bay. The Dismal Swamp Canal was chartered by the state in 1787, begun in 1793, and completed in 1805.[3] The good harbor and inlet near Cape Lookout were recognized early by the new state. Both were underutilized because the Newport River carried little traffic as it penetrated only a short distance into the country.

Other shippers did not want to hazard the shallow waters of Core Sound to connect Beaufort harbor with Pamlico and Albemarle Sounds. Therefore, the Clubfoot and Harlowe's Creek Canal Company was incorporated in 1795. This private venture connected the Neuse River with Beaufort. The canal was not opened until 1826.[4] The canal was not dug to the planned depth, was little used, and was abandoned before the Civil War.

Lighthouses to orient mariners to the location of both inlets and hazards were concerns of both the state and national governments. In 1784 the North Carolina General

Artist's rendition of the original Cape Hatteras lighthouse, based on descriptions and contemporary drawings. Courtesy Jerry Jennette.

Assembly levied a special duty on ships entering the Cape Fear River, the money to be used for a lighthouse on Bald Head Island at the Cape Fear's mouth. The 1789 General Assembly continued funding the Cape Fear light and authorized another duty on ships using the ports of the northern banks by an "Act to Erect a Light-House on Ocacock Island."[5] In that same year the Congress of the United States passed an act "for the establishment and support of light-houses, beacons, buoys and public piers."[6] Since 1789 aids to navigation have been a national, not a state responsibility.

The Ocracoke lighthouse, a fifty-five foot high wooden pyramid, was actually sited on Shell Castle, a privately owned island shaped like a crooked snake, and located just inside the inlet.[7] It was followed by a ninety foot octagonal sandstone tower at Cape Hatteras, which was completed in 1802.[8] The Cape Lookout light was next, a ninety-six foot wood-sheathed brick tower, completed in 1812. As the old wooden lighthouse on Shell Castle had been struck by lightning and burned in 1818, the Congress appropriated fourteen thousand dollars for a new one in 1820, followed by an additional twenty thousand dollars in 1822. The new Ocracoke lighthouse, sixty-five feet tall to the level of the light, was erected on Ocracoke Island and illuminated in 1823. Other lighthouses followed; Bodie Island light was built in 1845 and a new taller tower was erected at Cape Lookout in 1859.[9]

In addition to lighthouses for guiding mariners, the Federal government was concerned with means to repel enemy mariners. "A comprehensive system of defense stressing complete and adequate coastal fortifications was developed by 1819 for our maritime frontier. As a component part of this system, surveys and plans for a new fort on Bogue Point were completed between 1822 and 1824."[10] The new fort, of the most modern design, and costing $350,000, was completed in 1834. It was named Fort Macon in honor of Senator Nathaniel Macon.[11] Beaufort harbor was secure against any invader, if garrisoned and backed by supporting troops.

The industrial revolution clanked along with increasing velocity and power throughout the whole country, but with little initial effect along the coast. However, its offspring, the transportation revolution, had an enormous impact. The advent of steam navigation wrought changes throughout the coastal region. Steam-propelled vessels soon dominated the commerce of the narrow upper rivers, and steam towboats hauled more traffic through the Dismal Swamp Canal. Though the coastal and West Indian trades were still carried under sail, the Bankers all along the coast witnessed more frequent passage of steam boats. This increasing maritime traffic directed the state's attention to possible improvements, in addition to federal projects, in Ocracoke Inlet. The General Assembly in its 1827–1828 session passed "An act to incorporate the Occacock Navigation Company." This private venture was to improve navigation over the swash and to charge tolls to pay for the work. Nothing was ever done. The army's Corps of Engineers surveyed the inlet in 1821 and 1827 and began dredging the channels in 1830. This work was abandoned after 1837.[12] Ocracoke Inlet was never inclined to favor men's efforts to trifle with its bottom.

Ocracoke Inlet remained the state's premier port north of Wilmington. Portsmouth village commenced its slow decline in importance when the channels began to fill with sand, and ships used Ocracoke, just across the inlet, as an anchorage. Ocracoke Inlet had been declared a port of entry in 1806. The collector was authorized to draw government funds to pay for the care of sick or disabled seamen. Little was done until the next collector, Joshua Taylor (or Tayloe), was able to attract a physician to Portsmouth in 1828. Collector Taylor rented a small house for the first hospital.[13]

Ships and seamen passed through the inlet in increasing numbers, for the state had now left "Rip van Winkle" far behind. On the mainland of the eastern counties, trade was booming in naval stores and other forest products. One study of shipping records states: "Naval stores were the most important single export in North Carolina from its earliest days until after the Civil War."[14]

A patented lamp fuel, *Camphene*, developed in the 1830s, was manufactured from turpentine, wood alcohol, and camphor; consequently, the price of turpentine jumped. From 1835 through the 1840s, according to James Cox's study: "turpentine literally provided new fuel for the North Carolina economy and the upward trend in shipping."[15]

The bulk of the shipping passed through Ocracoke Inlet. The Committee on Commerce of the United States Congress reported in 1842:

> Ocracoke Inlet is the outlet for all the commerce of the State of North
> Carolina from the ports of Newbern, Washington, Plymouth, Edenton,
> and Elizabeth City, and the whole extent of the country for many miles
> around them; ... more than two-thirds of the exports of the state pass out
> to sea at this point ... one thousand four hundred sail of loaded vessels
> pass through the aforesaid inlet in space of twelve months, bound to vari-
> ous ports ... [it is] not uncommon to see from thirty to sixty sail of ves-
> sels at anchor in the roads at a time.[16]

The next Federal building project on the Banks was to better succor sick and disabled mariners. The makeshift marine hospital started by Customs Collector Taylor had never been satisfactory. At one time the collector and the doctor even had to isolate some smallpox victims in an abandoned warehouse on Shell Castle Island.[17] The United States Congress appropriated $8,500.00 in 1842 for a new hospital building, which was completed in 1847. It was a substantial two-story building with a fireplace in each large room, a water supply, and separate quarters for the hospital physician and a medical student.[18] The fact that the plan and the elevation differ in some details indicates that more than one plan was submitted to the government.

Before the new hospital was quite completed, a change of great significance occurred, and it was not a government project. It was a geographical change and was nothing more than an act of God. On September 8, during the hurricane season of 1846 a storm screamed ashore to cut two new inlets through the Banks. Old Hatteras Inlet, shallow and little used, had begun filling in 1755. In subsequent years it clogged with sand, joining Ocracoke and Hatteras Islands. The new Hatteras Inlet made by this 1846 storm cut through eight miles to the northeast, making Ocracoke a separate island again, but longer than before. Oregon Inlet, a pre–1585 waterway that had been

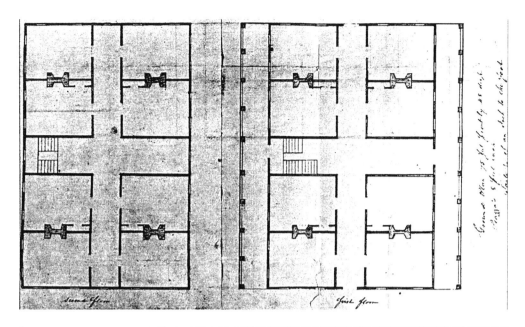

Two drawings of the Marine Hospital at Portsmouth, completed in 1847. *Top:* One of the plans submitted to the Department of the Treasury. *Above:* Side elevation of the same plan, showing substantial piers for support. Courtesy *North Carolina Medical Journal.*

sand filled for many years, was re-opened by the 1846 storm. Oregon Inlet had been seldom used by large vessels. "Hatteras Inlet, on the other hand, matured sufficiently by the middle 1850's to assume the position of supremacy among the inlets."[19] The complete birth record of the new inlets tells that the first vessel to transit Hatteras Inlet was the schooner *Asher C. Havens* on February 5, 1847. The first to pass through Oregon Inlet was the small steam boat *Oregon* in 1848, which gave the inlet its current name.[20] Though the change was not immediate, maritime traffic began to divert from Ocracoke to Hatteras Inlet, a serious loss for Ocracoke and Portsmouth.

A second geographical rearrangement occurred between the wars, this time an act of man. The Dismal Swamp Canal, chartered in 1790 to join Albemarle Sound and Chesapeake Bay, could no longer handle the increased traffic of the mid–nineteenth century. The old canal, twenty-one miles long, used seven locks to maintain an elevated water level. Operating the locks required a vast supply of water from a reservoir, which sometimes ran dry in arid weather. When the canal was originally constructed, no means existed to dig a sea level canal through the mass of roots, logs, and pre-historic stumps that underlay the Dismal Swamp. Steam engines made a new canal necessary and provided the means to dig it. Work began on the Albemarle and Chesapeake Canal in 1855, a sea-level canal which used only one lock to control the tides.[21]

Edmund Ruffin, a touring scientist, was impressed by the steam dredges. He described "the enormous beam with an iron scoop ... that made it seem as if it was the manual labor of a thinking being of colossal size and inconceivable physical power."[22]

The new canal opened in 1859. During the first full year, 1860, 116 steamers traveled through the canal as well as 393 schooners, the vessels most used. Counting small sloops, barges, and open boats, the total using the new canal was 999. During 1861, there were 671 steamers and 1,139 schooners, with a total count of 2,524.[23] A great deal of shipping was diverted from the state's inlets to these canals even before war came and the traffic became military.

Another improvement in transportation affected the coastal region, particularly Beaufort and Morehead City, though its results were less immediate. The North Carolina Railroad, connecting Goldsboro with Charlotte was completed in 1856. An extension of this line running from Goldsboro to the coast, with its eastern terminus at Morehead City was completed in 1860. The line was officially named the Atlantic and North Carolina Railroad, but it was fondly known as the Mullet Line. The counties of Carteret, Craven, and Lenoir owned 15.6 percent of its stock.[24]

The United States census records, taken each decade, give the best general picture of the Bankers' livelihood, and comparison of the censuses show the results of changes in their lives that occurred before the Civil War, and the great changes that occurred after. Even so, the occupations listed are not absolutely accurate. Historian Gary Dunbar explained why:

> The economy of the Bankers in the Federal Period was not vastly different from that of colonial times.... The typical Banker was still a man of varied talents. His garden and few head of stock did not occupy as much time as his marine pursuits.... The fact that a single occupational category could not describe the many means of subsistence of the Banker, together with the difference among census takers, make the old census occupation breakdowns difficult to use.
>
> The occupations listed in the census for a particular individual might have depended upon the time of the year or even the time of the day when the census enumerator called. In the old censuses it is difficult to separate "fisherman," "mariner," "boatman," "seaman," "sailor," and "laborer"....[25]

Though imperfect, the following tables show the occupations of the coastal dwellers as best we can do it.

CARTERET TOWNS

Occupations	Beaufort 1850	Beaufort 1860	Morehead City 1860	Carolina City 1860
Boatman	5	2		
Carpenter	18			
Ship Carpenter	25			
Cooper	9	8		
Gov't. Official	7	4		
Farmer	97	154		11
Fisherman	10	many		
Laborer	7	6		
Lighthouse Keeper	2	6		
Machinist				
Mariner	41	91	2	
Mason			4	
Mechanic		74	16	8
Merchant	29	32		2
Miller		6		
Minister	2	6		
Physician	4	4		1
Pilot ???				
Railroad Emp.		3	3	2
Ship Builder	4	1		
Sailmaker	4	3		
Soldier	1	2		
Smith		4		
Teacher	5	7		2
White Population		973	165	
Pop.-Free Black		59	4	
Pop. Slaves		579	147	
Pop. Total		1611	316	160, app.

Not all occupations are included, only those dealing with maritime affairs. No pilots were on the census rolls and there certainly were pilots in Beaufort. As Gary Dunbar noted, they probably appeared as mariners. The ship carpenters listed in 1850 did not all die or move by 1860, but were probably listed as mechanics. Not shown in this table are one silversmith and one gunsmith as well as seven musicians, a clockmaker and a shoemaker.

The 1860 census for Hyde County, Ocracoke and Hatteras Islands in the following table is also unreliable. Some of the tally sheets have no location shown and some have two different townships listed. Some known Islanders and occupations are missing, leading one to suspect that some sheets were lost or blown overboard, perhaps.

The graphs on page 19 depict shipping from North Carolina's seven minor ports. The graphs labeled "Registered Trade" show exports and those labeled "Enrolled Trade" show coastwise shipping. The great increase in enrolled shipping from Elizabeth City-Camden was due to the advent of steam tugs on the Dismal Swamp Canal which made

THE SAND BANKS
1860

Occupations	Portsmouth	Ocracoke	Hatteras	North Banks	Roanoke Island	Currituck Court House
Boatman				24	5	1
Carpenter		4		2	3	2
Customs	1		1			
Farmer	3	20			34**	
Fisherman	80	1	6	26	24	
Laborer						
Lighthouse K.	2	2	2		1	
Mariner	52	58	200+	6	9	1
Mason						
Mechanic	2			1		3
Merchant	3	?	?		?	
Miller				1		1
Minister		1	2			
Physician	2					3
Pilot	7	20	35			
Smith						
Teacher	2					
Misc.			3*	1^		3^^
White Pop.	445	500 app.		440 app.	427	400 app.
Free Blacks					25	
Slave	117	103				
Total	562	603?			XXX	

* One "Yappon" manufacturer, one herdsman, one canoe builder.
** 34 farmers were listed by the census taker, but only 20 produced enough to be included in the Agricultural Census, the only such listing on the Sand Banks.
^ Seine Maker.
^^ 2 Ship Captains, 1 Lawyer.

the Chesapeake Bay a convenient departure point for both registered and enrolled trade.[26] The quantities displayed represent ships, not voyages, which most likely would number considerably more. For example, a vessel enrolled for the coastwise trade could make several trips on the same enrollment certificate during that year. Any change in the vessel's rig or construction, or a change in captains or owners would, however, require a new certificate. Also, if the coasting vessel loaded a cargo for export, the captain surrendered the enrollment certificate and received a registration certificate for foreign trade which he held until changes arose.

The Bankers' names, their various occupations, their places of abode are all recorded facts, but their political beliefs were not listed, and national politics was trending toward trouble. In 1860 the political climate in the state was uncomfortable, for the old parties were fragmented into diverse splinter groups.[27] In early 1861 the state was still predominantly Unionist; when the General Assembly provided for a referendum on holding a secession convention, the Convention Act was defeated in the voting on February 28.[28] The delegates selected in each county for the convention that was not held

New Bern, Edenton, Washington, Beaufort, Elizabeth City-Camden, Plymouth, Ocracoke

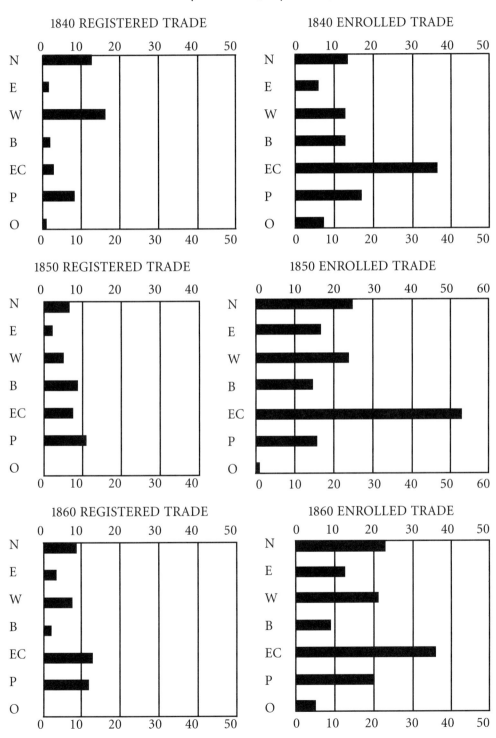

1840 REGISTERED TRADE

1840 ENROLLED TRADE

1850 REGISTERED TRADE

1850 ENROLLED TRADE

1860 REGISTERED TRADE

1860 ENROLLED TRADE

provide a means of assessing local feeling. Carteret County, which included Beaufort and Portsmouth island, elected conditional Union delegates, as did Beaufort, Washington, Currituck, and Hertford. Hyde County, which included Ocracoke and Hatteras islands, was unconditional Union along with Bertie, Chowan, Perquimans, Pasquotank, Camden, and Gates. Pitt County chose divided delegates. Onslow, Craven, Martin, and Tyrrel voted for secession. The counties surrounding the sounds were predominately Union.[29]

This strong Unionist feeling was considerably eroded by April of that year. On April 14 Fort Sumter in Charleston harbor surrendered to Confederate forces, pleasing the North Carolina secessionists, but saddening unionists. On April 15 the Lincoln government wired Governor Ellis to furnish two regiments of troops for suppression of the rebellion, to which the governor replied "You can get no troops from North Carolina." On this same day the governor ordered Colonel John L. Cantwell with his Wilmington volunteer companies to take possession of Forts Caswell and Johnson at the mouth of the Cape Fear River. This was the second occupation of the forts. In January a group of local citizens had marched into the forts, only to be ordered back out as soon as the governor was notified.[30]

Captain M. D. Craton with the *Goldsboro Rifles* received orders from the governor also on April 15 to occupy Fort Macon. When his men marched into the fort they found it already occupied. Captain Josiah Pender, with volunteers from Beaufort, had arrived there first. Fort Macon was twice taken, too, although both garrisons stayed.[31] The three coastal fortifications each had been garrisoned by an ordnance sergeant of the United States Army who surrendered the forts to the state troops in exchange for a receipt for the forts and their contents. The governor subsequently took over the mint in Charlotte on April 20 and the arsenal in Fayetteville on April 27, thus completing the occupation of Federal property in North Carolina.[32] All of the sites were taken without bloodshed or fighting, but certainly not in a friendly manner.

The next move was President Lincoln's. He ordered a blockade of the ports of the new Confederate States on April 19, and on April 27 he extended the blockade to include Virginia, which had seceded on April 17, and North Carolina, which was still officially in the Union.[33] This action could not have pleased the dwindling number of Unionists in the coastal counties, but it was not unexpected. A Wilmington, North Carolina, newspaper reported Lincoln's proclamation in a very low-key manner, coupled with the news that the Brazilian Minister demanded three months' notice before the blockade took effect.[34]

Preparations continued throughout the state. Generals were appointed, military companies organized, and a training camp was established near Raleigh. Volunteer troops mustered and marched. The Wilmington Committee of Safety borrowed gunpowder from South Carolina and asked what ordnance could be spared. "The work of such groups as the Wilmington 'Committee of Safety', coupled with the Governor's actions and the mad rush to the colors, put North Carolina on the road to war before the General Assembly met in special session on May 1."[35]

Chapter Three

Fifteen Weeks

HERE WAS NOTHING UNIQUE about the *Pearl*, a centerboard schooner of 247 tons, nor her cargo of white oak barrel staves under hatches and a deck cargo of sawn lumber. Neither was her voyage from New Bern, North Carolina, to the West Indies unusual. Dozens of similar vessels made similar voyages from North Carolina ports each month. What was new and unique was her flag, for the *Pearl* flew a preview of the Stars and Bars on March 5, 1861. Shipping with Captain Bob Robbins and his regular crew were two boys, C.H. Beale and John Hall, who had made the flag:

> At our main topmast we had unfurled the first Confederate flag that ever kissed the breeze of the Atlantic, so we claim and believe. The design of this flag was adopted in Montgomery and telegraphed throughout the country.... The design of this flag was a blue field with seven stars and the red and white bars and was made of oil calico.[1]

The *Pearl* crossed Hatteras bar on March 9 and three weeks later reached the island of Antigua. The Antiguans greeted the flag with curiosity and courtesy, but some captains of New England schooners jeered. When the boys displayed their flag on a pole ashore, it was torn down and destroyed by a mob of local Negroes incited by the New Englanders. Beale and Hall, undaunted, had a new flag made of bunting by some friendly English ladies. The *Pearl* spent several more weeks in the Caribbean selling her timber and loading a new cargo for the voyage home. She showed the flag in other English, French, and Danish island ports, meeting a friendly reception in all of them.

Fully loaded and homeward bound, the *Pearl* made her landfall at Hatteras in early July, where she stood off and signaled for a pilot. Through the captain's spyglass, the boys picked out more flags like the *Pearl*'s, with the Stars and Bars streaming over two forts on the island. However, Captain Robbins picked out a steamer bearing down on them flying the Stars and Stripes. When the steamer fired a gun, Captain Robbins crowded on sail and outran the steamer in the brisk wind to arrive at Ocracoke Inlet alone. Here the pilot, Captain Midyette, explained that the war had begun and all ports were blockaded. The *Pearl* proceeded to New Bern to unload her cargo and release the boys to tell all about their adventures.[2] More ships flying Confederate flags were at anchor or steaming in the sound as soldiers drilled and labored on the Sand Banks.

The war caught another Tar Heel schooner away from home. The *Paragon* of Ocracoke unloaded her cargo in Charleston, South Carolina, but was unable to find a return cargo for the Charlestonians had other things on their minds. When Captain Horatio Williams applied on April 12 to the harbor authorities for clearance, he was told he could not leave Charleston. "The Yankees will get you outside the harbor if you sail now, and besides, we may need your vessel ourselves." Captain Williams went back to his ship to consider the matter.[3]

The firing on Fort Sumter began that same day and settled the matter in the captain's mind. He determined that the Charlestonians were not going to get the *Paragon* and neither were the Yankees. He waited for the right weather and it came that night: moon dark, gusty wind, drizzling rain and even some fog. He pulled his crew out of their favorite tavern, hoisted anchor and sails and silently left the harbor. The boom and flash of the guns helped guide them out to sea. The gray dawn revealed no land and no ships. Williams sailed north and completed his plans as he steered for Ocracoke Inlet. Not needing a pilot, he conned the *Paragon* through the inlet, past the anchorage at the island, and across Pamlico Sound. When the crew asked questions, he told them he was keeping the *Paragon* safe from the war.

Captain Horatio Williams had not been captain of the *Paragon* long, just since Jobey Wahab had decided to take a job ashore and sold Williams a half-interest in the ship. Wahab had built the *Paragon* in 1838 at Ocracoke. He had framed her with live oak and red cedar cut on the island, and planked her with good white oak cut up the Roanoke River. And there, Williams told his crew, was where they were going.

Captain Horatio Williams sailed up the Roanoke to where the water was dark, deep, and fresh. He and Tom and Jeb removed the sails and spars and hid them ashore. Then they sank the *Paragon*. Live oak, red cedar, and good white oak last longer than the life of man when they are submerged in fresh water. Neither Yankees nor Confederates would have the *Paragon*. She would be neutral.[4] After the sinking they traveled overland to Washington and boarded a fishing sloop bound for Ocracoke.

While Captain Robbins was sailing the *Pearl* through the Caribbean and while Captain Williams was placing the *Paragon* in her submarine storage, soldiers arrived on the Banks and North Carolina ships steamed on the sounds. The state had entered wholeheartedly into the war. To create the instant navy necessary for defense of her waters, the state of North Carolina had to buy what vessels were available, while negotiating contracts to build new warships.

> After the ordinance of secession was passed, her sons, who were in the United States Navy, tendered their resignations, and placed their services at the disposal of their native state, prominent among them was William T. Muse, who was ordered by the Naval and Military Board, of which Warren Winslow was secretary, to Norfolk, Va., to take charge of, and fit out, as gunboats at the navy yard at Norfolk, the steamers purchased by the state.[5]

The first vessel thus acquired was the *J.E. Coffee*, a fast side-wheel steamer of 207 tons running between Norfolk and the eastern shore of Virginia. Her captain, Patrick McCarrick, was commissioned a Master in the state navy. She was armed with a thirty-two pounder gun and a small brass rifle. Her new commander was Lieutenant

Thomas M. Crossan, and she was renamed the *Winslow*. The second ship in the new navy was an iron-hull tug boat, formerly the eighty-five ton steam tug *Caledonia* of Edenton. She was bought in New Bern, and sent to Norfolk to be fitted out. She was commissioned as the *Beaufort*, armed with one long 32-pounder, and commanded by Lieutenant W.C. Duval.[6] Third was the steamer *Raleigh*, mounting one 32-pounder and commanded by Lieutenant J.W. Alexander. Next came the *Ellis*, a steam tug mounting two guns and commanded by Commander W.T. Muse.[7] Several of the Albemarle and Chesapeake Canal Company's tugs were requisitioned, beginning with the *Junaluska* of seventy-nine tons, which received two guns.[8] A few other vessels would come to the sounds to join the little flotilla that people soon called "The Mosquito Fleet."

Capt. Horatio Williams. Courtesy North Carolina Maritime Museum.

The soldiers came, too, some of them arriving before the naval vessels. Fort Macon had been occupied by local volunteers since April 15.[9] Josiah Pender's volunteers, soon to be formally organized as the Beaufort Harbor Guards, were mustered into service as Company G, Tenth Regiment North Carolina Artillery.[10] The early volunteer artillery companies were organized as the First North Carolina Artillery Battalion. Later in the summer they were permanently designated the Tenth Battalion. Company G of the Tenth stayed in the fort as others joined them.

Captain H.T. Guion arrived at the new Morehead City rail terminal on April 17 with sixty-one slaves and free Negroes. They boarded the schooner *George S. Handy* loaded with supplies donated by the citizens of New Bern, and proceeded to the fort. The next few weeks were frenzied as more troops arrived to use Fort Macon as a mustering point, until the resulting overcrowding interfered with the work on the fort. More slaves and free Negroes arrived, bringing the work force to 207 men other than the soldiers. Captain Craton who arrived at the fort on April 16 replaced Captain Pender as commanding officer and was in turn replaced by Colonel C.C. Tew. There was so much work to be done, for the fort had not been garrisoned since 1849 except for a lone ordnance sergeant.[11] During those years sand dunes shifted, iron rusted, wood decayed, and masonry cracked. Captain Guion, the engineer, put his laborers directly to work and the soldiers began small arms training and artillery training in mid–May when the gun carriages were repaired. Many deficiencies in ordnance and supplies were noted and requisitions forwarded. During the first week of May the garrison sponsored one of those ceremonies, beloved of the times, that were being held throughout the state. "Earlier in May, probably on the fifth or sixth, 'several ladies from Morehead City brought over a Southern Confederacy flag' which was unfurled to a salute of nine guns."[12]

Further up the coastline, more soldiers had arrived. In Washington a company of volunteers enlisted under the leadership of Thomas Sparrow, who was elected captain. They chose the name of Washington Grays and were assigned as Company A in the Seventh North Carolina Regiment (Artillery). The company was soon re-designated heavy artillery in the North Carolina Tenth Artillery Battalion (K of the Tenth). In early May an advance party of an ensign, two sergeants, two corporals and ten men was ordered to Portsmouth Island.[13] The early history of the Washington Grays is better known than many of the volunteer companies, as the memoirs of three of the soldiers and those of one interested civilian have been preserved.

Sergeant William Henry, the Baron von Eberstein, an unusual recruit, began his account first. He came of a noble German family with a military heritage. Young von Eberstein broke with tradition and went to sea. Starting as a midshipman in an East Indiaman, he progressed through mate, navigator, and captain in various types of ships in all the world's oceans. He sailed as a passenger with an old shipmate who commanded a trading schooner from Washington. He liked North Carolina, settled and married in Chocowinity, N.C., and continued at sea in Washington vessels. When war came, von Eberstein gave no reason for joining a local volunteer company instead of using his vast seagoing experience. However, his knowledge of naval gunnery was of great use to the Washington Grays. He consistently performed duties far beyond his nominal rank throughout his Confederate service.

The sergeant's memoirs described the departure of the advance party for the war:

> On the day of our departure our Detail was assembled and formed in front of the dwelling on Main Street of Samuel R. Fowle where we were presented with a beautiful bouquet accompanied by a very appropriate speech from Miss Martha M. Fowle. After which headed by the old colored Fifer Dennis to the air or tune of "Who'll Be King but Charlie," we moved off.[14]

The advance party boarded the schooner *Petral*, owned by Samuel R. Fowle, and set sail for Portsmouth. Led by Sergeant von Eberstein, the troops unloaded the schooner there by carrying their stores on their shoulders and wading through waist-deep water. Unloading took all night and most of the next day and was "very arduous duty." The

Grays then seized the Marine Hospital, stood sentry at the gates, and awaited the arrival of the rest of the company.[15]

Sergeant von Eberstein related that the rest of the company rejoined the advance party in a few days. His memoirs contain an extract from the local newspaper describing the ceremony of the Grays' departure on May 20, with many young ladies attending, many speeches given, and the presentation of a silk flag to the company. Four other volunteer companies watched the Grays march aboard the steamer *Post Boy* for the war.

Other troops were dispatched to the Banks as soon as possible. The Independent Greys of Pasquotank County enlisted at Elizabeth City on April 23 under the leadership of Captain John Thomas P.C. Cohoon. They were mustered into state service as Company A of the Seventeenth North Carolina.[16] The Greys were shipped to Hatteras sometime in mid–May. Work crews, too, were sent to the islands as soon as possible to build fortifications, though their contributions were not so clearly noted. The *Newbern Daily Progress*, in an article on the gathering state troops, mentioned the Beauregard Rifles and the Elizabeth City Rifles camping at the fairgrounds. The paper also noted that a company of free Negroes from Hillsboro, uniquely named the Orange Blacks, had come looking for work.[17] There was plenty of work for them along the coast.

Week One

Portsmouth, Ocracoke, and Hatteras Islands were under Confederate jurisdiction for just fifteen weeks, beginning with Secession Day, May 20, 1861. During week one the Washington Grays landed on Portsmouth Island and the Independent Greys arrived at Hatteras. The work of fortifying Hatteras Inlet and Ocracoke Inlet began at once, progressing faster as more men arrived. Building material, arms, munitions, all kinds of supplies, sometimes even water, had to be brought from the mainland. At Ocracoke Inlet soldiers and a small work gang labored on a fort on Beacon Island, that dot in the inlet that had been fortified too late to see service in 1812. A procession of steamers and schooners began during week one, growing as the weeks passed.

Week Two, May 26–June 1

The second week brought the first in a series of successes for the Mosquito Fleet. The North Carolina Ship Winslow steamed out of Ocracoke Inlet to look around. She sighted and captured the brig Lydia Frances of Bridgeport, Connecticut, laden with sugar from Cuba and bound for New York. A few days later, the Winslow brought in the bark Linwood, which was carrying coffee from Rio de Janeiro to New York.[18]

During this week, too, the soldiers and Negroes sweating on fortifications all along the coast could rejoice at the sight of a visiting general. Brigadier-General Walter Gwynn, North Carolina State Troops, inspected the various forts and reported progress to the governor. He began in New Bern where he reported twenty gun carriages nearly complete and large stores of lumber on hand which he recommended be used to manufacture wheelbarrows and wagons. He made other recommendations to Governor Ellis for ordering tents, shirting and light cassinette for soldiers' clothing, and advised, "I am hurrying on to Fort Macon."[19]

Gwynn reported that Fort Macon had only one heavy gun mounted as yet and no land defenses. The gun positions were exposed to enemy fire with no traverses or merlons to protect them. Translated from the general's sapper vocabulary, he meant that the individual gun positions had no walls on either side to absorb shell fragments and no solid walls in front on each side of the gun port. The general thought the grading and leveling of the adjacent sand dunes was "judicious, but most expensively conducted" as the earth moving was being done with handbarrows. He ordered more wheelbarrows and ten thousand two-bushel sand bags. He believed the fort would need thirty-seven heavy guns and not less than 2,000 men. In a supplementary report he termed the "discipline and drill of the men very imperfect." He exonerated Colonel Tew of any blame in this respect and suggested that he be provided with drill officers.

In his next report to Governor Ellis, datelined May 30, Raleigh, General Gwynn continued his recommendations for the Fort Macon area. He called for signal stations and field batteries along the Banks, as well as detachments of troops on Shackleford Banks and Bogue Island, Morehead City, and Beaufort. He steamed to Ocracoke Inlet where he found a battery being built on Beacon Island with five guns mounted and positions for twelve more that would be emplaced in a few days. He recommended a field battery, troops, and siege guns for the protection of Portsmouth Island.

Hatteras was his final stop, where he noted that two guns were mounted at the time of his visit and five more were expected to be emplaced by the time of writing, with six more a few days later. He intended to send five additional guns for the fort. General Gwynn postponed his visit to Oregon Inlet. He emphasized the need for more soldiers on this portion of the coast. "There will be required 5,000 men of all arms, infantry, rifles, cavalry, and artillery, to wit, two regiments of infantry, two of rifles, one of cavalry, and one of artillery."[20] Where would all the soldiers come from?

Week Three, June 2–8

This first full week of June brought another success for the navy. The *Winslow* captured another prize, the schooner *Willet S. Robbins*, and sent her to New Bern.[21]

On June 6 General Gwynn reported from Norfolk, Virginia. He had loaded his steamer with guns, ammunition, engineers, laborers, and tools for the forts at Oregon and New Inlets and at Roanoke Island. His next dispatch was June 9 on the steamer *Fairfield*. In it he appealed to the citizens of Currituck County to send laborers, slaves, or free Negroes to Major D.S. Walton at Roanoke Island. He asked that the laborers be given tools, axes, spades, shovels, picks, grubbing hoes, and cooking utensils. He promised that an account of the time would be kept, for which the state would pay. General Gwynn's final report was headed "Steamer *STAG*, Bound to Ocracoke, June 11, 1861." In his report the general stated that he had received a full supply of guns and shot at Norfolk, but only four thousand pounds of powder and small ordnance stores. He had stopped at Currituck Court House, found two companies of troops organized, and ordered them to Oregon Inlet. He stopped at Hatteras, where he ordered seventy-one hands to help build the fort at Oregon Inlet. He promised to stop in New Bern, then to hurry on to Raleigh to report in person to the governor.[22]

Week Four and Week Five, June 9–15 and June 16–22

The inlets around the banks saw little naval activity other than the arrival of a few supply vessels. Army activity, in addition to General Gwynn's island-hopping, however, increased. Reinforcements of soldiers landed from transports, not by regiments as Gwynn had hoped, but company by company. Sergeant von Eberstein reported the new arrivals.

> After sometime — a few weeks — several companies came down and joined us at Portsmouth, two from the North Counties and one from Greenville Pitt County. We were then organized into the 7th North Carolina Volunteers — Col. Martin. We did patrol duty on Portsmouth our men took turn and turn with the companies to garrison Beacon Island where Fort Ocracoke as the Yankees called it was situated. I was detailed to drill the different companies in Artillery drill. Whilst at Portsmouth we had quite a pleasant time fishing, crabing, clamming and oystering — nothing much to do but drill and keep guard. Whilst there we captured a schooner that came off the Barr from the West Indies. Col. Martin put me on board and gave me orders to get underway and proceed to New Bern and to deliver her up to the authorities there which I accomplished with the crew detailed for that purpose from the sailors which had volunteered in the Washington Grays.

The first of the companies to arrive was the Hertford Light Infantry, Captain Thomas H. Sharp (D of the Seventeenth), from Hertford County, who arrived on June 13. The Hyde County Rifles, Captain James J. Lieth (B of the Seventeenth) were next, arriving on June 18th. They were followed on June 20 by the Morris Guards, Captain Henry A. Gillam, from Washington County (H of the Seventeenth) and the Tar River Boys, Captain George W. Johnston, from Pitt County (C of the Seventeenth).[23]

A letter from Sergeant John Wheeler of the Hertford Light Infantry to his mother survives. The letter, dated June 14, 1861, announces their arrival at Portsmouth "yesterday" and mentions their gratitude to Murfreesboro for last Wednesday. Sergeant Wheeler says they had crabs, bluefish, spots, and mullets, besides ham for dinner, served on a rough board table with tin utensils, and that they saved their cake until later. The drinking water was "oh such stuff." He describes Portsmouth Island and asked that a few things be sent from home: a sponge, a mattress or a cover, and three silk handkerchiefs. Four weeks later Sergeant Wheeler, nineteen years old, was dead.[24]

Week Six, June 23–30

Action returned to the Mosquito Fleet during week six. The *Winslow* again was foremost. She captured the chartered transport *Transit*, which was returning to New London, Connecticut after resupplying the United States forces at Key West. The *Transit*, a schooner of 193 tons, and valued at $13,000, was taken into New Bern. The *Winslow* also captured the brig *Hannah Balch*, only to discover she was a Confederate vessel with a Yankee prize crew aboard. The *Winslow* released the Confederate crew and sent the vessel to her destination, Savannah.[25]

Week Seven, June 30–July 6

During week seven, the *Winslow* made another good catch. She took the schooner *Herbert Manton* of Barnstable, Massachusetts, loaded with sugar and molasses and valued at $30,000.[26] The schooner *Pearl*, with her eye-opening cargo of coffee and sugar was welcomed home during the week.

When the schooners *Herbert Manton* and *Transit* were auctioned by the New Bern prize court later in the summer, they sold for $5,000 and $2,960, respectively. Their chronometers sold for $77.50 and $92.50. A newspaper editor gave the opinion that the ship prices were low and the instruments, worth two hundred dollars, sold very cheap.[27] Perhaps supply exceeded demand for such items, a condition increasingly rare in the Southern Confederacy as the war endured.

Week Eight, June 7–13

The eighth week of activity was prizeless. The *Winslow*'s prize crew boarded the schooner *Charles Roberts* off Ocracoke bar, only to learn she was Confederate with a cargo of West Indian molasses headed for Wilmington. *Winslow* could do no less than escort her there. Next the *Winslow* captured the schooner *Priscilla* and sent her to New Bern. Here, *Priscilla*'s captain proved her Baltimore ownership and she was allowed to proceed.[28]

On July 9, the naval propeller *Beaufort* was commissioned at Norfolk, Lieutenant R.C. Duvall commanding. After taking aboard powder, shot, and other supplies, she proceeded through the Albemarle and Chesapeake Canal for the North Carolina sounds. *Beaufort*'s first station was Oregon Inlet, but later in July she steamed to Ocracoke.[29]

A surprise visitor to Hatteras on July 10 was the USS *Harriet Lane*. She had been a welcomed visitor before the war as the Revenue Cutter *Harriet Lane*. She was definitely not welcomed this time, for she let fly three salvoes from her guns aimed at the forts under construction. The shells did no great damage other than considerably upsetting the soldiers and Negroes working on the forts.[30] However, some of the Hatterasers thought her action was somehow traitorous because of her previous relationship to their city.

Week Nine, July 7–13

The middle of July was quiet for the ships, with no new prizes for the soldiers. Infantry drill continued on the parade ground near the church, and coast artillery-man's drill for great guns in the batteries that had been completed. Up North reactions to the Mosquito Fleet's captures began to bubble and boil. Collector Barney of the New York Customs House wrote Secretary of the Treasury Salmon P. Chase:

> … to Beaufort, Wilmington and New Bern or Ocracoke, the entrance is almost unobstructed, and no blockade has been enforced or even announced. Every day vessels are passing in or out of these ports, carrying whatever cargoes they choose … vessels are fitted out, armed and sent from Ocracoke to capture coasters and whatever other craft they may fall in with. These shore privateers do not wait for letters of marque, but act without even the semblance of authority. They find no difficulty in taking their prizes into their unblockaded ports.[31]

Collector Barney assured Secretary Chase his information was reliable and included a telegram from the collector at Newport reporting the brig *Mary E. Thompson* of Searsport, Maine, was robbed by a southern privateer. Chase forwarded the letter and enclosure to Secretary of the Navy Gideon Welles, who sent it to Flag Officer Silas H. Stringham, commanding the Atlantic Blockading Squadron.[32] Commodore Stringham had no one to whom he could pass the buck.

Week Ten, July 21–37

On Monday of the tenth week, the *Raleigh*, Lieutenant J.W. Alexander commanding, joined the Pamlico Sound squadron.[33] Two new privateers joined the naval vessels during the week as well. The *Mariner* was a small screw-steamer from Wilmington, captained by B.W. Berry, and mounted one 6-pounder rifle and two 12-pounder smooth bores. She captured one prize, the schooner *Nathaniel Chase*, on July 25. On that same day the other new arrival, the *Gordon*, towed in her first prize. This was the brig *William McGilvery* of Bangor, Maine, laden with molasses. The *Gordon* was a fast side-wheeler, formerly a packet of the Charleston-Fernandina line. She mounted three guns described as "very fair pieces of ordnance" and carried a crew of fifty. *Gordon*'s next prize, the schooner *Protector* from Mantanzas, Cuba, was to delight many people. She carried a cargo of luscious tropical fruit.[34]

Several more volunteer companies mustered on the Banks during July. The Roanoke Guards, Captain John C. Lamb (F of the Seventeenth), from Martin County arrived at Hatteras, and the Currituck Atlantic Rifles, Captain Daniel McD. Lindsey (E of the Seventeenth), from, naturally, Currituck County, reported at Oregon Inlet. The Hamilton Guards, Captain Lycurgus L. Clements, (G of the Seventeenth), also from Martin County, mustered at Hatteras. The John Harvey Guards, Captain Lucius J. Johnson (I of the Seventeenth) from Perquimans County reported at Oregon Inlet, as did the State Guards, Captain William F. Martin (L of the Seventeenth) also from Perquimans. The Confederate Guards, Captain James H. Swindell (K of the 17th) from Beaufort County arrived at Ocracoke Inlet in early August.[35] The Lenoir Braves, Captain William Sutton, from Lenoir County, was an artillery company temporarily assigned as Company K Thirty-second Regiment. The company was sent to Hatteras in August. Additional artillerymen were sent to Fort Macon in July and August. Guion's Battery (B of the Tenth) from Craven County arrived in Fort Macon on July 2, and Andrew's Battery (F of the Tenth), from Wayne County came to Beaufort on August 1.[36]

On July 21 the battle of Manassas (Bull Run) ended with a Confederate victory. The battle's effects were far-reaching in both the North and the South. More of North Carolina's troops were dispatched north to Virginia. There were now fewer troops than needed to defend the Sand Banks.

Week Eleven, July 28–August 3

The beginning of August was a busy one in the sounds, for the Confederate supply effort was increasing daily. The NCS *Beaufort* anchored off Ocracoke's old swash on July 19. A portion of *Beaufort*'s log survives, giving a detailed account of ship movements for the next two weeks. Early on July 30 a pilot boarded the *Beaufort* to move her to Wallace's channel opposite Portsmouth. The Confederate steamer *Post Boy* arrived from New Bern bringing a document for Captain Duval from the Confederate Secretary of the Navy. On July 31 the *Beaufort* picked up a pilot and took a look outside the inlet. On her return she sent a party ashore to set up a signal station in Ocracoke lighthouse. Next day the new lookout station "signalized" a man-of-war steamer to the southward. The strange warship proved to be the *Mariner*, which anchored near the fort. The *Mariner* was followed by CSS *Edwards*, another armed tug which was soon renamed *Forrest*. On August 3 *Beaufort*'s log reported CSS *Teaser*, another gunboat converted from tugboat, getting up steam and standing out of the inlet behind *Beaufort*. They sighted the *Gordon* and a schooner outside, and the supply ship *Col. Hill*.[37]

Across the sound and up the Pamlico River at Washington, Miss Martha Matilda Fowle packed her writing kit along with her clothes. Miss Fowle was the same young lady who had presented a bouquet of flowers to the advance party of the Washington Grays as they set forth to war. She wrote in her journal:

> In August, Father's health not being good, I accompanied him on a short
> trip to Hatteras in the schooner *Minot*, then commanded by Mr. Jarvis.
> We enjoyed it very much. We had an abundance of tropical fruit taken in
> prizes brought in by the privateers.[38]

Week Twelve, August 4–10

On August 4, the lighthouse post made confusing signals, causing all ships to go outside, then signaled a man-of-war in sight, which brought them back in. The *Beaufort* again sent a party ashore to re-instruct the signalmen and to re-rig the halyards for more distinct display of the flags. CSS *Ellis*, Commander W.T. Muse, arrived at Ocracoke in the evening. On August 5, the privateer *York* made port and the *Gordon* returned. Sadly, the log keeper observed, "No chance for the *Beaufort* as long as these fast steamers are here." *Gordon* and *Winslow* were the fastest ships present. On August 4 the *Gordon* had brought in two schooners, the *Henry Nutt* with logwood and mahogany, and the *Sea Witch* of New York with another cargo of tropical fruit from Baracoa, Cuba. The traffic grew even heavier, as *Beaufort*'s log recorded various ship movements. Confederate steamers *Post Boy*, *Curlew*, *Albemarle*, and the schooner *Crinoline* called at Portsmouth. The schooner *Isabella Ellis* discharged gun carriages at Beacon Island.[39] The buildup in the sounds continued, and in the North, plans were made for future fighting.

The planners in Raleigh, Richmond, and Washington, D.C., studied the same problems. The importance of controlling the North Carolina sounds was as apparent and urgent to the United States as their defense was to the Confederate States. The North Carolina sounds were viewed by Union naval officers as "safe and commodious anchorages," a protection against Atlantic storms. Most important, the sounds could become a base from which the inland communication of the Confederacy could be disrupted, and they were the "back door" to Norfolk and the lost Navy Yard.[40]

The prizes captured by the Confederates, while a bonus to the South and an annoyance to the North, were not major events in the war. The extent of northern reaction to these losses was unanticipated, although General Gwynn had warned of retribution. The anguished howls of insurance companies paying multiple claims joined the roars of under-insured ship owners. The din was committed to paper. Five presidents and one secretary of maritime insurers banded together to write United States Secretary of the Navy Gideon Welles on August 9:

> …He [the writer's informant] heard that eighteen privateers were out: three were at Hatteras Inlet-*York*, *Coffee* and *Gordon*…. We would respectfully request a careful consideration of the above narrated facts. The loss of property is and has been very heavy. The BTM (the brig *B.T. Martin*) and her cargo alone were worth $60,000.[41]

Secretary Welles wrote Commodore Stringham expanding on this subject on August 10. Welles realized the difficulty of blockading the North Carolina coast, but noted that "intercourse at the different ports and inlets … alarm our commercial community and cause embarrassment and distrust to the Department." He called the Confederates "nests of pirates" and stated that "vigilant attention and some stringent action" were required.[42] While strategic considerations called for the identical solution, it seemed that economic complaints would produce faster action.

While economic pressure continued to rise in the North, in the sounds the serene cruise of the schooner *Minot* continued. Martha Matilda Fowle and her father sailed to Portsmouth after a few days at Hatteras. The influx of civilians visiting the island demonstrates the support offered by the people at home to the volunteer soldiers and the confidence in victory. Apparently, many young ladies convinced their parents that a sea voyage was necessary. This influx is often called the "ladies invasion." The Outer Banks were recognized as healthful places to visit to escape the danger of miasmas rising from mainland swamps in hot weather. Most families rented houses from the islanders, as few of them had a private schooner as both conveyance and quarters. Miss Fowle, a daughter of one of Washington's "first families," could have taken such a trip only if chaperoned by a parent or other close relative. The schooner *Minot* was owned by her father. She was to meet other ladies of similar station and intent on Portsmouth Island. Though health was the stated reason for the voyage, an additional reason was social. The towns of the main had become very lonely places with most of the young men gone. Hence, if they could do so in a seemly manner, the young ladies followed the flag. Indeed, so much traffic developed between Washington and the islands that Captain B.F. Hanks put his steamer, *Col. Hill*, in service making regularly scheduled voyages to haul all the parcels and people awaiting passage.[43] The ladies, like Uriah the Hittite, rushed nigh the forefront of the battle. Miss Fowle's papers describe the visitors:

> We stopped at Portsmouth on our return and were joined by Mary, Magg, Anna Marsh and Mattie Telfair. Helen and Laura Shaw came down also. Clara Hoyt, Kate Carraway and Sallie Howard, and there were many other ladies in the house. Here we spent two weeks very pleasantly and formed

some agreeable acquaintances, of whom I would mention Lieuts. Perry and Moore of the Hertford Light Infantry. Lieut. Perry fell in love with Mary at first sight and there commenced his attentions to her.[44]

Weeks Thirteen and Fourteen, August 11–18 and August 19–25

Weeks thirteen and fourteen were rife with ship movements. On August 13, the *Gordon* anchored in the roads and departed next morning. The *Winslow* arrived, anchored, then sailed for Hatteras escorting the steamer *Col. Hill* and the schooner *Crinoline*. On August 14, the *Beaufort* stood out the old swash channel for New Bern, from whence she returned on the twenty-second and coaled from the schooner *Alexina*. On the same day the *Ellis* was freeing the inlet's lightship, aground on the swash, and hauling her outside.[45]

On the morning of August 20 the *Winslow* brought in the last of the prizes, the steamer *Itasca*. The Confederates, unaware that their day was drawing to a close, continued their forays." Prizes had now become rare. Few merchantmen flew the United States flag. Many were laid up for lack of cargoes and many had transferred their registry. Most of the ships overhauled were flying British colors. "After her two captures on the fourth, although remaining almost continuously at sea, the *Gordon* saw only two enemy merchantmen and they were under convoy of men-of-war.[46]

On the islands, Sergeant von Eberstein noted that more Confederate troops had arrived. He was given a new task, more consistent with his ability, which he was happy to perform, although he received no promotion.

> Captain James Leith with a company raised in Hyde County, and Captain James Swindell, with a company which was raised in Chocowinity, were ordered to join the Seventh [17th] Regiment at Portsmouth to Colonel Martin, which they did so. They were sent to garrison the fort on Beacon Island, for the defense of Beaufort....
>
> As the ordnance officer on Beacon Island, a Lieutenant Brantley, having been removed from his office for drunkenness and bad conduct, and at the investigation of Col. Morris the Chief Engineer of the Battery, Col. Martin ordered Cap't. Sparrow to send me forth to take and occupy Lieut. Brantley's place. I then proceeded to take charge of the heavy guns on the Battery and all ordnance. I was also to instruct Leith & Swindell's company in artillery service.[47]

Colonel Martin, the regimental commander, should have been more careful in his selection of companies to garrison Beacon Island, and in his instructions to their captains, as we shall see. He was probably distracted by other problems, for the Tar River Boys had mutinied. Sergeant von Eberstein, who was peripherally involved, noted: "there was one unpleasantness which happened while we were there. The Greenville company mutinied at the time I was on Beacon Island." Some lines in his manuscript are unclear, but the sense of them was that a gunboat was called upon to help quell the mutiny:

> Confederate gun boat in the roadstead commanded by Cap't Cook a brave naval commander ... got so high he [Captain Cook] received orders to

train his guns upon the House where that company was quartered. I also
at the fort received the same orders and I trained two ten inch Columbiads
upon the same house, and waited for the result, finally volunteers were
called for to go arrest the mutineers, the Washington Grays volunteered.[48]

There were other witnesses to the affair who recorded their observations. Miss
Fowle inscribed a more personal view of the mutiny:

> A mutiny broke out in the camp of the "Tar River Boys," Cap't. Johnson.
> In this company Howard Wiswell and John Boyd were orderly and 2nd
> sergeant. They seemed to possess more influence over the men than any of
> the other officers. It seemed that the officers were tyrannical, especially
> Lieut. Green. The men were dissatisfied and threatened to mutiny,
> Howard knew of this and used his influence to soothe them, but they did
> mutiny and claimed Howard and Mr. Boyd as their leaders; a mistaken
> sense of honor led these young men to stand by the men. It was a serious
> affair and at one time it was thought force would have to be used, but
> after many arguments from Cap't. Muse and others, Howard was per-
> suaded by father to lay down his arms and the others followed his example.
> The prisoners were confined and a court martial called, which was sitting
> at the time when orders came for them to go to Hatteras.[49]

Sergeant von Eberstein, thinking like a sea-captain, did not concern himself
with reasons for the mutiny. If the Tar River Boys did not surrender, he was prepared
to blast them into submission with 10-inch guns. Martha Matilda Fowle thought they
had ample reason, but poor judgment. She was anxious to excuse Sergeants Wiswell
and Boyd. A third source gives the best explanation of the Tar River Boys' mutiny.
William Augustus Parvin, a "sailor-boy" in the Washington Grays, left a memoir
telling of service at Portsmouth, capture at Hatteras, and escape from prison in Boston
Harbor. Private Parvin declared patriotism was the reason for the mutiny.

> We were getting along fine until the Battle of Bull Run and then everybody
> wanted to go to Virginia and there was so much dissatisfaction in the
> Company that Capt. Sparrow made a speech that if they wanted to go to
> Virginia they would have to go in the Confederate Army for the war …
> they had a election and 100 out of 112 voted for the war and those 12 Capt.
> Sparrow traded of to Capt. Gillam for 12 of his men that wanted to go for
> the war, after our company had an election captain Johnson's company
> wanted to have an election and Capt. Johnson would not let them … the
> company had a mutiny and part of them wanted to go in for the war and
> have Howard Wiswell as their captain....[50]

Miss Fowle and her father returned home on August 21, as did most of the other
ladies. The wives and daughters of the soldiers tarried. On August 27 the *Gordon*
sighted "ten ships in the offing, which were supposed to be United States vessels. Captain Lockwood thought it best to give such an assemblage a wide berth, and stood for a
southward cruise"[51] According to the log of the CSS *Ellis*, the *Gordon* came in from the
sea at 2:20 P.M. and went to sea again at 2:30.[52] The *Gordon* foamed out the inlet and

steamed hard for safety. The happy time for the privateers was over, the time for stringent action had come. The Union's weapon was at hand—the ships of the old Navy—
ships the young Confederacy could not hope to equal at the time.

According to Admiral David D. Porter, at the beginning of the war, the United
States Navy had only eight vessels that the government could use immediately, and
only four of them were steamers. The rest were laid up in yards, on foreign service, or
were old sailing vessels and generally useless. The twelve ships of the Home Squadron,
scattered in several Atlantic ports were assembled quickly, and those on foreign stations recalled as fast as possible. They came from the Mediterranean, the coast of
Africa, Brazil, and the East Indies, arriving all the summer through September.[53]

The Atlantic Blockading Squadron was commanded by Flag Officer Silas H.
Stringham, an old sailor of great experience. Commodore Stringham's efforts met with
no more success than the British Navy had had in the two previous wars against a long
coast with many inlets. The commodore knew what should be done, but had first to
convince Secretary Welles' office, who repeatedly ordered that old schooners loaded
with stone be sunk in the inlets to seal in the "pirates." Stringham, on July 22, wrote
the Secretary:

> I would suggest the capture and occupation of Bodie's Island as a very
> good point for commanding the extensive inland communication of Pat-
> apsco [Pamlico], Albemarle, and Roanoke sounds and interfering very
> materially with transportation of provisions, stores, etc., to Norfolk from
> this region through the Dismal Swamp Canal.[54]

Even though the commodore's inland geography was slightly skewed, his strategic sense was correct and he knew that sunken vessels would not plug an inlet. Before
mid-August he knew all about the various inlets and the forts the Confederates were
building. Two Yankee ship captains, Daniel A Campbell of the brig *Lydia Francis*, and
Henry W. Penny of the bark *Linwood*, had been captured by the Mosquito Fleet with
their ships. The captains were hauled by their captors to New Bern and Raleigh, then
to Ocracoke and Hatteras, and once more to New Bern where they were released. The
two captains, with a few other released masters, mates, and boys, purchased a boat and
sailed out to sea via Oregon Inlet. They were picked up by the USS *Quaker City* and
taken into Hampton Roads. There two sharp-witted Yankees carefully noted everything they had observed, were shown, heard, or were told and reported it all when they
arrived home. A copy of the report was sent to Stringham pointing out which inlet was
best and describing the two forts there in detail. The two-captain report noted the
number of guns emplaced, the estimated number of men, and the facts that the Confederates were short of ammunition and had only one hundred kegs of powder.[55]

Commodore Stringham reset his sights for Hatteras and by August 20 was conferring and corresponding with the army about the troops that would accompany the
expedition. On August 23 he wrote Secretary Welles that the Navy was ready and only
waiting for the weather to moderate. The Army, on August 25, ordered politician-
turned Major-General Benjamin F. Butler to prepare 860 troops with ten days' rations

and water and 140 rounds of ammunition. Butler was ordered to report his readiness to Flag Officer Stringham, and be ready to embark at 1:00 P.M. the 26th. Stringham reported to Secretary Welles on August 26, "I sail to-day at noon for Hatteras Inlet.... The expedition, I hope will be successful."[56]

Commodore Stringham's flagship was the big steam frigate *Minnesota*, mounting one 10-inch Dahlgren smoothbore gun, twenty-eight 9-inch Dahlgrens, and fourteen 8-inchers. Next came the *Wabash*, a similar frigate with similar armament. The side-wheel steam frigate *Susquehanna,* mounting twelve 9-inch Dahlgrens and two 150-pounder Parrot rifles, joined next morning. The big sailing frigate *Cumberland*, armed with twenty-two 9-inch guns, one 10-inch and one 100-pounder rifle, kept up with the steamers. Also, there were the steam-sloop *Pawnee* with eight 9-inch guns and the screw schooner *Monticello* with one 10-inch Dahlgren and two 32-pounders. The *Harriet Lane*, with four guns, and the tug *Fanny* accompanied the larger vessels. There were two troop transports, *Adelaide* and *George Peabody* carrying the 860 soldiers commanded by Major-General B.F. Butler.[57] All these ships and guns were to oppose two small forts. According to Confederate General Gwynn's report at the time the larger one, Fort Hatteras, mounted thirteen guns and Fort Clark, five guns. The Confederate guns were almost all 32-pounders, with smooth bores 6.4 inches in diameter. Both Fort Clark and Fort Hatteras had two 8-inch howitzers pointing seaward. As the spoils go to the victor, so should the first account of the battle. Since it was primarily a naval victory, Flag Officer Stringham's after action report best describes the naval battle.

Week Fifteen, August 26–September 1

The Commodore's first post-battle dispatch to Secretary Welles, dated August 30 was short. It announced: "We have been eminently successful in our expedition … I shall forward a full account immediately on my arrival at New York...."[58]

The full account followed on September 2. The fleet anchored south of Cape Hatteras at 5.00 P.M. on the 27th. An early breakfast on the 28th preceded loading a 12-pounder rifle and a 12-pounder howitzer on the surfboats already launched and sending them to the transport *Adelaide*. Major-General Butler and the *Minnesota*'s marines boarded the *Harriet Lane*. At 6:45 the Flag signaled "disembark troops." The *Wabash* towing the *Cumberland* and the *Minnesota* led in toward Fort Clark. The *Monticello*, *Pawnee*, *Harriet Lane* and the transports began to land the troops two miles east of the fort at 11:30. *Wabash*, *Cumberland*, and *Minnesota* began to fire on the fort about 10:00, sailing a circular course and firing as their guns bore on the target. The *Susquehanna* "made her number" at 11:00 A.M., and was directed to join in. At 12:25 P.M. the flags were down on the forts and lookouts saw men running from Fort Clark, which had stopped firing. The fleet ceased firing. Stringham noted that the fort's shot either fell short or passed over the ships. The Union soldiers marched up the beach and hoisted the United States flag at 2:00 P.M.

As Fort Hatteras was not displaying a flag, the commodore ordered Captain Gillis in *Monticello* to "feel his way into the inlet and take possession." Fort Hatteras, which had not hauled down its flag, as no flag had been hoisted, opened fire on the

Monticello. The flag officer signaled "engage batteries," the ships reopened fire, and *Monticello* threshed back out of the inlet, bumping, shoal dodging, and returning fire as she steamed. The *Monticello* took several hits that did no serious damage and did not slow her escape.

At 6:15 P.M. the commodore ordered the ships to cease firing and the larger vessels to haul offshore for the night. The *Pawnee, Harriet Lane,* and *Monticello* stayed inshore to protect the landing force.[59] Confederate reinforcements arrived from Portsmouth before dark. Thus ended the first day of battle.

The results were gratifying to the Union. A part of the soldiers had landed with the loss of only a few surf boats and barges, and the smaller of the forts had been taken. Flag Officer Stringham had accessed the accuracy and range of the Confederate's guns. The new maneuver of steaming in a circular pattern while firing on the forts was now made practical by steam propulsion. The navy would repeat it in later battles with Confederate forts.

Next morning, Thursday, August 29, with "Southwest winds and pleasant weather … sea more moderate" the large ships again moved toward the shore. At 8 A.M. the *Susquehanna* opened fire, with the *Wabash* and the *Minnesota* following. The three big ships anchored in a line just out of range of the Confederate guns. The *Cumberland*, a splendid sight, came in under full sail, furled, anchored near the *Minnesota*, and opened fire. "Handsomely handled," said the commodore. Firing ceased briefly as the flag officer signaled to adjust range and fuse settings, then recommenced firing, "our shot now falling in and around the battery with great effect." At 9:35 A.M. the *Harriet Lane* joined in with her rifled guns.

A white flag was displayed over the fort, so "Cease Firing" was signaled at 11:10 A.M. The troops on shore started marching toward Fort Hatteras, while "the officers and crews of the squadron gave three hearty cheers for our success."

At this point, Major-General Butler began to earn his pay. Butler, aboard the tug *Fanny* entered the inlet to the rear of the fort to take possession. The *Harriet Lane* followed and grounded. The chartered transports with the rest of the Federal troops went into the inlet to debark the soldiers. *Harriet Lane* steamed off the shoal to follow the transports, but soon grounded again, and here she stuck. Butler returned to the flagship at 2:30 P.M., bringing with him the three senior Confederate officers; Flag Officer Samuel Barron, Confederate States Navy, Colonel William F. Martin, commanding the Seventeenth North Carolina Volunteers, and Major William S.G. Andrews, commander of forts Hatteras and Clark. Stringham and Butler accepted the capitulation of the Confederates, as all five of the officers signed the articles.[60]

General Butler's report of the battle, longer than Stringham's, describes the troop movements and his own exploits. Butler reported in detail on the forts and their armament, and listed the booty from his victory. Major-General Butler stressed the importance of Hatteras to the United States, "it is a station second in importance only to Fortress Monroe on this coast." While Butler stated that all had done well, he laid especial commendations on many people in and with the landing force — Army, Navy, regulars, Marines, Coast Guard, and civilians. Butler also recommended that Fort

Hatteras be renamed Fort Stringham.[61] Having spread sufficient hyperbole and honey over self and subordinates, Major-General Butler departed the battlefield.

The transport *Adelaide* sailed on August 30 for Annapolis carrying thirteen wounded prisoners and Major-General Butler. After stopping by Fortress Monroe to report to Major-General John A. Wool, Butler continued to Annapolis with the wounded. Here, he requisitioned a train and rushed on to Washington, determined to be the first to report the victory. Heroically steaming on an uncleared track the last nineteen miles, Butler arrived in the capital, galloped to Postmaster-General Blair's house, then on to the White House to awake the sleeping president and announce the victory.[62] Major-General Butler was an amateur, usually an inept soldier, but he was a shrewd politician and an astute man. He decided to disobey his original orders that called for evacuation of his troops after the forts were destroyed. He could see no sense in giving away the results of the victory. He conferred briefly with Commodore Stringham, who was of like mind. The navy had instructed him to block the inlets and sail home after the forts' capture. Stringham knew the Union would need both the forts and the inlet. Hence, the troops were left in place along with a few of the ships. Within a few days, both the army and navy issued orders for the commanders to do what they had already done.

Colonel Max Weber, commanding the Twentieth New York Infantry Regiment reported the initial landing.

> On Wednesday morning, the 28th ultimo, at 10 o'clock, the landing of the troops commenced. The surf was running very high, and continued to run higher and higher, so that but 318 men could be landed. The condition of these troops was of course a very bad one. All of us were wet up to the shoulders, cut off entirely from the fleet, with wet ammunition, and without any provisions; but still all had but one thought — to advance.[63]

Weber had Acting-Adjutant von Doehn form and count the troops. They consisted of:

45 men of the Army's regular artillery from Fortress Monroe, commanded by
    Captain Larned.
45 Marines from *Minnesota*, Captain William L. Shuttleworth.
68 men of the Ninth New York Regiment, Captain Jardine.
102 men of the Twentieth New York Regiment.
28 men of the Union Coast Guard, Captain Nixon. [This was the name given to
    the Ninety-ninth New York Regiment.]
28 sailors (gunners) from the ships.

The force landed three miles from Fort Clark.

Colonel Weber, properly cautious initially, sent Lieutenant-Colonel Weiss forward with a twenty-man reconnaissance patrol. In due time a Lieutenant Wiegel returned to report that the patrol had taken (found) a dismounted gun and that the Confederates had begun to evacuate the fort. Weber dispatched two companies to reinforce Weiss and occupy the fort. As Weber followed with the rest of the men, the ships commenced to fire on his men and the fort. When Weber sent men out on the beach to wave the Stars and Stripes, the firing ceased. Captain Nixon and his twenty-eight Coast Guardsmen put out pickets and held the fort during the night. Captain Jardine with his company of the Ninth New York occupied the beach, while the rest of the men bivouacked at the landing place. The night passed quietly, with only scouts from each side peering through the dark. Some of Weber's men feasted during the night on roast goose and mutton, spoils from the Hatterasers' free ranging stock.[64]

Next morning, as soon as the fleet resumed firing, Weber ordered Captain Meyer's company of the Twentieth to cross the beach to the empty camp of the Confederates, where they captured a color and a cookstove. Lieutenant Johnson of the Union Coast Guard was ordered to advance with a 6-pounder rifle landed that morning. Johnson's gunners fired at Confederate steamers near Fort Hatteras. Weber continued: "We remained thus four hours in this position, the shells bursting over us, when at last the white flag was hoisted on the second fort." Captain Nixon and his hard working Coast Guardsmen were the first to enter the fort, followed by Weber and his staff and three Union surgeons, who assisted the Confederate doctors in dressing the wounded. Weber commended his junior officers and noted that all of his troops did their duty in every respect.[65] And so they did. Weber and his troops greeted Major-General Butler and the rest of the landing force.

Colonel Rush Hawkins, commanding the Ninth New York had no opportunity to enter the battle, nor even to participate in the occupation of Fort Hatteras. He was stranded on board the *Harriet Lane*, stuck fast on a shoal, and he did not land until August 30, when he took command as senior colonel after Butler's exodus. The *Harriet Lane*, after jettisoning stores, ammunition, and part of her guns, was hauled off the shoal by two tugs on August 31.

Reports from the Confederate side do not contradict the Federal records, but do clarify and explain some events. Colonel W.F. Martin, commanding the Seventh [Seventeenth] Regiment, wrote his report while being transported to prison in the North. His letter to the Adjutant-General of North Carolina is headed "Flagship *Minnesota* At Sea, August 31, 1861."[66] Colonel Martin's first order, after spying the enemy fleet through his glass on August 27, was to send for the men at Portsmouth. He had only a sailing pilot boat to dispatch, so the order was not delivered until the next morning. Before the message reached Portsmouth, the bombardment of Fort Clark started on the 28th. The Confederate accounts generally agree with the real time stated in Commodore Stringham's report, even though the hours creep by more slowly for those being shelled than for those doing the shelling.

Captain J.C. Lamb of the Roanoke Guards [E of the Seventeenth.] was senior officer in Fort Clark. His men kept up a steady fire and scored a few hits, though most of their shot fell short. When the last charge of powder and every primer were expended, the Confederates evacuated the fort. Before leaving they spiked the guns as best they could with nails, having no proper spikes. Captain Lamb, carrying the fort's colors with him, assembled the men posted in the woods and bivouac, and made for

Fort Hatteras — fast.[67] Bearing out Captain Lamb's claim of hits, Captain Saml. Mercer of the *Wabash* reported his ship was hit twice, once above and once below the water line. He did not state which day it happened, but reported both shot were buried in the hull. That most Confederate shot fell short was also confirmed by another observer: "Promptly, the fort had returned the fire, but a shout of 'derisive laughter' was heard from the *Minnesota*'s gundeck, when the shells fell half a mile short."[68]

The only satisfaction the Confederate gunners had on the first day was when the *Monticello* steamed in the inlet to see if Fort Hatteras had surrendered. The Confederates happily poured it on the hapless ship until she thrashed out of range. Colonel Martin, commenting on the lack of a flag over the fort stated: "I suppose [it] can only be accounted for from the flag having been torn to pieces by the winds … for when on the 29th the flag was ordered to be hoisted we had to use the one brought from Fort Clark." The reinforcements summoned from Portsmouth arrived after dark on Wednesday, August 28, numbering 257 officers and men. Commodore Samuel Barron, commanding the naval defenses of Virginia and North Carolina, arrived about this time with several other officers. Barron found Colonel Martin "very much exhausted." Major Andrews described him as "utterly prostrated." Martin and Andrews together asked Flag Officer Barron to take command, which he agreed to do. Barron and the other senior officers "designed an assault on Fort Clark" for that night, but decided to wait until another regiment expected from New Bern joined them.[69]

The delay was a mistake, as the hoped-for regiment never came. The Confederates' only chance would have been an attack that night with a part of the fort's garrison and the newly arrived men. The Federal soldiers, spread from Fort Clark to the original landing place were fatigued too, and only partly re-supplied. The night passed with only patrols and pickets sent out.

Captain Thomas Sparrow wrote the best account from the Confederate side of the final day's fighting. He started with the reactions to the news on Portsmouth Island.

> The privateer steamer *Gordon* ran into the inlet sometime in the afternoon and put David Ireland and two others of the crew on the shore. They reported in camp, the appearance of a fleet of United States steamers, seen off Hatteras, after they left that inlet. This news corresponded with a letter previously received by Captain W.T. Muse of the Navy, giving news of the expedition.[70]

A court-martial had been convened on Portsmouth to try the mutineers of the Tar River Boys. Two of the officers of the court, Captains Lamb and Clements, were from the Hatteras garrison, and upon hearing the news, wanted to return to their commands at once. Captain Sparrow detailed Privates Hanks and Woodley of his company to take the steamer *M.E. Downing* to rush them to Hatteras. That afternoon he inspected Fort Ocracoke on Beacon Island with Lieutenant-Colonel G.W. Johnson and Major H.A. Gillam. The officers took with them Sergeant von Eberstein and appointed him acting Ordnance Officer. The day was otherwise a normal one of drill and fatigue details. The following day was different after the pilot boat arrived. Captain (Major designate) Sparrow related it:

> August 28, Wednesday. I rose and dressed at reveille and went on drill with the company … Colonel Martin had sent a dispatch ordering all the forces at Ocracoke to Hatteras and requesting me to go. (I had been released from service in the Seventeenth Regiment, and was expecting orders … to Virginia.) I at once gave orders for the men to get breakfast, prepare two days' provisions, pack their knapsacks, take tent flys and prepare to embark....
>
> The Washington Grays, forty-nine in number, exclusive of commissioned officers, were in line, uniformed and equipped at 10 o'clock. I marched to the wharf, and embarked them for Hatteras, on the schooner Pantheon. The Morris Guards, Tar River Boys, and Hertford Light Infantry, embarked in other vessels.[71]

The entire garrison, save a few camp guards and special details and the two companies on Beacon Island, pressed on to the sound of the guns. The court-martial had been expunged by battle and never convened again. Fort Morgan, to use its proper name, though it was usually called Fort Ocracoke, was nearly complete, even though some stores were short. As late as week twelve, August 12, Captain Sparrow forwarded a list of "absolute needs" to Major John D. Whitford, the state's ordnance officer. The list was compiled by Sergeant von Eberstein and asked for much: from paint, brushes, and turpentine to gunners' tools, shot and shell, and ten thousand pounds of powder. He also ordered tangent sights for each of the fort's guns, carefully specifying the weight of the guns to ensure that the sights would fit the curve of the guns' breeches. The sight requisition gives the best inventory of the fort's guns. Besides the two 10-inch columbiads mentioned, there were two 8-inch columbiads, three 8-inch howitzers, and ten 32-pounders, a total of eighteen medium to heavy guns. Fort Morgan was better armed than the forts on Hatteras island. The sergeant also ordered ten new barbette gun carriages and one good spy glass.[72]

With the wind and tide against her, the Pantheon was behind the other vessels being towed by the Ellis. Sparrow and his men had a grand view of the whole panorama, the large ships off shore, the forts, and one ship in the inlet. They had arrived just in time to witness Fort Hatteras firing on the Monticello. "I had never before seen a shell explode," wrote Captain Sparrow, "beautiful little puffs of white, silvery smoke hanging over the fort." Seeing the Ellis grounded nearby, Captain Sparrow had himself rowed over to her, where he borrowed a pilot from Captain Muse. The Pantheon beat toward shore as rifled shot from the enemy flew overhead. Taking to his boat again, Sparrow landed, leaving orders for the Grays to disembark while he entered the fort for orders. He passed soldiers sitting outside the parapet, looking "fatigued and careworn," and others in the fort under arms and some with muskets stacked, and all looking glad that the day's fight was over.[73]

Captain Lamb, "cheerful as usual," greeted Sparrow and explained the situation. Colonel Martin and other officers were at the front of the fort, facing the ocean. "The

Colonel seemed feeble and worn out." These officers expected to be attacked that night by the eight hundred enemy in Fort Clark. By this time the Washington Grays had arrived, and Sparrow ordered cook Jesse Liverman to prepare bread and coffee for the men. "Everybody was in want of nourishment, including myself," Sparrow noted, but the little bread and coffee on hand could not feed them all.

After dark Commodore Barron arrived and assumed command. Sparrow was present at a consultation between Commodore Barron and the superior officers at which they decided the enemy was too strong to be attacked that night. Sparrow was ordered to select one hundred men from several companies to form a picket guard outside the fort, with Lieutenant James J. Whitehurst in charge. Next, Major Andrews ordered him to select another force to move a 10-inch columbiad from the sound shore into the fort. Captain Sparrow placed Private William B. Willis in charge of this group. Willis was a ship carpenter in the Grays who had experience in moving guns and other heavy weights. There was no equipment, no blocks and tackle, no shear legs, nothing but ropes, timbers, and manpower. They went to work, Sparrow included, sweating and cursing undoubtedly, to mount at least one gun that could reach the Federal ships. Major Andrews came back and ordered them to cease, saying there were no 10-inch shot nor shell in the fort. The men spent the rest of the night trying to sleep on the gun platforms or behind the traverses.

In the pre-dawn darkness the men in the fort were called to arms to repel an approaching force of the enemy, which turned out to be the returning Confederate pickets. Captain Sparrow formed four detachments of the Grays into eight-man squads, each under a gunner. They were assigned to a 32-pounder and an 8-inch how-itzer, bearing on the inlet. The Tar River Boys had two 32-pounders on their left and the Morris Guards manned an 8-inch howitzer and a 32-pounder facing the ocean, separated by a traverse. The rifled pieces in Fort Clark began to fire, their shells flying overhead. As the enemy fleet steamed into position, Sparrow stared at the broadside guns of the *Minnesota*, glaring back at him between two traverses. He immediately showed this to Barron and Martin, who ordered Engineer Allen to extend the traverse, but the work was not completed when the firing began.

> The action lasted three hours and twenty minutes. Such a bombardment is not on record in the annals of war. Not less than three thousand shells were fired by the enemy during the three hours. As many as twenty-eight in one minute were known to fall within and about the fort.

Sparrow compared the shelling to a hailstorm and credited Providence that so many escaped. He continued:

> The naval gun commanded by Lieutenant Murdaugh, and the guns com-manded by Lieutenants Johnson and Grimes returned the fire of the enemy, but it was discovered that with the greatest elevation we could get, our guns did not reach the enemy. It became a question of endurance on our part. Could we hold out during the day we would take the enemy in Fort Clark at night.[74]

Captain Sparrow moved from place to place behind his guns. A shell exploded on the parapet over his head and covered him with sand. Another shell fragment ripped his coat. As he stood talking to some other officers, a shell struck and exploded almost at their feet, but injured no one. Providence? A shell penetrated a ventilator in the bombproof shelter and exploded inside. Someone reported that the magazine was on fire, so the wounded were removed from the bomb shelter. It was smoke from the shell, not a fire.

> For the last hour the enemy seemed to have got our range exactly, and almost every shot fired from their ships fell into and about the fort. We had long ceased to fire, as we could not reach the enemy, and to man the guns was a useless exposure of the men. It became apparent that in an hour or so every man must be either killed or wounded.[75]

Commodore Barron called another council which decided to spike the guns and retreat. As the Confederate ships were a mile or more off shore in the sound and the garrison had no boats, this was impractical if not impossible. It was the reported fire in the magazine that became the deciding factor. Someone found a white sheet and waved it from the parapet. The enemy did not notice. Finally, a second flag, the white part of a large Confederate ensign did attract notice and the firing ceased. Raising the white flag caused various reactions from the garrison, raving rage from some, tears from others, and unauthorized escape to the ships by a few. Major-General Butler in the *Fanny* entered the inlet and fired at the departing *Winslow*. The other Confederate steamers departed. Federal soldiers from Fort Clark, carrying the Stars and Stripes, marched into the fort. Sparrow incorrectly stated they were led by Weber and Hawkins, "both Germans." Hawkins was neither German nor present. The chaplain from Fortress Monroe came in with Weber's men, collecting "relics," asking questions and taking notes. He stopped at a tent and prayed for a dying man, then resumed work. He told Sparrow he was a special correspondent of the *New York Tribune*. Like every man connected with the northern press, Sparrow observed, "he deals in falsehoods knowing them to be such." Colonel Max Weber, "a tall sharp-featured Dutchman, that could hardly speak English," returned with Butler's refusal of the Confederate terms. He demanded unconditional surrender. There was no alternative. Commodore Barron, Colonel Martin, and Major Andrews were carried to the *Minnesota* to arrange the details and surrender their swords to Commodore Stringham. Next came B.F. Butler.

> This worthy, with his blue coat and brass buttons, his lop-eyelids, and swaggering, fussy, waddling mien, came to receive the surrender of the fort and to embark the prisoners.
>
> I was introduced to General Butler at the door of the officers' tent. For-getting myself, and indulging in my usual politeness, I said, when shaking his hand, "I am glad to see you, sir." He replied in a familiar manner, "That is not true: you are not glad to see me. "Oh! no," said I, slapping him on the shoulder, "I forgot myself. I am not glad to see you. I beg your pardon."

> The General [Butler] inspected my men, as also the rest. I offered him
> my sword. He refused to receive it, and told me to hang it on the muskets,
> which I did.

One action of Butler's met Sparrow's approval that day. When asked if he wanted to march his men in before the Confederates marched out, he replied, "No, I will never take possession until the men who have made so gallant a defense have marched out." Sparrow emphasized, "I heard the remark." Captain Sparrow continued to the end of the surrender:

> My company was about the second that left the fort. We also formed in
> two ranks in the causeway from the sally-port to the sound. The gunboat
> *Fanny* was at the landing to receive us and take us to the *Adelaide*,
> anchored in the roadstead. General Butler superintended the embarkation
> himself — stood at the landing — passing and giving orders, boatswain's
> mate or boss workman totally destitute of all dignity or propriety.[76]

So ended the battle of Hatteras. The *Adelaide* steamed north with thirteen wounded Confederates and B.F. Butler. The *Minnesota* sailed for New York carrying 670 Confederate prisoners.[77] Major-General Butler reported "12 or 15" Confederates killed in his report to General Wool.[78] One Union soldier was wounded.

The Union victory over the Hatteras forts was complete, but other Confederate forts remained on the Banks. Fort Morgan might well be a tougher problem because of the range of its artillery pieces. The navy's large warships could neither enter the inlet nor come close enough to smother the fort with shellfire as at Hatteras. Sergeant von

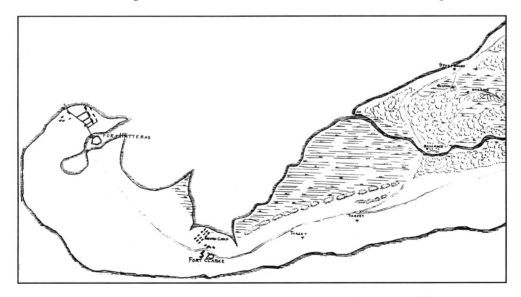

Hatteras Island. Courtesy National Archives Cartographic Section, from "Map of Part of Hatteras Island" 1864, by Capt. F.U. Farquhar, Chief Engineer, Dept. of Va. and N.C., and Pvt. Solon Allis, Co. K, 27th Mass. Map No. 143-23.

Eberstein related the "battle" of Beacon Island, which was fought in the mess room of the officer's quarters, after the officers of the garrison heard of events at Hatteras.

> When Captains Leith and Swindell heard of this, they called a conference of their officers, to be held in a big house which was on the island and which they used as officers quarters and mess room. I was invited by Captain Swindell and the officers to take part in the deliberations, which invitation was as Ordnance officer, being in charge of artillery, and Mr. Henry Brown the engineer of the works. We accepted.[79]

Captains Leith and Swindell next made the shocking proposal that the fort be evacuated before the next morning, as resistance to the Yankees was useless and they would all be captured. Sergeant von Eberstein was appalled at the suggestion. He remonstrated against evacuation as forcefully as a sergeant could against captains. He explained that the Yankees must come in small vessels and that the fort could be reinforced from New Bern. Even though Henry Brown, the engineer, and Lieutenants Frederick Harding and Henry Harding of Swindell's company supported him, he was overruled by Swindell and Leith and the rest of their officers. Captain Swindell seized two schooners at Portsmouth, one for each company, immediately scrambled the men aboard, and shoved off for the mainland. Von Eberstein called it "the most cowardly evacuation ever known … a most disorderly thing."[80]

Von Eberstein, Brown, and four Negro workmen were left in the fort, not enough for one gun crew, much less enough to defend a fort. Instead they did their best to destroy and burn and otherwise dismantle the fort. They set sail for New Bern to report the fort's evacuation and partial destruction to higher headquarters. The sergeant, still fuming, noted:

> We departed for Newbern. I took Capt. Swindell's flag with us. I would not disgrace it by leaving it there … and thus he abandoned the Flagg that had been presented to him to defend and which he had promised to do with the best of his ability — even with his life's blood. A more cowardly act I never knew.[81]

Headquarters in New Bern ordered the complete evacuation of the soldiers left on Portsmouth Island. CSS *Ellis*, towing a schooner removed the camp guards and the few remaining lady visitors from the ladies' invasion. One of *Ellis*'s officers, in a letter to the *Dispatch* newspaper of Washington, N.C., reported: "After finding the fort had surrendered and that we could be of no possible use, we left for Ocracoke to take on board the sad and weeping wives of the officers, now prisoners, and shall proceed to Washington, N.C."

Martha Matilda Fowle saw them land in Washington: "It was indeed a sad sight to see the remnants of those fine companies which we had so lately admired. I was affected almost to tears when I saw Lieut. Perry at the head of only six men."[82]

An additional evacuation, or more accurately, a mass migration, occurred at Portsmouth. One historian, Kenneth Burke, wrote:

The people of Roanoke Island were rather indifferent about the outcome of the War and just wanted to be left alone. But it was not so with the Portsmouthers. As has been shown earlier, they had a very keen financial interest in the maintenance of slavery, if not the Confederacy. With the abandonment of the fort on Beacon Island, the entire city of Portsmouth was evacuated for the duration of the War by the entire population, save one poor woman. She, too, earnestly desired to go, but while others were fleeing, she was compelled to remain, according to tradition, she was too fat to get through the door. However, when everyone returned after the War she stated that she had been very courteously treated by the Yankees.[83]

Burke was correct in his description of the evacuation of the island and the reasons for it, but he assigned improper weight to the reasons. The Portsmouthers did not abandon their homes for the preservation of slavery, nor for remembrance of past invasions, though these probably were factors. They left because of a condition more contagious than plague, faster spreading than fever. It was panic.

The Portsmouthers had witnessed the panic on Beacon Island, the "complete disorderly thing." They had seen Captain Swindell's frenzied commandeering of the schooners. They had heard rumors of disasters at Hatteras and, finally, they had observed the evacuation of the weeping wives and daughters and the camp guards.

They panicked themselves and fled in whatever boats were left to wherever they could go. Some of the islanders began to drift back in a few weeks, although some stayed away for the duration of the war. The Ocracokers, farther removed from the scene, did not panic, but a few did leave. The Hatterasers, in close contact with the first major battle on the Banks thus far, felt war's effects. Some moved to the mainland to farm or fish there, and some joined the armies — on both sides. With Portsmouth, Ocracoke, and half of Hatteras under Federal control, there was only one more fort on these islands to defend them, or one more domino to fall. The panic spread northward, along Hatteras Island to Oregon Inlet. On September 1, Fort Oregon became the next domino.

The fort was designed and built by Colonel of Engineers Elwood Morris and his assistant C.R. Barney. The labor was performed by 150 free Negroes sent to the site by General Gwynn, using tools bought or borrowed by the general. The fort mounted thirteen guns, with a sea battery of five more. Commander T.T. Hunter of the Confederate navy stated that the fort was a " beautiful piece of engineering work," but he thought it was improperly sited. The garrison consisted of three companies of the Seventeenth North Carolina, and included about twenty-five men who had just escaped from the Hatteras battle.[84]

Captain Lindsey, Currituck Atlantic Rifles, who commanded the fort called a council of war. The council voted to abandon the fort, with Chief Engineer Morris, Captain Lindsey, and Lieutenant Mercer dissenting. Abandon it they did!

Lindsey's report to Adjutant-General Martin explained: "The reasons given for our evacuation were the isolated situation of the island, the exposure to attack from sea and land, the scarcity of our ammunition, and the fact that it was in the power of the enemy to cut off entirely all supplies of provisions, ammunition, or men." Commander Hunter was present, but not voting. He did insist that the fort not be abandoned until every gun and all other public property was removed. He left four schooners and the *Raleigh* under Commander J.W. Alexander to haul men and ordnance to Roanoke Island. The soldiers only spiked the guns, although Captain Lindsey said they tried to move them and could not. In spite of Commander Alexander's efforts, only the men and a part of the supplies were evacuated to Roanoke Island.[85] Another account noted that the barracks were burned and three guns lost overboard, showing that Captain Lindsey had tried to move them.[86]

The Union victory on the Banks caused great jubilation in the North. Congratulations and praise flowed from the War and Navy Departments in Washington to the victorious commanders. Merchants and insurance company officials congratulated Commodore Stringham on destroying the nest of pirates. Northern newspapers exulted. Typical was a columnist in a New York paper, also quoted in the *Philadelphia Ledger*: The effect of the victory "contributes to the cheerful feeling that prevails, by encouraging the hope that the tide of victory is now turned from the rebels to the Union arms."[87]

In the South there was consternation mixed with anger. Governor Clark telegraphed Confederate Secretary of War L.P. Walker, "An extensive coast frontier now requires all the attention of the Confederate Government." General R.C. Gatlin, commanding the military district, wired Adjutant-General S. Cooper for four more regiments and light and heavy guns. The Confederate Congress passed a resolution calling for complete information, which President Jefferson Davis promised to transmit as soon as received. President Davis continued: "Preparations to put the coast of the State of North Carolina in a proper condition for defense are still in progress and will receive such additional attention as this occasion indicates to be necessary."[88]

One more event concluded the battle of Hatteras. When Colonel Rush Hawkins assumed command on the island after Butler's departure, he had Colonel Weber's Twentieth New York garrison the forts and their environs. His own Ninth New York camped outside the forts and in several outposts and established a picket line across the island to catch any roving Confederates. Weber's Germans were clad in the standard blue Union army uniforms, but Hawkins's Zouaves were a much more colorful lot. They wore a uniform patterned after some of the French colonial regiments. They wore bright blue trousers, cut very full, almost bloomers, a red sash, and a short, heavily embroidered jacket. They crowned this gaudy splendor with a red fez, which resembled an oversized nightcap topped with a long tassel.

Johnny Barnes lived with his widowed mother in the village of Kinnakeet. She was the only person who could understand the few sounds he could make, for he had been a deaf mute since birth. He was also a skilled woodworker and worked in a boatyard outside the village. When battle erupted and everyone left the yard, Johnny Barnes knew something bad was happening. Probably he saw the smoke and shellbursts, possibly he felt the concussion. His first thought was to go check on his mother. He set off for home at a run. If he saw the picket who challenged him, he might not even have recognized the strangely dressed man as a soldier. He did not hear the repeated command to halt. Johnny Barnes never knew why they shot him. His last thought was of his mother. No weathered red-cedar slab marks his grave, but if he had one, carved on it would be Johnny Barnes, Age 53, Died September 2, 1861.[89]

A blending of marital with martial history can strike a happier note to bring to an end this account of the Federal capture of the three islands: the pleasant aftermath of the ladies' invasion of Portsmouth. Before the year was out, Mary Fowle married Lieutenant Jesse Perry of the Hertford Light Infantry. Before the war was over, Martha Matilda Fowle married First Sergeant Howard Wiswell of the Tar River Boys.[90]

Chapter Four

Guns in the Sounds

$\mathcal{C}$OLONEL RUSH C. HAWKINS was left in command of the troops on Hatteras Island: there were detachments of the Ninth New York, his own regiment, and a larger part of Colonel Weber's Twentieth New York, plus the half-company of the Union Coast Guard. The naval ships *Pawnee*, the *Monticello*, and the tug *Fanny* remained on station.

Just before he sped off, Major-General Butler sent word to Hawkins to supply his troops from provisions aboard three schooners left by the Confederates. The Union soldiers who foraged through the vessels fared common according to their commander. The only rations left on these former Confederate prizes were the remnants of a cargo of tropical fruit, fast decaying. Otherwise, they lived on black coffee, fresh fish, and what they called sheet-iron pancakes, which were flour and saltwater patties or Johnny cake. The diet "produced unpleasant scorbutic results." Better rations came on September 10 when Lieutenant-Colonel George F. Betts arrived with five more companies of the Ninth New York and with supplies.[1] According to Ben Dixon MacNeil, five of the soldiers died of dysentery caused by eating those over ripe bananas. No further mention was made of roast goose and mutton. Perhaps the New Yorkers had eaten them all, but most likely the islanders learned to hide their stock from the invaders.

The steamer *Spaulding* returned to Fort Monroe the next day with Weber's regiment. She turned right around for Hatteras with Hawkin's remaining two companies and Brigadier-General John F. Reynolds, an artilleryman, and a load of building material.[2] The Twentieth New York, though able soldiers, had given Colonel Hawkins problems by their behavior toward the civilians on the island. As early as September 2, he had written Colonel Weber that his men "…continue to commit depredations against the property of the inhabitants of this island." He also informed Weber that he would use his artillery against the looters if necessary. He reported the "vandals" among Weber's Germans to Major-General John E. Wool, along with a report on his belief in the loyalty to the United States of many North Carolinians. Hawkins suggested that a Union convention should be called at once to bring the eastern counties back into the Union. He predicted that with such a convention, backed by more troops, "one third of the state of North Carolina would be back in the Union within two weeks."[3] Hawkins believed that the local people would enlist to fight for the Union, and continued to recommend such a course. Eventually, somebody listened, for

on September 16 President Lincoln authorized recruiting for a regiment (or a company) of North Carolinians at Fort Hatteras. The Adjutant-General, on September 17,
issued the order for the commanding officer at Hatteras Inlet to begin.[4] Thus were
born the North Carolina Union regiments later to be called Buffaloes.

The Confederate soldiers had left Ocracoke and Portsmouth Islands, sent north
as prisoners via Hatteras, or withdrawn to the towns of the mainland or on Roanoke
Island. The Mosquito Fleet, too, had withdrawn to Albemarle and the narrow sounds.
Roanoke Island became the center of Confederate defenses in the area, with a slow
buildup of troops. The Confederate authorities had intended to reinforce Fort Hatteras. On August 27, the Third Georgia Regiment had embarked on canal boats to
transit the Albemarle and Chesapeake Canal for the sounds. Commander William H.
Parker, CSN, hooked the launch he was sailing to Hatteras onto the procession of the
Georgian's canal boats, towed by Captain Thomas Hunter's steamer *Junaluska*. The
column met a schooner crossing Albemarle Sound whose captain gave the news of
Hatteras' fall. Instead, the Third Georgia landed on Roanoke Island, a welcome addition. Parker called them "A remarkably fine regiment."[5] The Confederate ships came
back south, steaming cautiously as they scouted. CSS *Albemarle* came first to Ocracoke
Inlet. She had been attached briefly to the Mosquito Fleet, but because of her age and
condition she had been relegated to service as a supply vessel. She docked at Beacon
Island where her captain inspected the half-ruined fort while her crew hoisted aboard
the two big 10-inch Columbiads, the most valuable guns in the fort. The captain surveyed the beach at Portsmouth, but did not land. Wheeling around, her paddle wheels
flailing, *Albemarle* steamed for New Bern to deliver the guns and Captain Roberts'
report to Major John Whitford, the state's Ordnance Officer.[6]

The next visitor to the islands was from the Union Navy. Commander S.C.
Rowan, aboard USS *Pawnee*, dispatched the steamer *Fanny* under command of Lieutenant J.G. Maxwell, *Pawnee*'s executive officer, to inspect the abandoned defenses of
Ocracoke Inlet. Maxwell sailed on the morning of September 16, towing *Pawnee*'s
launch loaded with more men. Captain Chauncey of the *Susquehanna* agreed to cooperate from outside the inlet and to send four boats loaded with Marines if necessary to
join Maxwell. Lieutenant Maxwell set his men to completing the destruction started by
Sergeant von Eberstein. They broke the trunnions off the guns and torched the
remaining gun platforms and other structures. Maxwell described the fort as well
made of earth covered barrels of sand with a large bomb-proof shelter and magazine
in the center.[7]

Lieutenant Eastman, in the launch, landed at Portsmouth and disabled four guns
lying on the beach. He reported most of the people had left, and the few remaining
ones "seem to be Union men and expressed satisfaction at our coming." Eastman did
not mention the fat lady. Lieutenant Maxwell reported that there were no entrenchments nor guns at Ocracoke and stated that the few pilots and fishermen who had fled
had returned. Maxwell also advised that the lightboat used to mark the channel past
Beacon Island was fired and set adrift to sink in the inlet. Maxwell's force returned
safely to Hatteras on September 18.[8]

Each side began to reinforce its troops on the Banks. The Confederates, with only fragments of the Seventeenth Regiment on Roanoke Island, needed the troops from Virginia. Colonel Ambrose Ransome Wright, the energetic commander of the Third Georgia was reporting from Roanoke Island on September 6 to Brigadier-General Benjamin Huger who commanded in Norfolk. Wright asked that his remaining two companies be sent to him if he was to be stationed at Roanoke Island permanently (he hoped not). He reported the North Carolina troops on the Island "in a state of disorganization." He stated that the troops were mounting guns and "we are all well, and the men are working cheerfully. No late news from the Hessians."[9] By the latest Confederate reorganization in the state, Roanoke Island was in the Department of Norfolk. Brigadier-General R.C. Gatlin commanded the rest of the state's coastline, with Brigadier-General Joseph R. Anderson in charge of the Wilmington District, leaving the defenses between Albemarle Sound, the several rivers of the area, and Pamlico Sound to a new arrival. After two tries, Governor Clark managed to extract Brigadier-General D.H. Hill from Virginia. Hill, a cold-eyed warrior, commenced work at once, inspecting, recommending, and commanding. By horse, afoot, and afloat, Hill went through his big district like a cannonball. From Fort Macon to Roanoke Island he looked at everything, not just towns and rivers, but most of the countryside, too. He noted: "Hyde, the richest county in the state, has ten landings and only one gun — an English 9-pounder of great age and venerable aspect." In a later report to General Gatlin, Hill pointed out that Roanoke Island and Fort Macon were the weak points in the district. Roanoke Island, he saw as the key to one-third of North Carolina. Four additional regiments were indispensable for that place. Hill ordered a continuous line of earthworks across the narrow neck of Roanoke Island. He recommended earthworks at most of the places he visited. "The spade has been set agoing wherever I have been," he wrote. Before he could make sure it was all done, General Joseph E. Johnston called him back to Virginia.[10] One more regiment was sent to Roanoke Island. The North Carolina Eighth Regiment, Colonel Henry M. Shaw, was dispatched from Camp Macon in Warren County on September 18. The regiment arrived on September 21, and was transferred from state to Confederate service while en route.[11]

On the Union side, Colonel W.L. Brown's Twentieth Indiana Regiment had arrived to replace Weber's Germans, along with one company of the First U.S. Artillery. General Reynolds stayed at Hatteras only briefly, before he was ordered back North, leaving Colonel Hawkins again in command.

Hawkins had too much energy and ambition to be content with a passive occupation of the forts. He was also concerned with returning the state to the Union. He decided to occupy more of the island. "I had already apprised General Wool of my intention to establish a post near Chicamacomico for the purpose of protecting the natives who had taken the oath, and also to prevent a surprise by the landing of a large force of the enemy to march down the island." Hawkins suspected such a move was planned by the Confederates, for one of his spies had told him so. Accordingly, the Twentieth Indiana embarked in the gunboats *Ceres* and *Putnam* and landed opposite Chicamacomico, about twenty-seven miles north of the Cape and thirty-six from the fort. On October 1 the steamer *Fanny* arrived at the new post and prepared to unload supplies.[12] The *Fanny*, not a naval vessel, had a master and mate and sufficient crew to operate her machinery, but she was manned largely, it is believed, by volunteers from the Twentieth Indiana, and the Ninth New York.

The Federal movement had not gone unnoticed by the Confederates. The Mosquito Fleet decided to go for the *Fanny*. Colonel A.R. Wright conferred with Commodore Lynch, who had commanded the vessels in North Carolina's waters since Commodore Barron's capture. Lynch selected the *Junaluska*, *Raleigh*, and *Curlew*. The largest ship, the *Curlew* was unarmed, so Wright furnished a long, rifled and banded 32-pounder from Fort Bartow. This was temporarily mounted on *Curlew*'s foredeck. She was additionally manned, like *Fanny*, by an ad-hoc crew of soldiers, these drawn from the Dawson Greys, the Governor's Guards, and the Athens Guards of the Third Georgia. The Georgians had practiced gun drill, but had never fired one. After two hours steaming, the flotilla sighted the *Fanny* near shore. She had just begun unloading when the Confederates arrived, for Colonel Brown was unprepared to help land the supplies earlier. The *Curlew* opened fire, the other ships followed suit. The *Fanny* returned the fire, with Sergeant-Major Peacock of the Zouaves in charge of the gun. A small part of *Fanny's* cargo was thrown overboard as she steamed for the shore. When a shell (probably from the long 32-pounder) exploded on her deck, a white flag was hoisted. The master and mate escaped ashore in small boats, but Captain Hart of the Twentieth Indiana surrendered the rest of his men when the Confederates boarded.[13] The captured cargo was welcomed.

> She carried two rifled guns, a crew of forty-nine men, besides a large amount of army stores valued by some as high as $100,000. Among the latter were 1,000 new overcoats, which were turned over to the Third Georgia regiment, and contributed greatly to their comfort during the ensuing winter…. [T]he *Fanny* became a part of the Mosquito Fleet….
> The victory was important in more respects than one. It was our first naval success in North Carolina and the first capture made by our arms of an armed war-vessel of the enemy, and dispelled the gloom of recent disasters.[14]

The Confederates learned from their prisoners the size of the Union force at Chicamacomico. Headquarters on Roanoke Island began to suspect a Federal move on them. The Mosquito Fleet ships were almost out of fuel, so all possible men, sailors and soldiers, were cutting wood on Roanoke Island while the commanders conferred.

Colonel Wright, seeing a crisis approaching, decided that an attack was his best defense. Commodore Lynch was willing, so preparations were made to attack the Federals at Chicamacomico. On the Federal side, the loss of the *Fanny* caused General Wool to speed Brigadier-General Joseph K.F. Mansfield to Hatteras to take command, and five hundred additional men for the garrison.

Lynch assembled the steamers *Curlew*, *Raleigh*, *Junaluska*, *Fanny*, *Empire*, and *Cotton Plant*, the latter a new arrival of shallow draft. Wright loaded Colonel Shaw's Eighth North Carolina and his own Third Georgia. Wright embarked on the *Cotton*

Plant with three of his companies and two 6-pounder boat howitzers. The little flotilla arrived off Chicamacomico just after sunrise. The *Cotton Plant* ran close inshore and Wright and his three companies waded ashore "in water up to their middles," the gun crews dragging the howitzers behind them. The ship's guns fired in support. While wading ashore, the Georgians opened as rapid a fire as they could against the Twentieth Indiana, drawn up on the beach. "The enemy stood in line of battle on the beach, twelve hundred strong according to their muster rolls. Soon after the firing commenced they began a retreat, moving hastily and in great disorder towards Fort Hatteras." [Brown retreated according to orders laid down by Colonel Hawkins.] Most of the inhabitants of the village joined the exodus. The rest of the Third Georgia landed to rejoin Wright and the chase began which was later styled the "Chicamacomico Races." Colonel Wright's horse was landed, so the mounted Colonel was able to lead his men trudging through the sand. Colonels should not take the point in an attack, even against fast retreating men. Wright caught up with the rear guard, who turned and fired on him. His horse was killed, but Wright, unharmed, drew his pistol, shielded himself with an undersized Union soldier, and captured Sergeant-Major Hart and four other men of the rear guard. The Confederates marched until exhaustion and nightfall halted them. They made camp at Kinnakeet.[15] The Federals made it to the lighthouse where they collapsed.

The flotilla, according to plan, continued down the shore to land the Eighth North Carolina between the retreating Indiana regiment and the forts. This part of the plan went awry, the trap failed to close, as one side developed lockjaw. The flotilla reached the chosen landing point in mid-afternoon, but the vessels grounded far out from shore. Shaw's men dropped over the side and started to wade only to encounter sloughs of deep water between them and the shore. The ships picked them up and returned to Roanoke Island. When Colonel Wright learned of this on the morning of the fifth, he began a countermarch back to Chicamacomico. At about one o'clock in the afternoon, as the Confederates emerged from the woods of Kinnakeet, the USS *Monticello* came into view. She commenced a furious cannonade of shell, grape, and canister on the column. She harried the Confederates all afternoon with gunfire. The sea was rough, preventing accurate aim, so little damage was done. The second of the Chicamacomico Races continued until dark.[16] Colonel Hawkins, with the Ninth New York, joined Brown's men at the lighthouse and chased the Confederates north, never quite catching up. After a thirteen mile march, the Federals returned to the Cape.

The official reports of the action varied. Historian J. Thomas Scharf wrote that Colonel Wright's seven hundred Georgians killed eight Indianians and captured forty-two of Brown's twelve hundred men. Federal General Mansfield reported Brown's losses as twenty-nine due to straggling. Colonel Hawkins, in his report to General Wool on October 8 did not state losses, as he said his information was incomplete due to the loss of the Twentieth Indiana's roll books. Colonel Wright's men probably had the roll book, as they stripped the Federal camp on their way coming and going. Hawkins did have much to say in his own defense when he was criticized for splitting his forces. He blamed the "recent disaster" on the "criminal neglect of the Government in not heeding my suggestions." He further stated that he did not want to be a Brigadier-General anyhow. "Brigadier-Generals are made of such queer stuff nowadays," he grumbled. General Wool endorsed Hawkin's report with a comment: "Colonel Hawkin's remarks in relation to the Government are highly insubordinate and ought not to pass unnoticed."[17]

The greatest variance in accounts comes from the report of Lieutenant D.L. Braine, commanding the *Monticello*. He reported the troops he shelled as being in great confusion and suffering greatly from the fire. In an exchange of fire with the Mosquito Fleet, Braine thought his guns hit the *Fanny*. The *Monticello* picked up one man from the beach, Private Warren O'Haver of the Indiana regiment. Private O'Haver had great tales to tell. He had seen two sloops loaded with Rebels blown up by shells and sunk, and all the men on shore in wild confusion. O'Haver claimed he had been captured, but had escaped after killing a Rebel captain. No doubt these stories colored Lieutenant Braine's report.[18] Scharf in his 1887 account, in comparison, said one man from the Governor Guards died from exhaustion, the only death during the retreat. Braine did good work keeping the retreating Confederates moving, but it was more like a wagon-master cracking the whip to keep the teams going than a grim reaper taking his toll.

According to Colonel Hawkins, "until October 13th we had peace at the inlet. That day Brigadier-General Thomas Williams relieved General Mansfield." With General Williams came a new captain for the Ninth New York, who was "a disreputable officer who had received an appointment from Governor E.D. Morgan." Hawkins refused to accept the captain in his regiment, so Williams promptly put Hawkins under arrest. Thus matters stood until Hawkins was sent on a mission to Washington, D.C. by General Wool.

Although Rush Hawkins was a prickly problem for his immediate superiors, he had the attention of some of the authorities, civil and military, in Washington, and he was esteemed by the soldiers of his regiment. Private Charles F. Johnson has left an account of his service in Hawkins' Zouaves in North Carolina.

Private Johnson arrived in time to join the last lap of the Races. "With the exhilarating idea of going to the rescue, all went merrily until about midnight, when the rapid march in the sand, which sank under us at every step to a depth of three or four inches, began to tell on us." Johnson thought it was a romantic march, but suffered much from thirst all night. The Zouaves were then quartered at Camp Wool, their name for the wooded part of the island near Hatteras village. The Indianians occupied Fort Clark. "My messmate and I have pitched our tent on a spot under some trees in front of a clear stream of water in the marsh, which is very pretty, though I presume not the healthiest in the world; but then, if one is after health, I think it best to get off the Island of Hatteras as speedily as possible." Johnson described another post at Trent where the men had thrown up a small breastwork in front of the church which was used as a barrack and guard house. The huts they built of pine logs and brush were warmer shelters than the church. Johnson, a talented artist, sketched many of the scenes on the island, some of which are included in his book.[19]

Johnson noted General Mansfield's transfer and the new General Williams's intense interest in building fortifications. The soldiers repaired and extended the walls of Fort Clark, only to see their work wash away during a heavy storm. This did not daunt General Williams, who had them start work on a new and bigger fort sited on the highest land in the vicinity. The usual schedule had half the men drilling at Camp Wool, while the other half wheelbarrowed sand and turf to the new fort. The work proceeded at a snail's pace, said Johnson, except when headquarters sent Lieutenant Flemming to inspect and report back. "We performed prodigies of labor for the half hour he was with us." Private Johnson wrote more:

> But that officer was scarcely out of sight when a number of the men were detailed to construct a few pitfalls near the walls, arranging boards and brush over them not strong enough to bear one's weight, yet sufficient for a cover of sand so as not to be perceptible. We hoped the General would fall into one of them while we were at dinner, for it was his custom to go out at that time, for the purpose of inspecting the work done, accompanied by his Staff and Orderly, the latter at precisely twelve paces behind him… It is a comical sight to see, and more so because the Orderly is a good fellow with an appreciation of the ludicrousness of his position, which he adds to by a well-guarded mimicry of the General's carriage and motions. Our plan worked better than we had hoped. It seems the General stumbled into one pitfall the very first thing, and had hardly been helped out of that before he fell into another. This was such a mortal affront to his state and dignity that he has hardly shown himself out of his quarters since. There was a report around that he was shot at the other evening through a window, but this is hardly probable, for General Williams is rather a vexatious than a cruel tyrant.[20]

General Williams must have been a remarkably patient and even-tempered man toward his citizen-soldiers, but equally determined to get some work out of them.

When the rumor circulated through the regiment that Hawkins had declined an appointment as brigadier-general in order to stay with the Zouaves, Private Johnson noted: "Our boys need but the confirmation of this to fairly worship the 'King of the Hawks.'"[21]

There was no military action on the islands after Chicamacomico for the rest of the year. The soldiers drilled and dug. In the sound the small vessels occasionally exchanged long-range cannon fire. The Federal Navy controlled the ocean, Hatteras Inlet and the bight inside the sound. The Mosquito Fleet still patrolled the rest of the sounds. However, there were other ships at sea besides the Americans'. Great Britain and France sent naval vessels on intelligence missions to see what those unruly Americans were doing. The British frigate *Rinaldo* was cruising off Beaufort in early November, and peering in Topsail Inlet at times. The French frigate *Catinet* had called at Norfolk. A French sail appeared off Ocracoke Inlet about the same time. The same kind of weather that had washed away part of Fort Clark moved in.

Federal ships steaming outside in the ocean reported "a terrible gale of wind … on the third instant." On November 5 the naval commander at Hatteras Inlet received the report that two enemy steamers were outside the inlet to the southward. He dispatched five ships to capture the extruders. "They did not discover the enemy but instead the French side-wheel steamer of war *Catinet*, ashore inside the bar at Ocracoke."[22] The USS *General Putnam* and *Ceres* arrived at Ocracoke Inlet together. The *Ceres* was the first to speak with the French when she picked up a French lieutenant who had rowed out in a whaleboat from the stranded vessel. He informed the *Ceres'* captain that his ship was the corvette *Prony*, not the *Catinet*, and that his captain hoped to get her off by jettisoning his guns, ammunition, and coal.[23]

The *Prony* was a steam corvette 190 feet in length, with an engine of 360 steam horses, as the French put it. She had a beam of 33 feet and, most important in this instance, a draft of 12 feet.[24] *Prony's* draft was too great for her to enter the inlet, and proved to be too great for her to approach closely the coast.

The senior naval officer at Hatteras, Lieutenant R.B. Lowry, arrived in USS *Underwriter*, sent the smaller ships back to Hatteras because of the worsening weather, and remained on station. *Underwriter* stood off and on, straining and leaking in the heavy seas, unable to close the French ship. The *Prony* fired signal guns and distress rockets during the night. Lieutenant Lowry decided the safety of his ship required him to return to harbor. He explained in his after-action report:

> It was only after the profound conviction at 7:30 A.M. this morning, that I could do nothing to aid the stranded Frenchman, that I bore up for this harbor and abandoned him to the attention of the rebels. The sea was running too high to permit me to approach within several miles, and the safety of my own vessel became a subject for serious consideration. ...If the rebels rescue the crew of the Frenchman, or save the vessel, and after treating them with interested kindness cause them to be returned to France, the event may have a most important bearing upon our political questions.[25]

Lieutenant Lowry condemned the rebels, who, because of their "insane barbarity" had extinguished all the lights along the coast, forgetting for the moment who had burned the Beacon Island lightship. The barbaric Rebels viewed the political questions exactly as Lowry had done.

The log of CSS *Ellis*, after noting strong gales and dragging anchors, recorded on November 5:

> At 1:30 P.M. came to anchor in Wale's [Wallace's] channel at Ocracoke, at which place we discovered a French man-of-war on shore. At 2:30 P.M. the CSS *Curlew* and *Albemarle* went out to rescue them which they succeeded in doing...[26]

The rescue actually took place on November 6. The *Curlew* and *Albemarle* managed to reach the Frenchman and rescued the entire crew and their baggage. CSS *Winslow*, steaming hard to assist them ran afoul of the wreck of the lightship and holed herself so badly that she sank in the inlet. The Confederate steamers *Beaufort* and *Ellis* rescued the *Winslow's* crew and salvaged what they could from her wreck. All that remained above water of both *Prony* and *Winslow* was burned.[27] It was a haz-ardous operation to even approach a wrecked vessel in that gale-swept, treacherous inlet, much more so to take off the crew and baggage. In fairness to Lieutenant Lowry, it was probably a smidgen easier to conduct the rescue from inside the inlet, rather than from outside. The Confederates risked it and lost the *Winslow*. A shift in the wind also helped.

The *Ellis* carried the officers, men, and baggage from the *Prony* to Norfolk under a flag of truce and delivered them into the care of the French Consul. The irate comman-der of the *Prony*, Captain N. de Fontanges, complained to Flag Officer L.M. Goldsboro of the United States Navy that the Union ships had not responded to his distress signals.[28]

The Confederates publicized the rescue as Lieutenant Lowry had feared. Captain de Fontanges sent his thanks to Colonel Singletary, "Commandant of the District of Portsmouth." It was published in the Norfolk, Virginia *Day Book* and copied by other newspapers, including the *Newbern Daily Progress*. De Fontanges lauded the Confeder-ates thus: "I cannot forget such services: you may be certain that the government of the Emperor shall know the persons to whom France owes the safety of 140 of her sailors." Leon Misano, the Vice-Consul of France, also wrote in like manner.[29]

Two more wrecks littered the channels of Ocracoke Inlet and more were to come. Naval headquarters in Washington were still intent on closing the inlets. Hat-teras Inlet was to remain navigable, but all the rest were to be blocked. Some naval officers recommended that Ocracoke Inlet remain open as an alternate route after the Confederates abandoned Beacon Island, but in mid–September Secretary Welles issued firm orders to close Ocracoke also.[30] Commander R.S. Stellwagen in USS *Monticello* assembled twenty-two old schooners loaded with stone at Hatteras for blocking all other inlets and canals. Considerable correspondence passed between various officers and headquarters concerning how and exactly where to sink the schooners. The solu-tion that evolved was to sink them across the inner bar — the swash.[31]

One letter from Jacob Westervelt, pilot of the *Ceres*, with Thomas Smith, pilot, concurring, sounds remarkably like a late twentieth-century geologist-hydrographer. After pointing out the volume of water pouring through the inlet, he predicted that any blocking attempt by sunken vessels would not last thirty days. He cited examples and concluded: "from my experience and knowledge of the bottom, which is shifting sand, I deem it entirely impractical."[32] Admiral Goldsborough was weary of discus-sion. He snapped at the commander at Hatteras: "What the department wishes is to have its orders executed if possible. I attach, myself, but little consequence to the opin-ions of pilots or other persons."[33] And so it was done. On November 15, Lieutenant William M. Jeffers, commanding *Underwriter*, reported that three schooners chained together were sunk athwart the channel in nine feet of water.[34]

While military and naval actions were winding down in those last months of 1861, political action was brewing. It might be said that it was a different kind of ill wind that blew Marble Nash Taylor and Charles Henry Foster to North Carolina. However, that is not a fair description of the North Carolina Methodist Conference that sent the Reverend Taylor to Hatteras in 1860. One account stated Taylor was rejected as a minister by both the Baptist and Methodist churches in 1850, but that the Methodists relented on his second application and licensed him. He was described as being below average height, having pale blue eyes, and of unprepossessing appearance. A Boston newspaper correspondent later regarded him as "a well meaning and unpretending sort of man, one of the last to lay claim to that which he did not believe himself entitled to."[35]

His colleague in their campaign for office proclaimed that Taylor was "a man of age and experience, incorruptible, and of true fidelity to the Union."[36] That is what his friends said. The other side took a different view. A correspondent of a Fayetteville newspaper wrote: "Marble Nash Taylor is emphatically a small man — small in stature, small in mind, small in morals. His tallow complexion resembles a whited sepulchre, and his eyes, mouth, and chin resemble dead men's bones."[37] The first official notice the Federal forces took of Taylor was on September 5, when Commander S.C. Rowan reported that two of the Hatterasers planned to cross to the mainland to induce the people to secede from the state. "I told one of them, their parson, that would not do. The Government of the United States was fighting against secession and could not sustain them in such a course: that their best course was to cultivate the Union sentiment and bring the State back to her allegiance."[38] Taylor took this advice and decided to overwhelm the Confederacy by ballots. On October 12 Taylor called for a meeting in the church at Trent to organize a new government for North Carolina. One of the speakers at the meeting was Charles Henry Foster who told the gathering that the Confederacy would become either a monarchy or a military despotism.[39]

Foster, born in Maine, had come South as a newspaper editor. In 1859 he bought *The Citizen*, in Murfreesboro, North Carolina and became a Breckinridge supporter and a strong Southern rights champion. He sold his paper in 1860 and left for Washington to work for the Post Office Department. During July, 1861, Foster contrived a series of bogus letters from supporters in various Tar Heel towns as a means of entering the Congress as a Union Representative from North Carolina.[40] When this effort failed, Foster, with a keen job-seeker's instinct, sped South again to Hatteras to join Marble Nash Taylor. They were ready, a matched pair of scoundrels — or patriots — ready to take over the government of the Old North State. Foster was the more impressive in appearance of the pair. In later years he described himself as: "5'9"," weighing 145 pounds, with sallow complexion, dark brown hair, an dark gray eyes."[41]

Two of the Hatterasmen, R.B. Ballance and Alonzo J. Stowe presided over the meeting, front men for Taylor and Foster. A committee composed of Taylor with two more Hatterasers, William O'Neil and Caleb B. Stowe, prepared a statement of grievances against the Confederacy, written in the form of the original Declaration of Independence. Favorable publicity was given by the correspondent of the *New York Herald*.[42]

Foster went North after the meeting to enlist more support for the new government. Marble Nash Taylor followed later in October, with a new recruit from Hatteras. It is not certain if Taylor or Foster conferred with Colonel Rush Hawkins about their mutual idea of separating the eastern counties from the Confederacy, but the pair did enlist Hawkins' regimental chaplain, T.W. Conway, who accompanied Taylor to New York.

It was a grand meeting that the threesome attended at the Cooper Union in New York City on November 7. Taylor and Conway brought endorsements from General Wool, Simon Cameron, Secretary of War, and even President Lincoln. Foster had been busy enlisting help and scheming to further their plan. George Bancroft, the historian, presided over the meeting. Others attending were William Cullen Bryant, William E. Dodge, John J. Astor, and General Ambrose P. Burnside, plus several eminent clergymen. Chaplain Conway described the population of Chicamacomico fleeing from the Rebels "without shoes and hats and almost in rags." Marble Nash Taylor asserted that the people of Hatteras, because of their loyalty, had no bread and no salt for their fish. He claimed that the whole population of the island, "four thousand persons flocked down to Colonel Hawkins and gladly took the oath of allegiance." [Hatteras had a population of less than fifteen hundred in 1860.]

A Committee of Relief was appointed at the conclusion of the appeals to collect funds to purchase and ship all the things needed by the war-stricken Hatterasers.[43]

Satisfied with the results, Taylor and Foster returned to Hatteras. Foster obtained permission from Secretary of State Seward and from Major-General George B. McClellan to travel by army transport vessels.[44] A schooner laden with the relief supplies sailed soon thereafter.

Taylor and Foster had campaigned from Hatteras to Washington to New York for their scheme. Back on Hatteras they called the Hatteras Convention on November 18, 1861. The delegates assembled with due solemnity, supported by local and military authorities. The hall was filled to less than capacity, as but six or eight delegates appeared. Foster had prepared for this by collecting proxies while he was in Washington and New York. The proxies were signed by individuals, in most cases, who had once lived in the state. The Convention claimed to represent forty-five counties.[45]

A sample proxy from New York appeared thus:

Lima, N.Y. November 15, 1861.

Dear Sir:—I address you this line to request you to represent the Union men of Onslow County, North Carolina, in the State convention to organize a provincial government, having once been a resident of the county and knowing something of the feeling there existing.
Rev. M.N. Taylor   I am, respectively
                                                        J.W. BAILEY[46]

The first business of the Convention was to proclaim Marble Nash Taylor the new governor of the state, and the next was to declare the Ordinance of Secession null and void. After being sworn in by a Justice of the Peace, Governor Taylor proclaimed an election for the Second Congressional District on November 28. The new governor, using his new state seal, began to churn out a flood of documents concerning the idealistic aims of his government. On election day none other than Charles Henry Foster received all of the 268 votes cast, all on Hatteras Island. The second district at that time contained more than nine thousand voters. The convention and the election garnered much publicity: acclaim by the press in the North and scorn in the South.

Representative Foster steamed north with his certificate of election signed and sealed by Governor Taylor, to claim a seat in the Thirty-Seventh Congress. The Committee on Elections and the Congress at large rejected his claim. The pair tried again with another election on January 30, 1862, with the same results. Neither Foster nor Taylor was recognized by the United States government.[47]

Taylor remained on the island for some time before moving back to the mainland. He was probably a well-intentioned man, though ineffectual. He sank into obscurity where he blended well. Foster went back North to rethink his strategy. He remained determined to promote himself somehow during the war, either by civil or military means. When the relief schooner arrived, according to historian Evert A. Duyckinct, most of the Hatterasers who needed help had jobs working for the Union forces. The supplies not distributed were sold and the money returned to the donors.

During the summer and fall of 1861 recruiting continued in the eastern counties for Confederate regiments. Some of the Bankers of the three islands crossed the sound to enlist. Companies B, F, and H of the newly organized Thirty-Third North Carolina were assembling and recruiting in Hyde County. In mid–October some thirty Ocracokers crossed over and enlisted. Included were a half-dozen boys under the age of eighteen. A few Ocracokers living in Forsythe County came back to Hyde County to enlist.[48]

Some Portsmouthers enlisted, also, in those early weeks, though they are harder to identify than their Ocracoke neighbors. With the dispersal of all its inhabitants, any Portsmouth family history has become diffused and diluted. It is known, however, that one prominent Portsmouth resident lost no time in joining the Confederacy. Doctor Spiers Singleton, Superintendent of the Marine Hospital, left with his wife and three small children for the mainland. He accepted a commission as surgeon of the Thirty-Sixth North Carolina and served all through the war at Fort Fisher.[49] A comparison of the census rolls of military-age Portsmouthers with the rosters listed in Manarin yields matching names of probable Confederates.

Hatteras Island, like Ocracoke and Portsmouth, furnished young men for the Confederate Army and Navy. The same comparison of the troop rosters in *N.C. Regiments* and the 1860 census rolls matches some of the names. There are fewer names of Hatteras men so listed than there are for Ocracoke in spite of Hatteras having a larger population. This may indicate more Union sentiment at Hatteras, or it may just indicate an incomplete listing. No central roster for the Confederate Navy has been compiled, so the Bankers who joined the Navy are difficult to identify. A few men are shown in the Confederate Army rosters as having transferred to the Confederate Navy. Since many of the Bankers were seamen, it seems probable that more would volunteer for the sea service than the army. These are included in the appendix with those from Ocracoke. (The appended rosters are not complete for either service nor for either side.)

On the other side men from the three islands did join the Union Army and Navy. Federal naval officers made efforts to hire local men as civilian pilots, but only a few can be identified individually. Hatteras furnished more soldiers for the Union than the other islands, possibly because it was occupied first and recruiting was more intensive. After all, Rush Hawkins did predict that one-third of the state would come back in the Union if a Union convention were called, and they would "take up arms to defend themselves if necessary." The lists of Union soldiers from the three islands shown in the appendices were compiled from the roster of the First North Carolina Union Volunteer Regiment.

The year ended quietly on the Sand Banks, both on the battle front and on the political front. The new year, however, would bring further stringent action to the coast.

Chapter Five

Burnside and Roanoke Island

"I WILL INVITE YOUR SPECIAL attention to Roanoke Island." These words were written by the Governor of North Carolina in a letter to President Jefferson Davis on December 16, 1861.

The thought was echoed up north by Major-General George B. McClellan in his instructions to Brigadier-General Ambrose E. Burnside. Burnside, who had been one of the successful Federal regimental commanders at the first battle of Bull Run, had been promoted and given command of a new division being formed to exploit the Union toehold in North Carolina. McClellan's orders stated, "Your first point of attack will be Roanoke Island and its dependencies."[1] Brigadier-General Burnside, a large man, nearly bald, with soulful eyes and serious side whiskers, was both serious and able in his work. He set about organizing and training his regiments. He had plenty of good volunteers to form his division and sufficient money to buy equipment.

When Governor Ellis died a few weeks before the battle of Hatteras, Speaker of the Senate Henry T. Clark succeeded him in office and inherited the problem of the Federal occupation of Hatteras. His letter to President Davis continued. "The possession of Hatteras affords the enemy a position or nucleus to form expeditions, almost without observation, to radiate to different points, even in opposite directions." The new governor believed that fifteen thousand men were insufficient to guard all the other towns, rivers, and sounds since Hatteras was lost. "I must urge the fortification of Roanoke Island to defend one-half of the exposed territory."[2]

D.H. Hill, the previous October, had made a similar report. "I fear for Roanoke Island. That place and this [written at Fort Macon] are the weak points in my department. Two more regiments should immediately be sent to Roanoke Island, and one with a battery to Shackleford Banks." He ordered the lower fort on the island moved so that it could cooperate with the other two, as well as ordering other extensive earthworks.[3]

Roanoke Island spreads itself in the center of the grand confluence of Pamlico and Albemarle sounds, controlling the maritime traffic between them. To the east lies Croatan Sound, between Roanoke Island and Bodie Island. It is narrow and shallow, but open to small vessels. On the west is Roanoke Sound, separating Roanoke Island from the mainland. This is wider and contains the main ship channel between Pamlico Sound to the south and Albemarle Sound to the north. The island is hourglass-shaped, pinched in at the waist by Shallowbag Bay on the east side. The southern half is swampy,

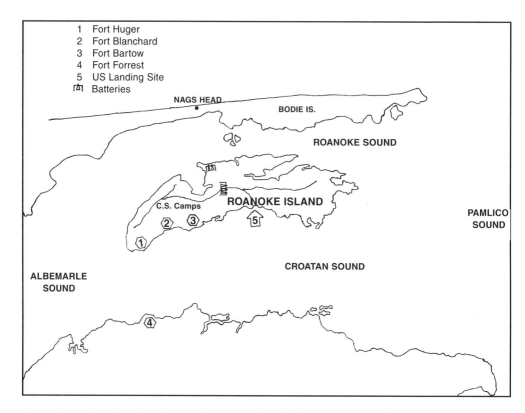

1   Fort Huger
2   Fort Blanchard
3   Fort Bartow
4   Fort Forrest
5   US Landing Site
     Batteries

NAGS HEAD

BODIE IS.

ROANOKE SOUND

C.S. Camps   ROANOKE ISLAND

PAMLICO
SOUND

CROATAN SOUND

ALBEMARLE
SOUND

Map of Roanoke Island showing the location of the island's many forts and batteries. Sketched from North Carolina DOT map of Dare County and John K. Burlingame, *History of the Fifth Regiment of Rhode Island Heavy Artillery* (Providence: Snow & Farnham, 1892), 20.

but with a ridge of higher ground running along its spine, the route of the main road, running north to south on a causeway. The southern half was unfortified. No overall plan of forts and batteries was made. Successive commanders built them where they thought best.

The first formed troops on the island were the two companies of the Seventeenth N.C. who had eluded capture after the battle of Hatteras, plus a few individual soldiers who had escaped. Colonel A.R. "Ranse" Wright and his 3rd Georgia, re-assigned from Hatteras, came next in the last days of August. The Eighth Regiment of North Carolina State Troops, Colonel Henry M. Shaw, was mustered at Camp Macon near Warrenton. This regiment was ordered to Roanoke Island, left camp on September 18 and arrived at the island on September 21, changing from state to Confederate service while en route. The men began to work on fortifications and barracks, dig wells, and drill. They participated in the unsuccessful second phase of the Chicamacomico Races, then returned to the work details. In late October Company H garrisoned Battery Huger, while the other nine companies remained in camp near Fort Bartow. Some of the ten companies of the Eighth bore their special names. Company B, raised in nearby Currituck County were the Shaw Guards. Company E from Cumberland County selected Manchester Guards and Company G, mustered in Pitt County chose General Bragg Guards.[4]

In early December General Huger summoned the Third Georgia Regiment back to Norfolk. To replace them, the state sent the Thirty-first North Carolina Regiment, Colonel John V. Jordan. This regiment was mustered at Fort Hill on the Pamlico River below Washington. When ordered to Roanoke Island it was half-trained, dressed in part uniform and part civilian clothing, and armed with the scrapings of the state's arsenals. The regiment marched to Plymouth where it boarded transports on December 10 and arrived at Roanoke Island on December 12. Here the men joined the men of the 8th in building barracks and fortifications, and driving piling and filling schooners with sand to block the ship channel in Croatan Sound. The Thirty-first included only one company with a special name listed. Company I from Harnett County was labeled the Cape Fear Boys.[5]

More help was coming. On December 21, 1861, Brigadier-General Henry A. Wise was assigned the command of the military district in North Carolina lying east of the Chowan River and the counties of Washington and Tyrrell. General Wise arrived at Roanoke Island on January 6, 1862, where he immediately began inspecting the works and conferring with his subordinates. He busied himself expediting the arrival of his Legion, which was supposed to be rushing to join him.[6]

General Wise, both able and energetic, was in almost perpetual motion for the following month. He inspected Roanoke Island minutely, crossed Roanoke Sound to Bodie Island where he selected Nags Head as his headquarters because Roanoke Island had no suitable building. The hotel at Nags Head did suit him. He inspected the shores of Currituck Sound, the Albemarle and Chesapeake Canal, and the route to Norfolk. When he was not inspecting he was corresponding. His after-action report, including copies of letters, would be 143 pages long (General Huger's count).[7] There was much that the general felt was needed besides his regiments. Rations, ammunition, and ordnance stores ordered by Colonel Shaw had not been sent, so Wise tried to expedite those items with additional requisitions of his own. He needed a small steamer for his own use, but Norfolk headquarters could not furnish a vessel. In one instance, Wise and Flag Officer Lynch of the Confederate Navy were bidding against each other for a steam tug belonging to the Albemarle and Chesapeake Canal Company. The Navy got the tug.

Wise ordered timber and pilings for docks and fortifications. He needed pile drivers to build a dock and wharf and to obstruct the channel through Croatan Sound. He needed a steam dredge to build batteries in the marsh on the mainland side of Croatan Sound, and he needed axes, spades, shovels, and hoes. He asked the War Department in Richmond to supply field guns, caissons, and horses as well as artillerymen. General Wise took the steam cars from Norfolk to Richmond to hurry along his own regiments and to harass the War Department into filling his requisitions. The Secretary of War agreed to do what he could and ordered Wise back to Roanoke Island.[8]

Wise believed the need for his full legion was imperative. He had little confidence in the two North Carolina regiments on the island, nor in the Mosquito Fleet. He described them:

> The infantry were undrilled, unpaid, not sufficiently clothed and quar-
> tered, and were miserably armed with old flint muskets in bad order. In a
> word, the defenses were a sad farce of ignorance and neglect combined,
> inexcusable in any or all who were responsible for them.
> Captain Lynch was energetic, zealous, and active, but he gave too much
> consequence entirely to his fleet of gunboats, which hindered transporta-
> tion of piles, lumber, forage, supplies of all kinds, and of troops, by taking
> away the steam-tugs and converting them into perfectly imbecile gun-
> boats.[9]

While General Wise was recording his displeasure with his North Carolina regiments and expressing his ire because Flag Officer Lynch would not let him have a
steam tug, rumors and reports of a Yankee expedition to the Banks were proving true.

Brigadier-General Burnside, before the war, had been both a friend and business
associate of the new General-in-Chief, George B. McClellan. Therefore, when Burnside
presented his plan for organizing a Coast Division it was quickly approved by General
McClellan and the Federal War Department. It was to be manned and equipped "so
that it could be rapidly thrown from point to point on the coast with a view to estab-
lishing lodgments on the Southern coast."[10] There was one major difference between
Burnside and his old buddy McClellan. Burnside would fight, while McClellan would
maneuver. Burnside was far ahead of Wise in his preparations. Before the first of Wise's
own regiments had arrived, the Burnside expedition has sailed for Hatteras. Burnside
had, of course, started much earlier, and received more help from his superiors.

On October 23, 1861, Burnside established his headquarters at Annapolis, Maryland where he commenced organizing and training his regiments as they arrived.
When the drill and discipline of the troops were far enough advanced that they could
be left to his subordinate officers, Burnside went to New York to fit out his fleet. There
was much competition and difficulty in procuring enough steam boats and other vessels, all of light draft.

> It was a motley fleet. North River barges and propellers had been strength-
> ened from deck to keelson by heavy oak planks, and water-tight compart-
> ments had been built in them: they were so arranged that parapets of sand
> bags or bales of hay could be built on their decks, and each one carried
> from four to six guns. Sailing vessels, formerly belonging to the coasting
> trade, had been fitted up in the same manner. Several large passenger
> steamers, which were guaranteed to draw less than eight feet of water,
> together with tug and ferry boats, served to make up the fleet, which gave
> a capacity to transport 15,000 troops, with baggage, camp equipage,
> rations, etc.[11]

Burnside also chartered store ships, transports, and coal and water vessels. The
ships were ordered to rendezvous at Fort Monroe except the transports, which were
sent to Annapolis harbor, where they arrived "after most mortifying and vexatious
delays" on January 4, 1862. The troops embarked on January 5, and sailed on the ninth
for Chesapeake Bay where they joined the other vessels.

The combined fleet of more than eighty ships sailed for Hatteras Inlet where they would join the naval vessels already on station. General Burnside's headquarters and staff were aboard the large steamer *George Peabody*, but he transferred to the army steamer *Picket*, the smallest vessel in the fleet. She was a fast and handy little ship of humble origin, and though her qualities were useful in a command ship, Burnside selected her for public relations reasons. Both President Lincoln and General McClellan had been warned that his ships were unfit for the sea, so Burnside chose the smallest to confound the critics and to encourage his soldiers during the rough weather ahead. His plan worked and his men admired him for it.

The weather worsened. A gale blew up as the fleet rounded Cape Hatteras. Everything loose on the *Picket*'s deck washed away and furniture and crockery were smashed below decks. The next night the wind again rose, "and within a short time it increased to a terrible gale…. At times, it seemed as if the waves, which appeared to us mountain high, would ingulf [sic] us, but then the little vessel would ride them and stagger forward in her course."[12] The terrible weather continued on through the rest of January.

Both naval and army vessels anchored or stood off in the crowded roadstead outside the outer bar waiting for the gale to subside before attempting to enter the inlet. The large army transport, *City of New York*, loaded with supplies and ordnance, grounded on the outer bar and was a total loss. Her crew clung to the rigging all night and were rescued next morning. The army gunboat *Zouave* ran afoul of her anchor and sank, but with no loss of life. The army steamer *Pocahontas* went ashore above the Cape, with her crew saved, but only nineteen of her load of 103 horses rescued.[13]

By January 18 all of the Navy's ships had crossed the bar and the swash, though with many groundings, and were in the sound harbor in the bight of Hatteras Island. On January 19 the first of the army's ships, the *Picket*, carrying General Burnside, crossed the swash towing a schooner loaded with troops. Burnside's vessels, one by one, came through, often towed by naval ships.

The storm-tossed soldiers waiting their turn told their own stories. The Twenty-Fourth Massachusetts Regiment sailed aboard the steamers *Guide* and *Vidette*. The regiment's history claims that "no description was ever able to do justice to the tribulation through which the cooped-up soldiers on board those creaking vessels had to pass." Further, "if officers and men had concluded that Neptune himself had made a hard and fast contract with the Confederacy to do all in his power to render useless the efforts of General Burnside and his followers … there was reason in their thoughts." Burnside, they said, was nearly ubiquitous, constantly checking his ships in the little *Picket*, through and around the fleet at anchor. They thought "Burnside a name to conjure with among all who participated in this expedition."

The *Vidette* entered first on the 19th, grounded on a shoal, and was tugged through the following day. The larger *Guide* stuck fast, had to jettison her coal, and did not reach harbor until January 26. The soldiers landed to regain their land-legs, to drill and to form for inspections. One company, quite against orders, killed and cooked some "starveling sheep." They were caught and pled that it was done as a kindness to the poor starving animals.[14]

The Fifth Rhode Island Heavy Artillery Regiment, aboard the large transport *Kitty Simpson*, had problems from the start. The men, mostly seasick, had to help throw seventy tons of ballast overboard when it was realized that the ship drew fourteen feet of water. Even so, when she started through, towed by the propeller *Virginia*, she struck bottom, the tow hawser broke, and the ship lay pounding on the bar. Several more tugs came, but *Kitty Simpson* was immovable. The tide ebbed, further efforts were deferred until the next high tide when the pounding began again. The situation looked solemn, one man said, as the wreck of the *New York* was only a hundred yards away. "It seemed like being deathly sick with a grave-yard right under the window." Another steamer came to try to take off the men, but the sea was too rough to transfer them. Up steamed Burnside in the *Picket*. The general ended an argument between the two ship captains, ordered the steamer to pass a tow line and to try again.

Even after the Fifth Rhode Island crossed the swash and anchored inside, the regiment's troubles did not end. Measles broke out among the close packed troops. The surgeon immediately removed five sick soldiers to the hospital ship. The disease did not spread, but one man died.[15]

Water was short on many of the ships during those long, stormy days and awnings and sails were spread during rain storms to catch more. The troops of the Twenty-seventh Massachusetts ran short of rations, too. The men ate raw salt pork and hardtack, except some clever but unknown soldiers who managed to find and devour the brigade commander's cabin stores. General Foster was quoted as saying that he hoped the regiment made as clean work of the Rebels as they had of his supplies.

The regiment's two vessels, the *Pilot Boy* and the *Ranger* passed the swash on January 20 and 22. The *Pilot Boy* was infested with lice below decks, and soon everyone was. There was no water to wash clothes. During the next period of sunshine, the top decks were covered with naked men, their clothes turned wrong side out, skirmishing through the seams with lice.[16]

The Confederates were aware of the gathering invaders. From time to time, ships of the Mosquito Fleet approached closely enough to count the vessels inside the inlet and to exchange long range gunfire before skedaddling away. Civilians knew about them, too. The *Newbern Daily Progress* on January 18 reported that although the editor had not believed the expedition was a serious menace to the coast, he was now a believer. "We have at last, after several day's painful suspense, learned something definite.... Capt. Salyer in command of the steamer *Johnson* ... reports positively that 42 gun-boats and 2 sailing vessels were in the harbor at Hatteras." On January 25 the *Progress* ran an article titled "An attack thought to be certain." After learning more about the storms and the shipwrecks, the editor was more optimistic. The January 27 *Progress* lead article was "The Burnside Expedition — A Failure."[17]

As the ships filtered through the inlet during those stormy weeks, a few small craft crossed the sound from the mainland. Some few were fishermen or deserters from the county militias, but most were escaped slaves. Black or white, they were all examined by Union officers. Most of the fishermen declined to serve as pilots, but several of the slaves proved to be very useful as guides. One Negro named Ben and his brother (unnamed in the record) came from Roanoke Island and had much local information of use to the navy. General Burnside also used an intelligent Negro youth named Tom in such a manner. He had somehow crossed Oregon Inlet and walked down the island to the Federal camp near the forts. General Williams sent him to General Burnside, who interviewed him at length. Tom described the batteries he had seen, including a strong one in the center of the island. He recommended Ashby's Harbor as a good landing place and said there was a "pretty good road" from Ashby's to the rebel battery. Burnside kept Tom close by and later carried him North.[18]

By the end of January most of the ships were inside, with the navy tugging and towing the last stragglers across the bar and the swash. Considering the ferocity of the storms and the number of small vessels, remarkably few ships or lives were lost. The worst loss of lives occurred because of an unnecessary small boat entry by men from the Ninth New Jersey Regiment. The Colonel, Lieutenant-Colonel, Adjutant, and Surgeon of the regiment, along with the ship's captain, second mate, and six sailors, set out in a very small ship's boat to report their arrival to General Burnside in the *Picket*. They arrived at the *Picket* safely and started back out to their ship. The schooner *Highlander*, towed by the *Hussar* and carrying the Twenty-third Massachusetts Regiment, was just then crossing the bar. Commissary-Sergeant George Driver of the Twenty-third described the incident in a letter. "Just before we went in a number of men were seen apparently standing, sitting and lying in nothing but water. We stopped and three boats … were lowered and sent to them. Eleven men were picked up and put on board. Two were found to be dead although everything was done for them." One of the dead men was the Colonel, who was floating on his back. Sergeant Driver said he was very fat. The other dead man was the Surgeon. The body of the mate was never found. The other nine men recovered. They told Driver that the breakers unshipped their rudder, the boat became unmanageable, capsized and swamped. "It was the saddest night I ever saw in my life and I shall never forget it."[19]

Once inside the harbor, the ships landed the men to recover from their days or weeks battened down. Whether they landed in shifts or all together, there were several thousand of them needing space, water, and firewood. The Twentieth Indiana and Hawkins's Zouaves had been living in tents or in buildings left vacant by departed Hatterasers. There were too many newcomers to move in with the two garrison regiments. The newcomers first drank the islanders' cisterns dry, and then they commenced to tear down the vacant buildings for firewood. One man of the Sixth New Hampshire Regiment, trying in vain to start a campfire, recorded that green live oak and willow burned just as good as ice. They ate up all the sheep and cattle they could capture and might have started on the Banker ponies if they had stayed long enough. Ben Dixon MacNeil says the Hatterasmen who were left, who had signed an Oath of Allegiance in an effort to get along with the invaders, watched in numb silence. The troop's actions, MacNeil claimed, "would evolve a bitter hatred that continued unabated, even down to the year 1936 when the native Southern Methodist churches, seven in number, refused flatly to be reunited with their Northern brethren in the

Methodist Church of the United States."[20] It should be noted that no major crimes were charged against Burnside's men, only the minor ones of foraging for food and harvesting houses for firewood, things soldiers have been known to do before. There were a lot of soldiers and a lot of campfires in the tiny village.

By February 3 the fleet and the army were ready to advance on Roanoke Island. General Wise and the Confederates had been given three weeks grace to prepare. Wise did the best he could.

The first regiment of his Legion arrived in Norfolk on January 15: nine companies, a total of 405 privates plus officers and non-commissioned officers. Wise's First Regiment was also known as the Forty-sixth Regiment of Virginia Volunteers. Some of the companies present were

> Company A — Richmond Light Infantry Blues, Captain O. Jennings Wise, who was General Wise's son. The Blues was an old Virginia militia company.
> The Ben McCulloch Rangers, Captain F.M. Imboden.
> Albemarle Rangers or Albemarle Jackson Avengers, Captain Coles.
> Red Sulphur Yankee Hunters and possibly the Blue Sulphur Yankee Killers.[21]

General Wise continued to hunt for his other regiments. His Third Regiment under Lieutenant-Colonel Wharton J. Greene was summoned from Wilmington, N.C. where it was wintering and recruiting. When Greene notified Brigadier-General J.R. Anderson, commanding, of his orders, Anderson objected and began to delay by correspondence. Wise sent Colonel Charles Frederick Henningsen, commanding his Second Regiment on a mission to the Governor of North Carolina, to present a letter asking for the governor's help. Wise had previously stated that he would be glad to incorporate the "fragments" of the Seventeenth North Carolina in his Legion. The missing Second Regiment, 350 men in eight companies, arrived at Nags Head on January 27. Henningsen himself arrived in Norfolk on January 28, bringing with him one hundred men and six field guns of Wise's artillery. Wise had left orders for them to proceed at once down the seashore route to Nags Head, by the "land bridge" as he called it. This was the shortest route, depending on the weather and Yankee gunboats. General Huger thought it was unsafe and sent the artillery by land to Powell's Point, from whence they would cross to Roanoke Island by ferry. Wise was infuriated at Huger's interference. The artillery finally joined Wise at Currituck Court House eight days after the battle. The lagging Third Regiment did but little better, landing on Roanoke Island on the very day of battle, too late to help. Wise continued his frantic efforts until February 1 when he was stricken. "I was seized with a violent and acute attack of pleurisy, with high fever and spitting of blood, threatening pneumonia." He was confined to bed at Nags Head, leaving Colonel Shaw in command on the island.[22]

The fortifications on Roanoke Island had begun six months earlier, in June of 1861, when General Gwynn had D.S. Walton commissioned as an engineering officer and left him in charge of erecting batteries at Oregon Inlet and Roanoke Island. Each senior officer since then had added his own accretions. Colonel A.R. Wright built the only inland fortification, the three-gun battery commanding the road along the cause-way. This was the only fortified part of the continuous line recommended by D.H. Hill. This battery contained the only mobile field artillery on the island: a heavy brass 18-pounder, a Mexican War relic, a 24-pounder boat howitzer, and a 6-pounder boat gun. Only the 6-pounder had proper ammunition. The larger guns had to make do with 12-pounder ammunition. General Wise assigned three officers to instruct the men of the Thirty-first Regiment in gunnery. Wright also built the two gun earthwork facing Roanoke Sound. General Wise commenced to build a battery across Croatan Sound in the marsh near the entrance to the channel. High water and lack of a steam dredge prevented its completion. As most of the works were coastal anti-gunboat batteries, a naval officer's view of them is most apt.

Captain William Harwar Parker in the gunboat *Beaufort* joined the Mosquito Fleet in mid–January and examined the batteries:

> Three forts had been constructed on the island to protect the channel. The upper one was on Weir's Point and was named Fort Huger. It mounted twelve guns, principally 32-pounders of 33 cwt., and was commanded by Major John Taylor, formerly of the Navy. About 1¾ miles below, on Pork Point, was Fort Bartow; it mounted seven guns, five of which were 32-pounders of 33 cwt., and two were rifled 32-pounders [actually eight guns]. This fort, which was the only one subsequently engaged in the defense, was in charge of Lieutenant B.P. Loyall, of the Navy. Between these two points was a small battery. On the mainland opposite the island, at Redstone Point, was a battery called Fort Forrest. The guns, which were 32-pounders, were mounted on the deck of a canal-boat which had been hauled up in the mud and placed so the guns would command the channel. The channel itself was obstructed a little above Fort Huger by piling.... The fortifications and vessels should have been at the "marshes" a few miles below, where the channel is very narrow...[23]

The ships of the squadron in which Parker served, commanded by Commodore Lynch were

Seabird, Captain McCarrick, Flagship,
Curlew, Captain Hunter,
Ellis, Captain Cook,
Appomattox, Captain Sims,
Beaufort, Captain Parker,
Raleigh, Captain Alexander,
Fanny, Captain Tayloe,
Forrest, Captain Hoole,
Black Warrior, Lieutenant Harris, schooner.

Each vessel mounted one 32-pounder rifle except the *Seabird*, which had a 32-pounder smoothbore forward and a 30-pounder Parrot rifle aft. As Parker counted, there were eight vessels with nine guns to oppose the whole Federal fleet.

That fleet was ready and the Federal army was, too. Their plans were complete. The soldiers marched back aboard the gunboats and transports. The naval ships were not the big steam frigates and sloops that had attacked the Hatteras forts, but smaller vessels that could navigate the shallow sounds, and could still carry heavy ordnance, heavier than those of Lynch's squadron. They were:

Philadelphia (Flag steamer) 500 tons, 2 12-pdr. rifles,

Delaware (Cmdr. Rowan) 357 tons, 4 32-pdrs., 1 12-pdr. rifle,

Stars and Stripes 407 tons, 4 8-inch Dahlgren smoothbores, 1 20-pdr. rifle, 1 12-pdr. rifle,

Louisiana 295 tons, 1 8-inch Dahl., 2 32-pdrs., 1 12-pdr. rifle,

Hetzel 200 tons, 1 9-inch Dahl., 1 80-pdr. rifle,

Valley City 190 tons, 4 32-pdr. SB, 1 12-pdr. rifle,

Underwriter 341 tons, 1 8-inch Dahl., 1 80-pdr. rifle,

Commodore Perry 512 tons, 2 9-inch Dahl., 2 32-pdr SB, 1 12-pdr. howitzer,

Commodore Barney 512 tons, 3 9-inch Dahl., 1 100-pdr. rifle,

Southfield 781 tons, 3 9-inch Dahl., 1 100-pdr. rifle,

Hunchback 518 tons, 3 9-inch Dahl., 1 100-pdr. rifle,

Morse, 513 tons, 2 9-inch Dahlgrens,

Lockwood 180 tons, 1 80-pdr. rifle, 1 12-pdr. rifle, 1 12-pdr. howitzer,

Ceres 150 tons, 1 32-pdr. SB, 1 30-pdr. rifle,

Putnam 149 tons, 1 32-pdr. SB, 1 20-pdr. rifle,

Seymore 140 tons, 1 30-pdr. rifle, 1 12-pdr. rifle,

Whitehead 139 tons, 1 9-inch Dahlgren,

Henry Brinker 108 tons, 1 30-pdr. rifle,

Shawsheen 180 tons, 2 20-pdr. rifles,

Granite (sailing sloop) 75 tons, 1 32-pdr. rifle.

The ships carried altogether twenty-one 8 & 9 inch smoothbore guns, twelve 32-pdr. (6.4 inch) guns, eleven rifled guns of 30 to 100-pounders, and ten smaller rifles from 12- to 20-pounders.[24]

Those were the naval vessels, plus chartered supply ships and colliers. There were also the army's vessels, the ones General Burnside had bought or chartered in New York. There were

Steam propeller gunboats

Chasseur 330 tons, 2 12-pdr. rifles

Zouave 200 tons, 1 30-pdr. Parrott rifle, 2 12-pdr. fieldpieces, rifled

Vidette 275 tons, 1 30-pdr.Parrott, 2 12-pdr. rifles

Pioneer 338 tons, 1 30-pdr. Parrott, 2 12-pdr. mountain howitzers

Sentinel 312 tons, 1 30-pdr. Parrott, 2 12-pdr. rifles

Picket 200 tons, 1 30-pdr. Parrott, 2 other light guns. This vessel was of less than 200 tons by note.

Ranger 348 tons, 1 30-pdr. Parrott, 2 6-pdr. rifles
Lancer 400 tons, 1 30-pdr. Parrott, 2 6-pdr. rifles
Hussar 350 tons, 1 30-pdr. Parrott, 2 6-pdr. rifles.
Bombshell, *Grapeshot*, *Grenade*, *Rocket*, and *Shrapnel* were towed floating batteries armed with 2 to 4 rifled boat guns.[25]

These were the ships assigned to the Regiment of Marine Artillery. The troop transports listed by Burnside were

S.R. Spaulding 400 men,
Guide 700 men,
Cossack 700 men,
Geo. Peabody 800 men,
Northerner 1,000 men,
New Brunswick 700 men,
New York 700 men,
Virginia 500 men,
Eastern Queen 875 men,
Brig Dragoon 300 men.

Additional transports not on Burnside's list were the *Pilot Boy*, *Curlew*, *Eagle*, *Pautuxent*, twenty to thirty schooners and the *Union*.[26] If the soldiers had a favorite ship, she was the *Union*, judging by the number of times she was mentioned in letters and regimental histories. Private Johnson of Hawkins's Zouaves described the *Union*: "The 'Union' is an exceedingly rickety stern-wheeler river steamer, but of very light draught, not drawing more than eighteen inches of water." Johnson explained that the boys of his regiment, not being familiar with such boats re-christened her with a name that stuck. She became known throughout the fleet as the *Wheelbarrow*. When the Zouaves boarded the transports to sail for Roanoke Island, part of them were quartered on the *Virginia*, but he was with the fatigue party and boarded late. "I will sleep aboard the 'Wheelbarrow' tonight," he proudly noted.[27]

Burnside organized his Coast Division into three brigades. The First Brigade, commanded by Brigadier-General John G. Foster included the following regiments:

Tenth Connecticut, Colonel Charles L. Russell,
Twenty-third Massachusetts, Colonel John Kurtz,
Twenty-fourth Massachusetts, Colonel Thomas G. Stevenson,
Twenty-fifth Massachusetts, Colonel Edwin Upton,
Twenty-seventh Massachusetts, Colonel Horace C. Lee.

The Second Brigade, Brigadier-General Jesse L. Reno included:
Twenty-first Massachusetts, Lieutenant-Colonel Alberto C. Maggi,
Ninth New Jersey, Lieutenant-Colonel Charles A. Heckman,

Fifty-first New York, Colonel Edward Ferrero,
Fifty-first Pennsylvania, Colonel John F. Hartranft.

The Third Brigade, Brigadier-General John G. Parke included:
Eighth Connecticut, Colonel Edward Harland,
Ninth New York, Colonel Rush C. Hawkins, and the company of the Ninety-
    ninth New York,
Fifty-third New York, Colonel L.J. D'Epineuil,
Fourth Rhode Island, Colonel I.P. Rodman,
Fifth Rhode Island Battalion, Major John Wright.
The Fifty-third New York was unable to land as its transport, the bark *John
    Trucks*, drew far too much water to enter the harbor. Lieutenant-Colonel
    J.A.V. DeMonteil alone accompanied the brigade.

Williams' Brigade, Brigadier-General Thomas Williams, stayed on Hatteras as
a reserve.
Eleventh Connecticut, Lieutenant-Colonel C. Mathewson,
Sixth New Hampshire, Colonel Nelson Converse,
Eighty-ninth New York, Colonel H.S. Fairchild,
Forty-eighth Pennsylvania, Colonel James Nagle,
First Rhode Island Artillery, Battery F, Captain James Belger,
First U.S. Artillery, Battery C, Captain Lewis O. Morris.[28]
The Regiment of Marine Artillery was not brigaded, as the men were distributed
to the army gunboats.

At 8 A.M. on February 5, the Federal armada sailed. The naval ships took the
lead, steaming in three columns, the army vessels following. After some delay caused
by the army steamer *Spaulding*, the expedition continued. About 5:30 P.M. the fleet
anchored off Stumpy Point, ten miles south of Roanoke Island. Generals Burnside and
Foster took supper with Commodore Goldsborough aboard the flagship. Early the next
morning the fleet again got underway. The commodore, accompanied by General
Burnside shifted his flag to the smaller and handier *Southfield*. The *Ceres* and *Putnam*,
scouting ahead reported they had sighted the enemy, but the fleet had to anchor at
10:40 A.M. because of increasing rain and fog. The fog was still heavy on the morning
of February 7, but dispersed by 9 A.M. when the fleet again steamed ahead. The flagship
hoisted the not entirely original signal "Our country expects every man to do his
duty." A little more than an hour later, one of the forts fired a heavy gun. The flagship
signaled "Steamers with 9-inch guns close up." The battle was joined.[29]
    The first objective of the Federal fleet was to sink or beat back the enemy ships
and to silence the shore batteries in order to clear the way for troop landing. The Confederate plan was to lure the Federal ships into the obstructions and within range of
the upper shore batteries. Hence, the first position of Lynch's squadron was just above
the line of piling and scuttled schooners. As the *Appomattox* had been sent to Edenton
at dawn and the armed schooner took no part in this fight, the Confederate force was

seven ships and eight guns. The battle began at long range. By early afternoon the firing was hot and heavy. Captain Parker in *Beaufort* said the Confederate fire was too rapid and not particularly accurate due to lack of practice. Even so, USS *Hetzel* was struck below the water line and forced to withdraw and repair. CSS *Forrest* was hit, her machinery damaged, and Lieutenant Hoole, her young captain badly wounded. She withdrew. The Confederate battery on Pork Point — Fort Bartow — kept up a constant fire on the Federal ships even though the buildings within and near the fort were burning furiously. At about 4:00 P.M. a heavy shell struck CSS *Curlew*, penetrating her decks and blowing a hole in her bottom. Captain Hunter steamed for shore as fast as he could, hailing the *Beaufort* as he passed. *Curlew* was obviously sinking, so Captain Parker followed to rescue the crew. *Curlew* struck bottom and sank close in front of Fort Forrest, effectively masking the fort's guns so they could fire no more. Parker noted that he could not remove the wreck by burning it for fear of burning the fort's canal boat base. About 4:00 P.M. the remaining five Confederate ships ran closer to the Union fleet, firing as they steamed, but were forced to withdraw. The Union vessels did not take the bait and pursue them into the piling across the channel. Firing continued until sunset, when both sides ceased fire. Several of the Federal ships were low on ammunition, the Confederates were almost completely out of it. For this reason Commodore Lynch sent Captain Parker on the unpleasant mission to notify Colonel Shaw that the squadron was withdrawing to Elizabeth City that night to resupply with ammunition brought from Norfolk through the canal.[30]

Parker was compelled to append a story to his account of the battle about his friend "Tornado" Hunter of the *Curlew*. Hunter himself related that during the fight he discovered he was wearing no trousers. He could not understand it as he distinctly remembered putting them on that morning. Parker replied that he had heard of a fellow being frightened out of his boots, but never out of his trousers.

Burnside had joined the battle. Early in the afternoon, Burnside had sent Lieutenant Andrews of the Ninth New York with a boat's crew from the Fifth Rhode Island to take soundings close inshore at Ashby's Harbor. Andrews, contrary to his orders, started to land when a patrol of the Thirty-first North Carolina under Captain Edward R. Liles of Company B rose from the bulrushes and fired a volley, wounding one man. Andrew's boat's crew returned fire and shoved off with speed. Lieutenant Andrews reported to Burnside that the depth of water was suitable for a landing. Corporal Charles Vail, shot in the jaw, was treated by Surgeon Potter of the Fifth Rhode Island. After the operation he was able to speak. "Damn the Rebels," he first exclaimed, then, "Doctor, my jaw is spoilt for hardtack, isn't it?"[31]

Brigadier-General John G. Foster led the landing party with the First Brigade. Foster spotted an ambush behind the landing of Confederate infantry and guns and sheered off to land a little beyond Ashby's house. The gunboats *Delaware* of the navy and *Picket* of the army volleyed into the woods, flushing the enemy. The Confederates, with a poor team of two horses and two mules hauled and man-handled their three guns back to the redoubt covering the causeway. Colonel Jordan was apparently more concerned with saving his guns than with firing them at the enemy. Foster's landing proceeded according to the plan made in conference with General Burnside. It was an operation finely planned and beautifully executed, worthy of comparison with landing operations of later wars. Each of the brigadier-generals had a fast light-draft steamer towing a long line of some twenty surf-boats packed with men. On a signal the boats cast off the tow lines, and with their residual velocity curved to the shore, prolonging white arcs in the cold green waters. Troop transports followed them to the beach. Less than twenty minutes later, four thousand men were ashore and moving inland.[32]

Burnside and staff landed with the Fourth Rhode Island. Finding Foster gone to bring up the rest of his brigade, Burnside returned to the flagship to coordinate with Commodore Goldsborough. By midnight the entire division was ashore, with the exception of the Twenty-fourth Massachusetts. This regiment, in the steamer *Guide*, was stuck fast on a mudbank and awaiting rescue. Foster returned and with Generals Reno and Parke reconnoitered the landing site and made dispositions for the night.

At daybreak of February 8, the advance up the corduroy road to the center of the island began. The Twenty-fifth Massachusetts led, General Foster with them, and drove in the Confederate pickets. With skirmishers out ahead, the chief body reached the main road and moved along it until the Confederate fort came in view. "The road at this point was a causeway, flanked on each side by an almost impassable marsh, with thick underbrush on either side. In front of the battery the trees were cut down, so as to give a clear sweep of their guns for a distance of 700 yards in front."[33] The key words in Foster's description of the marsh were "almost impassible." Some of the Southerners, too, referred to an "impenetrable swamp." They should have known better, for they lived in the state. Swamps in eastern North Carolina may be tough to traverse, but they are not impenetrable. Foster's next two regiments came up and formed a battle line. The general emplaced six of the boat howitzers that Midshipman Porter's men had dragged along on the causeway. Musketry had grown spiteful, artillery on both sides roared. The Twenty-fifth Massachusetts fired the last of their ammunition, so the Tenth Connecticut passed through them while they re-supplied themselves. The Twenty-third and Twenty-seventh Massachusetts arrived. Foster directed them to form in the swamp on the right of the causeway. Reno's brigade followed. After conferring with Foster, Reno directed them into the swamp on the left — on the Confederate's right. Reno's regiments were the Twenty-first Massachusetts and the Fifty-first New York, followed by the Ninth New Jersey and the Fifty-first Pennsylvania.[34]

Burnside was ashore early, first conferring with Brigadier Parke at the landing. He directed Parke to leave a regiment to guard the north side of the site and a force in Ashby's house. Parke selected the Eighth Connecticut to guard and the Fifth Rhode Island to take the house. Burnside sent Captain D'Wolf of his staff with a boat's crew borrowed from the *Delaware* to reconnoiter the shore line in both directions to discover any possible enemy penetration. The commanding general left the direction of the battle in front to Foster, his senior brigadier, who was performing well, while he directed and coordinated from the rear. As wounded were being sent to the rear, Burnside's brigade surgeon, Dr. William Henry Church, established hospitals in both the Ashby and Hammond houses.[35]

Those Federal regiments were determined. They slogged and sloshed on in water waist deep in places. The soldiers hung their cartridge boxes around their necks and held their rifles high, as Wright's men had done at Chicamacomico. Men were hit and were carried to the rear, but the lines advanced. The Fourth Rhode Island and the Ninth New York followed Reno's brigade to the boat howitzers on the road. The Rhode Islanders waded in behind the Twenty-seventh Massachusetts on the right. Hawkins's Ninth started after them, but were called back by Parke and formed on the causeway by Major Kimball. The situation was changing and Colonel Hawkins was at the head of the regiment in the swamp.

The battle had lasted three and one-half hours when Foster saw that Reno's men, led by the Twenty-fifth Massachusetts, had lapped around the Confederate's right and were charging toward the fort. Parke's lead regiment, the Twenty-third Massachusetts, had reached the other flank. At this point the generals ordered the Ninth New York to charge up the causeway. The Zouaves, bayonets fixed, charged ahead yelling their special battle cry "Zou-Zou!" Reno's men swarmed into the battery from the flank, with the Zouaves only a pace or two after them, leaping over the front. Both regiments claimed to be first. The Confederates rushed out the back of the fort, leaving their dead and wounded behind. Lieutenant Selden, one of Wise's gunners-on-loan, was dead. He had kept the 6-pounder firing furiously until he was shot through the head. Captain Jennings Wise was mortally wounded and carried away by his men. The battle was essentially over.[36]

The Twenty-fourth Massachusetts, tardy through no fault of its own, arrived just as the charge began. The men had been rescued from their mud-bound transport by the *Wheelbarrow*. The first two companies were set to humping ammunition to resupply the leading regiments. The rest of the regiment marched with General Foster straight past the captured battery in pursuit of Reno's regiments and the Confederates. Foster tarried only long enough to send a report to Burnside before marching past Reno who was gathering in the Confederates who were fleeing toward Nags Head. He met Lieutenant-Colonel Fowle of the Thirty-first North Carolina who carried a flag of truce and was sent by Colonel Shaw, commanding officer of the Confederates. Foster marched to the enemy's main camp and received the unconditional surrender of Colonel Shaw. Reno and Parke's men secured the camps and occupied the shore batteries. Hawkins and the Zouaves marched east, capturing more prisoners including Captain Wise and other wounded, and secured the two-gun battery facing Roanoke Sound, whose guns had been turned to fire inland. The garrison of this battery managed to escape across the sound. Wise's third regiment, also known as the Second North Carolina Battalion, under Lieutenant-Colonel Green, landed toward the end of the battle. Suddenly coming upon Federal troops, men of the Twenty-first Massachusetts, Green wheeled his men into line. The two regiments exchanged volleys, each suffering a few casualties, and dropped back to reform. Lieutenant-Colonel Fowle came up and informed Green of the surrender. The great victory was won. Only the tabulation of casualties, prisoners and spoils remained.[37]

Burnside's final report of the battle, dated February 14, noted complete possession of the island, with five forts, thirty-two guns, small arms, much building material and tools, barracks and a large hospital building, and about 2,500 prisoners.[38]

Federal losses were 37 killed, 214 wounded, and 13 missing. Confederate losses were 22 killed, 58 wounded, and 62 missing — probably escaped — plus the prisoners.[39]

Burnside's Acting Medical Director, W.H. Church, established his hospitals in "three unusually large, commodious, and well ventilated buildings erected on the island for hospital purposes," and put a regimental surgeon in charge of each.[40] Surgeon Potter of the Fifth Rhode Island continued to operate his hospital in the Ashby house for some time. The regimental history noted that few supplies or special food for the wounded were available at the time. The book especially cites Surgeon Potter's colored servant named Diggs. Doctor Diggs, as they called him, "showed his ability as caterer and cook." In modern parlance, Diggs was a scrounger, an important and useful, though unofficial, position in any army. He turned up a sack of corn meal and made gruel and johnny cakes. He searched a Confederate camp and brought back cooking utensils and bacon. He arranged to have a soldier assigned to him to shoot a steer. Diggs dressed the animal himself and produced beef tea, beef soup, and roasts. He found two barrels of flour hidden in the swamp. By the second day of his operations, Doctor Diggs had arranged to have five boxes of hard bread and two barrels of steeped coffee sent from the ships. Doctor Diggs' patients ate better than any others on the island, so were doubtless sorry to be moved to the central hospital.[41]

The island was secure, but there was more fighting to be done. The next task was the navy's — to destroy the remnants of the Mosquito Fleet. Commodore Lynch's squadron, five steamers and one schooner, were gathered near the little fort on Cobb's Point, two miles below Elizabeth City. The fort, according to Captain Parker was a wretched affair, with a magazine resembling an African ant-hill, its door fronting on the river. The guns, 32-pounder smoothbores, were so poorly mounted that only one could fire across the river. The other three pointed down the channel only. As the Dismal Swamp Canal was out of order, Captain Hunter sped to Norfolk to get more ammunition and men to repair the lock. The naval officers found Colonel Henningsen of Wise's Legion with six field guns and orders to do his best to defend Elizabeth City.

Henningsen agreed with Parker's view of the fort's worth and tried to improve it. He could obtain only thirty Negro laborers to erect traverses and strengthen the walls. Needing more soldiers, he requested that the militia be called out and was told that seven magistrates had to approve. He obtained all seven requisitions on February 9. Henningsen placed four of his guns in the rear of the battery where he intended to form the militia, and left two in Elizabeth City with his wagon train. He was sent three hundred pounds of powder which he began to make into cartridges. Little time was left.[42]

Having found a few more rounds of ammunition for his guns, Commodore Lynch in the *Seabird*, accompanied by the *Appomattox*, set forth to reconnoiter Roanoke Island. He returned at sunset, having met and been chased by a flotilla of the enemy. Commander Rowan steamed up the Pasquotank River for Elizabeth City, hot after Lynch's vessels. Rowan brought USS *Delaware, Underwriter, Valley City, Louisiana, Hetzel, Lockwood, Seymore, Morse, Shawsheen, Brinker, Perry, Ceres,* and

Whitehead, enough force to carry out his orders to destroy the enemy's gunboats. Rowan anchored for the night ten miles below the city.

Commodore Lynch had formed his gunboats in a line across the river a little above the fort, with the schooner *Black Warrior* moored close to shore opposite the battery. Upon hearing that the enemy had landed a force below the fort, and seeing them steaming upriver, Lynch landed to put the fort in order. Here he met Colonel Henningsen and learned that only seven militiamen were left in the fort. The others had vanished. Lynch sent orders to Lieutenant-Commanding Parker in the *Beaufort* to bring his crew to the fort to man the guns and to send the *Beaufort* on to safety with a skeleton crew. Parker arrived to help the seven militiamen at the fort. Briefly, Parker had enough men to man three guns. When the seven militiamen deserted, Parker's sailors fired two guns only. Lynch was stranded in the fort as a shot had smashed his boat. The Federal squadron came on fast. Rowan, without plentiful ammunition himself, had ordered his captains to ram or board the enemy, and not to depend on gunnery alone. "Dash the enemy" he ordered. The *Commodore Perry* rammed the *Seabird* and sank her. The *Black Warrior* was set on fire, her crew escaped to shore. The *Fanny*'s commander ran her ashore and blew her up. The *Ellis* was boarded and a desperate battle ensued between Lieutenant James W. Cook, cutlass in hand, and the boarders. Cook was wounded by a bayonet thrust and a musket shot. An old shipmate rescued him and sent him to the Federal flagship for treatment. Two Confederate vessels, *Beaufort* and *Appomattox,* escaped destruction in the battle. The *Beaufort* escaped to Norfolk by the canal. *Appomattox* was two inches too wide to pass through the canal locks and had to be burned. The *Forrest,* under repair at Elizabeth City was also burned. Thus died the Mosquito Fleet.[43]

When the Federal ships had passed the battery on their way to the town, Henningsen and his artillerymen marched overland to Elizabeth City, hoping to beat the enemy there. They had spiked the guns in the fort, but hauled Henningsen's horse drawn field artillery with them. They barely won the race. When they arrived at the edge of town, the Union vessels were at the docks. Henningsen's other two guns and his wagons were formed, ready to move. Several prominent citizens asked the colonel for help in burning the town before the enemy entered. He detached Sergeant Scroggs with a detail to assist them. Henningsen ordered the sergeant to catch up and marched off on the Edenton road. The column halted at Newby's Bridge, near Hertford, where the militia had established a guard post. Sergeant Scroggs was captured by Federal soldiers, put in irons and charged as an incendiary.[44]

The Elizabethans of the city had engaged in much discussion about what to do if the Yankees came. A popular view, among some, was to torch the entire city. "Burn the town," they said, "leave nothing for the invaders." From this came the request to Colonel Henningsen for help in ignition. According to the colonel, only two blocks and a few outlying houses were torched. Most of the citizens of "Old Betsey" emulated the Portsmouthers and left town. By carriage, wagon, and on foot they scattered through the countryside to whatever shelter they could find. Some made a miserable march through rain and mud.

Henningsen collected the wagon train of the Fifty-ninth Virginia from near Edenton and conferred with Colonel Moore of the local militia. The militia, he learned, could not be assembled until the enemy was "dangerously near." Then the militiamen delayed until they could move family and property to safety. After that they came out if there were any troops to support them. "Generally the population appear to be very true; there are, of course, some traitors, but far less disloyalty than in Western Virginia." Henningsen mentioned one such rabid Unionist near Elizabeth City who shot one of his men, then barricaded himself in his house. When called upon to surrender himself, the man fired several more times. The house was set afire and an artilleryman shot the man through a window. Henningsen marched on, picking up en route forty men of the Seventeenth North Carolina under Lieutenant Lyons. This was Company E, the Currituck Atlantic Rifles. They had escaped from Fort Oregon before its capture and landed on Roanoke Island. Here they manned one of the coastal batteries during the battle. After the firing ceased, but before the official news of the surrender reached them, Lieutenant John B. Lyon led them out of the fort and into the boats by which they escaped capture again. They had become adept at escaping. They marched with Henningsen to Winton where they formed with Colonel A.R. Wright's Georgians. On February 12 Henningsen reported his arrival in Winton to General Huger in Norfolk. He asked Huger to notify the Federal forces that Sergeant Scroggs was acting under his orders and that he, Henningsen, bore the responsibility for Scroggs' actions.[45]

Commodore Lynch and Captain Parker, with their contingent of sailor-gunners, trudged out of the river battery in the wake of Henningsen's artillerymen. The shipless mariners passed by Elizabeth City at noon without capture and began to feel safe. Lynch found a horse and galloped ahead to report to Norfolk. Parker organized transportation and had his men mounted in country wagons. They passed the smoking ruins of the house where the Unionist had fired on Henningsen's column. The scenes along the road were distressing yet sometimes comical, said Parker, though he did not describe anything comical. He reported, "the kindness and hospitality of the people along the route was unbounded." They were fed supper by a gentleman in the vicinity, all 150 of them, and quartered in his house and barn. They were waited on by refugee-ladies from Elizabeth City. "To supply us all was no light tax," he wrote.

They started again at 3:00 A.M., breakfasted at a tavern whose owner would take no pay, and continued on the road. They caught up with Commodore Lynch at 3:00 P.M. They took refreshments, rested an hour, and arrived in Suffolk, Virginia at 9:00 P.M. From there they took a special train to Norfolk where Parker reported on the battle of Elizabeth City and learned that the *Beaufort* had arrived safely. Lynch, having taken a wrong road, arrived next day.[46]

On Roanoke Island, after the fighting ended and the prisoners were rounded up, conversation and fraternization began between captors and captives. The men of the Twenty-fourth Massachusetts, clad in their neat, serviceable, blue uniforms expressed surprise at the mixed clothing of the Confederates, homespun and mill-knit, civilian and military. Only two companies, Private Lyon wrote home, were well uniformed; the

McColloch Rangers and the Richmond Blues. Lyon noted that most of the prisoners were sociable and entered into amusements together with the New Englanders. They said the Yankees were not as bad a people as they expected, although the Virginia soldiers spoke harshly of the North. All of the Union men who wanted them found souvenirs to send home, dirks, daggers, or knives stamped "Yankee Slayer." They also enjoyed foraging.[47]

The other regiments foraged, too. The record of the Twenty-seventh Massachusetts stated: "About noon, the 9th, permission was given the entire force to forage for the remainder of the day. With rifles in hand the troops invaded the remotest parts of the island, the Minie balls chi-ie-ing from every direction, rendering life about as uncertain as the contest of the previous day." The men returned that afternoon, shouting "Hurrah" and staggering under loads of carcasses of beef, pork, veal, and mutton: with squawking turkeys, geese, ducks, and chickens, and with sweet potatoes, other root crops, and vegetables dug up from winter store and bagged in overcoats. "It was a scene for an epicure," the record said.[48] One lieutenant of the Eighth North Carolina expressed joy at the slaughter of all the livestock, as he thought the inhabitants deserved it for acting as pilots and spies for the Yankees.[49] There were some Unionists on the island, but most did as the Hatterasers had done, whatever they could, to continue to live with swarms of enemy soldiers on their island.

Life was not all souvenir hunting and banqueting for Burnside's men after the battle. There was still work to be done cleaning up the island. Various expeditions set forth to the surrounding territory, by both the army and the navy. The first such sortie occurred on February 9, foraging day, when Burnside sent Rush Hawkins with a part of his regiment to capture Nags Head. Here, Hawkins learned that General Wise, still sick in bed, had withdrawn with his few men to Currituck Court House. Wise's men had burned the headquarters hotel, some warehouses, and a few private houses. Hawkins damned Wise as a "Vandal and Barbarian."[50]

The next expedition was the navy's, when on February 11 Lieutenant A. Murray, commanding USS *Louisiana* and three other gunboats, proceeded to Edenton. A few Confederate troops quickly left town, followed by most of the inhabitants. Murray's men landed to destroy eight antique cannon and to burn a schooner on the stocks. They remained two hours, talked to some inhabitants who claimed to be Unionist, and left after loading six bales of cotton found on the customshouse wharf. The flotilla captured two schooners in the sound, one laden with four thousand bushels of corn. The navy then steamed north to block the entrance to the Albemarle and Chesapeake Canal. Lieutenant Commanding William N. Jeffers led in the *Lockwood*, along with the *Shawsheen* and *Whitehead* and two towed schooners. Two steamers and three schooners were visible up the canal, but the Confederates had already blocked the entrance. A Confederate picket fired muskets as a signal, so the *Whitehead* returned the courtesy with her 9-inch gun, whereupon the Confederates, ships and soldiers, left. The obstructions consisted of piling and a just-scuttled, large dredge. Jeffers added his two schooners to the bottom of the canal, captured some axes, canteens, and clothing and returned to his station in the mouth of the North River.[51]

It became the army's turn for a trip. The Fifth Rhode Island Regiment in the good old *Wheelbarrow*, escorted by a detachment of the fleet under Captain Jeffers steamed up Currituck Sound to destroy a reported salt works. They entered a channel so shallow and so narrow that even the *Wheelbarrow* could not traverse it. The vessel stuck, her bow in the bushes on one bank, her stern wheel throwing up gobs of mud on the other. Using anchors, cables, and winch, they turned her around and anchored in the sound for the night, the salt works unfound. On the way back to Roanoke the expedition landed to capture a small schooner and to buy some chickens and eggs. Flushed with success, they returned.[52]

On the same day, February 18, Colonel Rush Hawkins and his Zouaves sailed on a joint expedition with the navy. They embarked on the *Hunchback* and *Barney* and proceeded to a rendezvous with Commander S.C. Rowan off Edenton. Rowan had risen to command of the Federal flotilla when Flag Officer Goldsborough was appointed the commander of the North Atlantic Blockading Squadron. Hawkins joined Rowan aboard the *Delaware*, and together with the *Commodore Perry*, they steamed, full speed, past Edenton, far up the Chowan River toward Winton, followed by the *Louisiana*, *Morse*, *Hunchback*, *Whitehead*, *Barney*, and *Lockwood*. The reconnaissance was to verify reports of men loyal to the Union under arms at Winton and to seek and destroy two railroad bridges above Winton. The voyage became more than a reconnaissance.

The town was hidden behind a high bluff, covered with trees, but a wharf and some houses were visible. Standing on the landing was a mulatto woman waving a handkerchief. Expecting no danger, the *Delaware* slowed to approach the dock. Colonel Hawkins, who had appointed himself lookout, was perched in the crosstrees of the vessel's foremast. Hawkins saw the glint of musket barrels atop the bluff and two pieces of artillery. He immediately yelled to the helmsman, "Ring on, sheer off, rebels on shore!" The men under arms were loyal to the Confederacy. They opened a rapid fire. Hawkins described his descent of the mast as "rapid and not graceful." The volleys of musketry hit the *Delaware* 125 times, though the artillery overshot. The ship was too close under the bluff for her guns to bear on the enemy, but the *Perry* fired shrapnel shell at them. *Delaware* twisted and turned to extricate herself from the narrow river and steamed full ahead downstream, firing as her guns bore on possible targets. The two ships anchored seven miles below the town. Not a man on the ships was injured, only Hawkins's dignity, which may have had some effect on his actions that followed. Rowan and Hawkins decided to return to Winton the next day.

The Confederate troops who surprised the expedition were the First Battalion of North Carolina Volunteers supported by Nichols's Battery of artillery, both commanded by Lieutenant-Colonel William T. Williams. In Winton soldiers and civilians celebrated the victory.[53]

By the dawn's early light, Commander Rowan's first two ships, with the others of his squadron closed up, steamed back up to Winton. The leading vessels fired shrapnel shells on the shore and bluff to cover the landing of Hawkins's troops and two boat howitzers from the navy. Colonel William's Confederates retreated at first sight of the

Federal regiment. They crossed Potecasi Creek and did not stop until they reached Mt. Tabor Church five miles from Winton. Hawkins and his men marched unopposed into the town, where Hawkins personally inspected the buildings. He noted that many of them contained much military property left behind by the Rebels and all of the houses had been occupied by them. Then he burned the town — all twenty houses and the courthouse.[54]

Hawkins attempted to justify his action in his official report to Brigadier-General Parke. Colonel Hawkins found and interviewed the woman who had waved from the dock. She was Martha Keen, a resident married to a brickmason. She probably saved her own life by baffling Hawkins during her interrogation and convincing him she was the slave of a Confederate officer. He tried to quote her exactly, both words and accent in his report: "'Dey said dat dey wan't goin' to let anybody lib at all, but was goin' to kill ebery one of 'em.' I infer from this," Hawkins reported, "that we were to receive no quarter." Secondly, Hawkins said the Rebels used all the buildings "for the purpose of subverting the Constitution and the laws of the United States." This was the first time, he claimed, "on our side where fire has accompanied the sword."[55]

Hawkins had no mercy on Winton. He had barrels of tar rolled into the courthouse and set afire as his men torched the rest. The few inhabitants left took to the woods. Hawkins's men looted everything that was not burning. Southern reaction to the "vile incendiary" was predictable, and reports of it spread to the North where the action brought disapproval. One New York newspaper had started a collection to strike a medal for the Zouaves, honoring their bayonet charge at Roanoke Island. Contributions ceased, the men never got their medals, but the money already collected was used to buy Hawkins a sword for his war service. On the Confederate side, Colonel Williams' conduct was disapproved, and he was released from further service in 1863.[56] The railroad bridges dismissed as unreachable, Hawkins's soldiers returned to Roanoke Island and the ships to the sounds.

Another Federal tentacle was extended to probe the Scuppernong River in Tyrrell County. Part of the Sixth New Hampshire Regiment, just arrived at Roanoke Island, embarked on the gunboats to look for a Confederate regiment rumored to be forming in the village of Columbia. No Confederate troops were found, but the troops destroyed some public property and searched public offices. They also found liquor in abandoned houses. Every smokehouse in the town was ransacked.[57] The raiders returned to Roanoke Island feeling rather high on the hog.

In addition to commanding a large military force, General Burnside became increasingly involved in the civil affairs of the expanding territory he controlled. He administered the Oath of Allegiance to many of the Roanoke Islanders, and assumed responsibility for the growing number of escaped slaves who fled to the Union lines. Black people, often with their families, had begun arriving soon after the Federal victory at Hatteras. The numbers multiplied on Roanoke Island. The general appointed Vincent Colyer of New York, a member of his staff, to take charge of them.[58]

Colyer wrote that he began his work "with the free people of color in North Carolina" soon after the battle. He noted that a party of fifteen to twenty arrived from up the Chowan River when he first took the job. By late spring there were a thousand free Negroes in the vicinity. Colyer put all the able-bodied people to work, paying each eight dollars a month, clothes, and one ration per day. The new labor force built the docks at Roanoke Island and a new fort, Fort Burnside, at the northern end of the island. They unloaded steamers, and the artisans among them did general repair work. Colyer said there were never enough of them initially, and later the surplus were moved to the mainland in the wake of the army.[59]

Burnside was preparing for the next phase of his campaign, and the 2,500 Confederate prisoners remained a problem. He had to feed and guard them as he did not have enough transports to send them North as was done with the Hatteras prisoners. The obvious solution was to parole and exchange them. The captured Confederates were the largest bag of prisoners in the eastern war zone and they could be exchanged for Union men captured at Bull Run and earlier battles. A prisoner exchange was made on an honor system, respected by both sides, and had been customary in previous wars. The prisoners were paroled and sent to their own lines, pledged not to fight again until formally exchanged for prisoners held by their own side. The exchangees could not rejoin the service, but they could farm or work at anything else. The system worked well for two years until General U.S. Grant, realizing how it favored the manpower-short Confederacy, stopped the practice.

Generals Burnside and Wise had corresponded since the battle concerning care of the wounded, and then the return of the bodies of the slain, including Wise's son. The navy had previously paroled and released thirty-nine prisoners.[60] Burnside proposed an exchange, Wise concurred and forwarded the letter to General Huger, who also agreed.[61] On February 16 General Burnside appointed Lieutenant-Colonel Francis A. Osborn of the Twenty-fourth Massachusetts and a proper Bostonian as the officer in charge of the negotiations. Osborn, carrying dispatches for General Huger, sailed for Elizabeth City under a flag of truce. He contacted Major Lee of the Third Georgia, who forwarded the dispatches to Huger. Osborn returned the next day with Huger's answer, and the exchange commenced. The prisoners boarded five steamers on February 20, steamed to Elizabeth City and marched ashore the next day. Some 2,580 men were paroled. The historian of the Twenty-fourth Massachusetts noted that the regimental music, the famous Gilmore's Band, gave the Rebels loading at Roanoke Island a fine send-off. "Need anyone wonder that the Confederate prisoners at Roanoke fairly went wild when, as they were filing down to the transports that were to take them to their own Rebeldom, Gilmore and his men struck up 'Dixie'?" Gilmore was chastised later for his action, but the writer thought he took pleasure in knowing he had given the enemy "one precious moment."[62]

What were the results of the battle? In the South gloom and doom prevailed and the finger-pointing began. The *Newbern Daily Progress* blamed sand and mud forts and short range guns in its February 12 issue. On February 14, the *Progress* blamed the Confederate Navy for the disaster. The paper announced that Commodore Lynch was a prisoner and added, meanly, that while not rejoicing, "we know of no one more deserving of such a misfortune."

Some Tar Heels thought the responsibility for the defeat was Colonel Shaw's, who was "disliked by his men, some even cursing him to his face" and General Huger's, who was "entirely unfit for business" due to drink.[63] While Shaw was not as outstanding a regimental leader as Colonel A.R. Wright of the Third Georgia, or as Rush Hawkins of the Ninth Zouaves, he did not lack courage. He performed satisfactorily for two more years until he was killed at the head of his regiment at the battle of Batchelder's Bridge near New Bern. Shaw's problem at Roanoke Island seems to have been chronic inertia, leaving the tasks of getting the correct ammunition for his field artillery and better arms and uniforms for his infantry to others. He might have prolonged the battle and inflicted more casualties on the enemy, but there was no way he could have successfully defended the island against such odds.

Governor Clark was blamed by the Secession Convention in Raleigh for his "total incapacity." The governor himself thought Burnside's invasion had stimulated recruiting in the state.[64] One such example, not cited by the governor, was former Second-Lieutenant Thomas Capehart of the First North Carolina Volunteers. Capehart left the University at Chapel Hill to join a company being raised in Edenton. The company joined Colonel D.H. Hill's "Bethel" regiment and Capehart was elected lieutenant. He fought at Big Bethel and marched under Brigadier-General John Magruder all over the peninsula around Yorktown. He was discharged at the expiration of his six-month enlistment. He returned home and immediately began to raise another company. Federal troops had begun to spread from Roanoke Island, catching many of Capehart's recruits outside Confederate lines. Using the extra time granted him waiting for his men to filter through the lines, Capehart got married. When his company was fully recruited, they traveled to Richmond with the North Carolina Third Battalion and fought in the battle of Seven Pines.[65]

The official verdict on the disaster at Roanoke Island was contained in the report of the Investigating Committee of the Confederate House of Representatives, a long document recounting everything about Roanoke island. The report concluded: "whatever of blame and responsibility is justly attributable to any one for the defeat of our troops at Roanoke Island on February 8, 1862, should attach to Maj. Gen. B. Huger and the late Secretary of War, J.P. Benjamin."[66]

In the North there was jubilation. Biographer Augustus Woodbury fairly foamed with joy himself in relating the North's reaction:

> Appreciative letters were sent from the President and the War and Navy Departments to the triumphant leaders. The Mayor of the city of New York issued a proclamation of congratulation. The Legislatures of Massachusetts and Ohio passed votes of felicitation. The General Assembly of Rhode Island, upon the recommendation of Governor Sprague, voted its thanks and a sword to General Burnside. Salutes were fired in the principal northern cities.[67]

Two letters from Burnside's old friend and mentor, General McClellan, probably pleased him as much as anything else. The first, sent just after the battle, began "My

Dear Old Burn" and ended with "God bless you, old fellow, and give you success. Ever yours." McClellan had heard only rumors about the battle, but he was sure Burnside had done all that a gallant and skillful soldier could do. The second letter, written two days later on February 12, was more formal. It was congratulatory also, and spoke of decisive and brilliant success and "Everything goes well with us, but your success seems to be the most brilliant yet. I expect still more from you."[68]

Burnside had indeed done well. Although there was little chance of losing the battle with his preponderance of forces, he had won the brilliant and decisive battle with minimum losses. He had shown himself to his soldiers and intervened personally when necessary during those rough weeks at sea. He had planned well with the navy and with his brigadiers for the landing and the battle. Once the battle began and he was assured that Foster, his senior brigade commander, was handling the fight skill-fully, he left the tactical command to him while he coordinated the whole battle-ground. After the surrender Burnside administered the whole island; including his men, the prisoners, the civilians and the refugees, while dispatching the joint expeditions to the surrounding towns. In his official reports he gave full credit to Generals Foster, Reno, and Parke, as well as the regimental commanders and the men. He continued to do well. He also planned for the next battle. He had his orders for crossing the sound.

Chapter Six

New Bern and Fort Macon

𝓐 SWOOP ACROSS THE SOUND to New Bern was Burnside's next campaign according to his original orders from General McClellan. It would be another joint operation with the navy, for the Neuse River opened the way to the town. The river was navigable to shallow draft vessels upstream from New Bern as far as Kinston. Any naval support much above Kinston would be restricted to flatboats or dugout canoes. Beyond New Bern, however, McClellan's instructions became more of a wish list than orders. McClellan spoke of seizing the railroad as far west as Goldsboro and possibly seizing and holding Raleigh.

According to Colonel Rush Hawkins the next objective, New Bern, was an open secret to the troops. A letter sent home by Sergeant George Driver, Company F, Twenty-third Massachusetts, confirms this. After a success at Roanoke Island, he speculated, they would have "Newberne and Goldsborough, on the railroad in our possession; and even perhaps more. Raleigh on another railroad..." Sergeant Driver duplicated the commanding generals strategy.[1]

On the day before Burnside departed, Hawkins related, he was appointed to the command of a new formation, the Fourth Brigade, for the protection of Roanoke Island. The brigade consisted of Hawkins's Ninth New York, and the two new regiments, the Sixth New Hampshire, and the Eighty-ninth New York. Hawkins also noted that on March 9 he heard distinctly the roar of gunfire from the battle eighty miles away between the *Merrimac* and the *Monitor* and the rest of the Federal fleet.[2]

Burnside's men had been loading supplies and ordnance for several days in preparation for the new movement. The general's last act before sailing was to divest himself of his most troublesome colonel by leaving Hawkins in charge on Roanoke Island, much to Hawkins' delight. Burnside embarked his three brigades, about eleven thousand rank and file, aboard his gunboats and transports on March 11. They joined the naval vessels at Hatteras, from whence the combined fleet sailed early on March 12 for the Neuse River. The weather was with Burnside this time. The sound was "Smooth as a mirror," one of the Rhode Islanders said, or a flat ca'm as the Bankers called it.

Commander Rowan was senior officer in the sounds, as Flag Officer Goldsborough had rushed back to the Chesapeake to confront the threat of the *Merrimac-Virginia*. Rowan, in the flagship *Philadelphia*, had with him the *Stars and Stripes*, the *Louisiana*, the *Hetzel*, the *Delaware*, the *Commodore Perry*, the *Valley City*, the

Underwriter, the *Commodore Barney*, the *Hunchback*, the *Southfield*, the *Morse*, the *Henry Brinker*, and the *Lockwood*. Since the death of the Mosquito Fleet no Confederate opposition was expected afloat. By 2 P.M. the fleet entered the mouth of the Neuse River, where Rowan halted the advance to concentrate his ships. Burnside came alongside the flagship to report that he had received intelligence of two enemy steamers in the Pamlico River. Rowan dispatched the *Lockwood* to guard the Pamlico. Burnside made his headquarters aboard the *Alice Price*, larger and more comfortable than the jaunty little *Picket* had been, but the *Picket* was there, leading the army's gunboats. The ships continued upriver, the navy leading, the transports in the rear. The fleet anchored at 6:10 P.M. off Slocum's Creek, twelve miles below the town by water, more by road.[3]

Confederate troops at New Bern numbered about four thousand, and were commanded by Brigadier-General Lawrence O'Brian Branch. Born in Halifax County, Branch was graduated from Princeton, after which he practiced law in Florida. His previous military experience was service in the Seminole War in 1841. He returned to North Carolina, married, and was elected to Congress in 1855 and served until 1861. Again in the state, after brief service as state Quartermaster and Paymaster, he enlisted as a private in the Raleigh Rifles. In September 1861 Branch was elected Colonel of the Thirty-third North Carolina Regiment, in which rank he demonstrated sufficient ability to be appointed Brigadier-General in the provisional army of the Confederate States and assume command of the District of the Pamlico.[4]

General Branch took over a large district with too few troops, the usual problem in the state. Branch's superior was Brigadier-General Gatlin, with headquarters in Goldsboro. Branch began to concentrate what soldiers he controlled and to inspect and improve the fortifications previously built. The return of his district for January, 1862 listed 379 officers and 5,955 men. However, the district spread from Fort Macon to Harker's Island and from the New Bern area to Washington and Hyde County.[5] A portion of some regiments were absent on re-enlistment furloughs. The regiment in the post of Washington, the Twenty-fifth Georgia, Colonel McMillan, would have been a welcome addition to the New Bern garrison, but it was removed from Branch's command before the battle. Secretary of War Benjamin, on March 2, ordered General Gatlin to withdraw the troops from Washington, North Carolina, and send them to Suffolk, Virginia.[6] A smaller garrison below Washington manning the forts on the Pamlico River was overlooked by the War Department. These artillerymen and their guns were ordered to New Bern, but it was a long trip by land.

Sergeant von Eberstein had come to the Swan's Point Battery by a circuitous route. After reporting the "cowardly evacuation" of Beacon Island, he was ordered by General Gatlin to Washington to serve Colonel McMillan as drillmaster. From there, he accompanied Lieutenant Obenchain of the Engineers to assist him in supervising the erection of the Swan's Point fort, and to drill Captain W.B. Rodman's company in heavy artillery. The sergeant related the next movement:

> After the fall of Roanoke Island, we commenced to remove the guns and abandon the battery on Swan Point. Captain Daniel Reid and myself

commenced dismantling the heavy Ordnance. We placed it upon a flat and the Ordnance stores in a small schooner, commanded by Benjamin Gautier... A steamer was provided me to tow the schooner and the flat up the river to Tarboro. We accomplished the duty by the 12th day of March, though we got across some logs two or three times. We landed the Ordnance and also the Ordnance stores safe in Tarboro, on the 13th day of March....

   I was then ordered by Major Anderson to take the Ordnance stores ... at once down to New Bern, N.C. with an infantry company, which was to get on board at Goldsborough, to go to the assistance of General Branch.... We left the night of the 13th.[7]

The artillerymen in the forts, Rodman's Battery (later Company C of the Fortieth N.C. Artillery Regiment), the McMillan Artillery or Tripp's Company (B of the Fortieth), and Whitehurst's Artillery (I of the Fortieth) were also ordered to New Bern. Unable to cross the Neuse River at New Bern, they too traveled the long way around via Kinston. The Branch Artillery or Latham's Battery (H of the Fortieth) recruited in Beaufort and Craven Counties and mustered closer to New Bern. This battery, strengthened by a contingent of the Twenty-seventh North Carolina arrived in time to garrison Fort Thompson on the river.[8]

General Branch drew all the troops he had from their training camps and bivouacs around New Bern and on the coast and mustered them across the Trent River to work on fortifications. A strong fortified line had been built before Branch assumed command in November, 1861. This fortification, called the Croatan breastwork ran from the mouth of Otter Creek three-fourths of a mile inland to an "impracticable swamp." It was, Branch reported, "well-planned and well-constructed" and could resist a very large force if garrisoned with two thousand men and two field batteries. Branch had the men to defend this line, but he did not have enough to hold the six miles of river shore between the Croatan line and Fort Thompson, the nearest of the river batteries. Several other water batteries had been built between the fort and the town, but only one, unoccupied and unarmed was downstream. He had rifle pits dug on the river shore near the Croatan line at Fisher's Landing on top of the twenty-five feet high river bank. He had another fortified line anchored on Fort Thompson and running one mile inland to the railroad. Branch decided to extend and improve this work as his main line of resistance.[9]

Branch needed laborers to complete his land defenses. He circulated handbills calling on the people to assist him, which brought in only a small party of free Negroes with no tools. He advertised in the newspaper for slave owners to hire out their slaves with implements for a few days, but "I got but a single Negro." The soldiers worked as best they could with half enough shovels and axes and no picks nor grubbing-hoes. The line from Fort Thompson ended at a brickyard on the rail line. Branch turned a corner with his additional breastwork to conform to the contours of the ground. The line dropped back about 150 yards to cross a small branch, then turned again in the breastworks original direction, or away from the river. This extension was defended by a series of small redans, or fortlets. These were still under construction when the battle began. The corner at the brickyard, almost a salient, was a weak point in the line. Branch ordered his men to cut loopholes in the thick masonry walls of the kiln buildings for rifle firing, and ordered a battery of two 24-pounder field guns brought up to reinforce the position. He intended to make a strong point out of the dangerous salient. All along the line from the fort on the river to the railroad Branch's men felled the trees with the tops toward the direction the enemy would appear. The thickets thus formed would impede a charging enemy without offering him cover. The men were still working when scouts brought word that the enemy's fleet was approaching and anchoring below Otter Creek, with more ships still coming.[10] Branch had the following present for duty:

> Seventh Regiment North Carolina State Troops, Colonel Reubin P. Campbell, Lieutenant-Colonel Edward Graham Haywood.
> Twenty-sixth North Carolina Regiment, Colonel Zebulon B. Vance.
> Twenty-seventh North Carolina Regiment, Major John A. Gilmer
> Thirty-third North Carolina Regiment, Colonel Clark M. Avery, Lieutenant-Colonel Robert F. Hoke.
> Thirty-fifth North Carolina Regiment, Colonel James Sinclair, Lieutenant-Colonel Marshall D. Craton.
> Thirty-seventh North Carolina Regiment, Colonel Charles C. Lee, Lieutenant-Colonel William M. Barbour.
> Brem's Battery, Tenth Regiment North Carolina Artillery.
> Latham's Battery, Fortieth North Carolina Regiment Artillery.
> Whitehurst's Company, Fortieth North Carolina Regiment Artillery, part of the garrison of Fort Thompson.
> Nineteenth North Carolina Cavalry, Colonel Samuel B. Spruill, Companies E and F, dismounted joined Colonel Vance's men, other men served as videttes.[11]

The individual companies still carried their fanciful names, often embroidered on the company's banner, but the men had begun to think of themselves as members of a regiment.

In addition to the line troops, there was a battalion of local militia, just called up and hardly trained. Colonel H.J.B. Clark did the best he could with his 309 men, armed with shotguns and sporting rifles. He detached forty-five men to assist the artillerymen in placing guns before marching the rest into their assigned place in the line — inside the brick works at the salient corner.

These made up Branch's men, just over four thousand of them, as closely as can be counted. He organized them into two ad hoc brigades by appointing Colonel Lee of the Thirty-seventh Regiment to command the left wing of the line, and Colonel Campbell of the Seventh to command the right. The battleground selected was a neck with the Neuse River on one side and Bryce Creek on the other, with the Trent River in the rear. The Trent was spanned by a railroad bridge and a road bridge. Bryce Creek had no bridge and was too deep to ford.

As soon as word of the enemy arrived, General Branch sent three of his regiments to meet them and fight a delaying action before retreating to the main line. Colonel Sinclair with the Thirty-fifth rode the steam cars for nine miles, dismounted and marched to the Fisher's Landing rifle pits. Sinclair noted that he could hear the enemy's band music and the soldiers' singing. Colonel Avery's Thirty-third and Lieutenant-Colonel Haywood's Seventh moved forward to the intersection of the Beaufort road and the railroad. During the remainder of the night Branch moved the rest of his regiments and companies, the field guns, and the ordnance supplies and materials into position. Early on Thursday morning, as Branch was riding toward Colonel Campbell's headquarters, he heard from Colonel Sinclair and from Captain Evans's pickets that Federal troops were landing below Otter Creek. He dispatched Vance's Twenty-sixth, led by Lieutenant-Colonel Burgwyn, to occupy the Croatan line of works. He sent engines and cars down the railroad in case the advanced regiments had to withdraw quickly. The two forward regiments might have offered the leading Union regiments a sharp check. Instead, Colonel Vance, hurrying to join his regiment met Colonel Sinclair retreating with his men. Sinclair had evacuated Fisher's Landing at the first shots from the enemy's gunboats. Vance then met his own regiment, ordered back by Colonel Campbell when Sinclair's retreat uncovered its flank. Branch placed all his troops in the Fort Thompson line.[12]

Burnside's regiments landed, not at Fisher's nor at Otter Creek, but lower down the shore at the mouth of Slocomb's Creek, where the shore was low and wooded. After the naval vessels and the *Picket* shelled the woods the troops began to land. They repeated the landing maneuver with towed surf-boats, which had worked so well at Roanoke Island, and landed three regiments in twenty minutes. The Twenty-fourth Massachusetts, the last ashore at Roanoke, was the first to land at New Bern. Beside them was the Twenty-first Massachusetts, which took the lead in the advance inland, with the Twenty-fourth in close support. No Confederates opposed them.

Except for the Ninth New York, all of Burnside's old Roanoke Island regiments were there, veterans now, morale high and the recollection of their past victory spurring them on. The same ships were there, too. The *Pilot Boy*, the *Guide*, *Lancer*, and the rest. The transport *Wheelbarrow* nudged the low river bank to unload the Fourth Rhode Island in the well-trodden mud. The regiments moved inland, behind the Twenty-first and Twenty-fourth Massachusetts.

The march of the Twenty-fourth as related in the regimental history was typical. After traversing two miles of woods showing signs of the shelling, the regiment came upon some Negro houses. Here the sudden unearthly-sounding screech of a peacock brought muskets to the ready until the country boys told the city boys what it was. Rain began as the troops approached the railroad, where they halted for lunch. They slogged on, up the railroad and the highway, toward New Bern. They passed the line of abandoned earthworks—the Croatan line. Foster's First Brigade, the Twenty-fourth still leading, marched along the road, while Reno's Second Brigade followed the railroad. Parke's Third Brigade came last as the reserve. They marched for ten miles through worsening rain and mud, then filed off the road to camp for the night. Those who

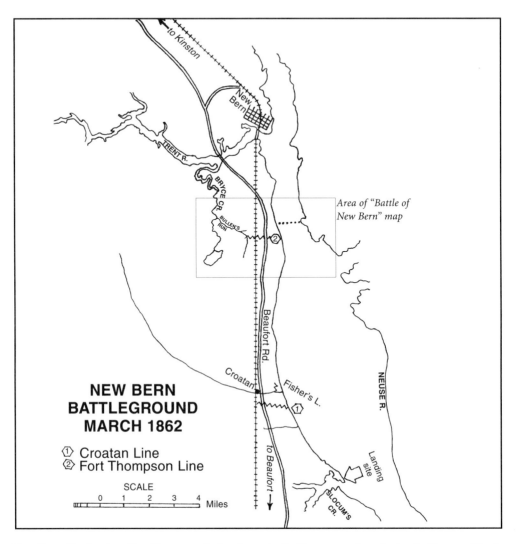

New Bern: The battle at New Bern was obviously controlled by geography — lack of bridges and fords made attacks and retreats a challenge. From North Carolina DOT map of Craven County with features added from Burlingame, *Fifth Rhode Island* and other contemporary histories. Overall sketch by author.

could slept in the mud, but it was a miserable night. The regimental history quoted a parody:

> *Now I lay me down to sleep*
> *In mud that's many fathoms deep*
> *If I'm not here when you awake,*
> *Just hunt me up with an oyster rake.*[13]

The deep mud and clay were wearing to infantry, but were impossible to the naval detachment manhandling their six boat howitzers. Lieutenant R.S. McCook had to ask the infantry for help. Gunners and riflemen alike sweated at the drag ropes and strained

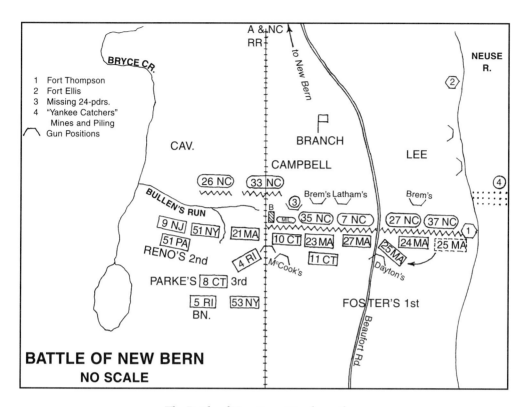

1 Fort Thompson
2 Fort Ellis
3 Missing 24-pdrs.
4 "Yankee Catchers"
  Mines and Piling
  Gun Positions

A & NC RR

to New Bern

NEUSE R.

BRYCE CR.

CAV.

BRANCH

CAMPBELL

LEE

26 NC   33 NC

Brem's Latham's   Brem's

BULLEN'S RUN

9 NJ   51 NY   21 MA

35 NC   7 NC   27 NC   37 NC

51 PA

RENO'S 2nd

10 CT   23 MA   27 MA   24 MA   25 MA

4 RI   McCook's   11 CT

25 MA

Dayton's

PARKE'S 8 CT 3rd

5 RI   53 NY
BN.

FOSTER'S 1st

Beaufort Rd.

BATTLE OF NEW BERN
NO SCALE

The Battle of New Bern. Map by author.

round the mud slimed wheels. The soldiers may have complained then, but later were glad they helped.

The same rain drenched Branch's men laboring to complete the extension of their line. It soaked the Thirty-fifth North Carolina and Colonel Sinclair in rifle pits overlooking Fisher's Landing and added to the colonel's feeling of forlorn isolation.

The Federal march resumed next morning at 6 A.M. through a heavy fog, but with no rain. Scouts reported the Confederate line, well fortified and manned, just a few hundred yards ahead. Foster and Reno formed their brigades in line of battle, Foster on the right, brushing the river shore, and Reno on the left, extending across the railroad. Parke's Brigade, still in reserve, closed up along the railroad.

Branch's line was anchored on his left on Fort Thompson, the largest of the river batteries. Much labor and material had been expended on the river batteries and on obstructions in the Neuse River. Fort Thompson mounted twelve or thirteen guns, most of them smoothbore 32-pounders, but two were 6-inch rifles. Only three of the guns were emplaced to fire on the land side, and none could be aimed to shell the road and railroad along which Burnside's regiments approached. Upstream from the main fort were Fort Dixie with four guns, Fort Ellis with eight guns, an unnamed two-gun casemated work, and Fort Lane with four guns. Besides these, two batteries of two guns each guarded the river shore inside the town.

According to Commander Rowan, "The obstructions in the river were very formidable and had evidently been prepared with great care." An intruding vessel would first strike a row of staunch piling cut off below the surface of the water. Behind these were a row of sharpened piling with iron caps driven at an angle of forty-five degrees downstream. If an enemy got through these, he faced thirty torpedoes [mines], containing two hundred pounds of gunpowder fired by percussion locks and trigger lines fastened to the pointed piling.[14]

Branch posted Lieutenant-Colonel Barbour's Thirty-seventh Regiment and Major Gilmer's Twenty-seventh in the line from the fort to the Beaufort road. Lieutenant-Colonel Haywood's Seventh and Colonel Sinclair's Thirty-fifth manned the line between the Beaufort road and the railroad. Colonel Clark's militia battalion occupied the brick kiln corner. Branch did not explain why he assigned this important position to his least-trained troops. Perhaps he thought the protection offered by the buildings would make the militiamen feel more secure. Colonel Avery's Thirty-third Regiment held the switch part of the line behind the little stream called Bullen's Run. Avery's men were posted on both sides of the railroad, and Colonel Vance's Twenty-sixth held the right flank beyond Avery, with the two companies of dismounted cavalry on his right. The few independent companies on the field filled in between the assigned regiments. Branch directed that a battery of 24-pounder field guns be emplaced behind the right center of the line to reinforce the militia and Vance's flank. He assigned Captain W.B. Rodman and his company who had just arrived from the Pamlico to man the guns. As the guns were not emplaced in time, Rodman's men fought as infantry. Latham's Battery took position between the county road and the railroad, as did two sections of Brem's Battery. Brem's other section was nearer the right of the line. Branch's headquarters was in the center of the line, two hundred yards behind the fortifications, and the cavalry reserve another two hundred yards back.

At 7:30 A.M. on March 14 firing began on the left of the line, from the river to the railroad. Branch thought it was a feint.

General Foster sent forward his Massachusetts Regiments first. The Twenty-fifth Massachusetts advanced in line of battle on the extreme right, opposite the Thirty-seventh North Carolina. Next to them, extending to the Beaufort road, came the Twenty-fourth Massachusetts. Captain Dayton, with a howitzer from the schooner *Highlander* wheeled around and went into action between the 24th and the Twenty-seventh Massachusetts, the next in line. The Twenty-third Massachusetts filed into the line, with the Tenth Connecticut on its left and reaching to the railroad. Lieutenant McCook with his six boat howitzers, his men daubed from their mud march, went into action adjacent to Dayton's howitzer.

The Federal regiments opened rifle fire as they came into line and the Confederates responded with rafales of artillery and musketry. "The firing was incessant and very severe from the breastwork and within a very short range."[15] It was not exactly a feint, but the attack was not pressed further along this line. The three guns in Fort Thompson bearing inland kept up a rapid fire at the Union lines, but generally shot high. The early morning fog was thickened by clouds of powder smoke. Exact aiming was difficult for everyone. The guns of the fleet exchanged long range fire with Fort

Thompson and tried to shell the Confederate lines, with mixed results. The front of the Twenty-fifth Massachusetts, close up to Fort Thompson was too hot to hold, shells from the naval guns aimed at the Confederates began to crash on the Twenty-fifth.[16] General Foster had the regiment sidestep to re-enter the battle line to the left of the Twenty-fourth Massachusetts. The firing continued on both sides, while the Federal's main thrust developed near the railroad.[17] Commander Rowan, in an unofficial letter to Flag Officer Goldsborough regarding the supporting naval gunfire, made an astonishing comment: "I commenced throwing 5, 10, 15 second shells inshore and notwithstanding the risk, I determined to continue until the general sent me word. I know the persuasive effect of a 9-inch, and thought it better to kill a Union man or two than to lose the effect of my moral suasion."[18] The general sent an officer with the word.

Further on the left, the Twenty-seventh Massachusetts fired almost all their ammunition. The Eleventh Connecticut was in reserve to relieve them, whereupon the Twenty-seventh fell back, fixed bayonets, and lay down in a fold of ground to await their next orders.

General Reno sent his brigade into line on the left, just across the railroad. The Twenty-first Massachusetts formed a battleline next to the track, with the Fifty-first New York beside them. The Ninth New Jersey prolonged the line on the Federal left flank, with the Fifty-first Pennsylvania in reserve. Parke's Third Brigade, the general reserve of the whole force, marched up close behind Reno and waited. Firing grew just as heavy on the left as it had on the right. Several pieces of Confederate field artillery were visible, pouring a fierce fire on Reno's regiments. One boat howitzer of the naval detachment was put out of action, the other guns were nearly out of ammunition. Infantry action was required.

Lieutenant-Colonel William S. Clark's Twenty-first Massachusetts lapped around the corner at the railroad where the Confederate line dropped back across Bullen's Run. Clark's men were in front of the Thirty-third North Carolina in their redoubts and on the flank of Colonel H.J.B. Clark's North Carolina Militia. The broken ground afforded them some cover, from which they could see men unloading a rail car further up the track. They opened fire, whereupon the working party fled into the brickyard. The riflemen of the Twenty-first Massachusetts spattered the walls of the buildings with minié balls. Sharpshooters fired into the loopholes in the walls. Four companies of the Twenty-first, led by General Reno and their Colonel, charged across the railroad and into the brick yard. Reno returned to the Federal line to send forward more men, while Clark and his two hundred men penetrated deeper into the Confederate lines to capture the nearest artillery piece. Before they could turn the gun and fire it, they saw Confederate infantry advancing on them as enemy musketry intensified.[19]

The Confederate Colonel Clark ordered his militiamen to fire three volleys as soon as the Federals were in range of his short-range weapons. When the smoke cleared he saw the enemy were penetrating his flank and rear, "and just as Colonel Vance [Twenty-sixth North Carolina] poured his first fire into the enemy, a panic seized my command and part of them broke ranks." Clark then ordered the rest to retreat and tried to reform them in a brush wood in the rear. The panic was renewed, he was left with only twenty men, so decided not to re-enter the fight with so few.[20]

The other Colonel Clark, with his stalwart two hundred, was confronted with Confederates from two regiments, advancing with bayonets fixed. He ordered his men to spring back over the parapet as fast as they could, cross the railroad, and retreat by the ditch to Union lines. The Confederates, instead of halting and firing a volley at the retreating foe, continued their charge. Thus, most of the four companies escaped. Lieutenant-Colonel Clark sought a senior officer as soon as he reached the Federal battle line. He did not find either brigade commander and had no time to look further. He did find the right man, Colonel Isaac P. Rodman with his Fourth Rhode Island. He told Rodman about entering the Confederate line, the flight of the militia, and his forced retreat. He told Rodman a new assault in the same place, with more men, would be successful. Colonel Isaac Rodman made the decision that won the battle. He notified one of General Parke's aides of what he intended, and, on his own initiative, led his regiment through the brickyard and into the Confederate's rear. The Eighth Connecticut, Colonel Harland, followed him, as did the Fifth Rhode Island Battalion. This mass of fresh troops in their rear was more than the thinly stretched Confederates could expel, especially as Colonel Sinclair's Thirty-fifth North Carolina crumpled.[21]

When the militia fled from the field, Colonel Sinclair reported, his second-in command [Lieutenant-Colonel Marshall D. Craton of the *Goldsboro Rifles*] ordered the four right wing companies to fall back. Sinclair tried to rally the men, but Craton again ordered them back. At this, Sinclair reported to Colonel Campbell, commanding the right of the line, that he was flanked. Campbell stated that Sinclair was "in much excitement," and when ordered to leave the trench and form to restore the line with a bayonet charge, instead left the trench and charged to the rear. Sinclair admitted that the death of an officer and several men "created somewhat of a panic." The regiment retreated to the road junction in the rear, then to the bridge across the Neuse.[22]

General Branch and Colonel Campbell attempted again to repair the break. The Seventh North Carolina, the next in line to the evaporating Thirty-fifth, rushed toward the gap as did Colonel Avery's Thirty-third North Carolina from the other side of the brickyard. Branch asked Colonel Lee to send the Thirty-seventh North Carolina to help. Foster renewed his assault on the part of the line held by Lee's left wing, so only half of the Thirty-seventh could leave the line. They were not enough. Reno and Parke pushed more fresh regiments into the battle. The break was irreparable. Branch realized he could only save his men if he retreated at once.

Conducting an orderly retreat was a critical operation, as the Federal regiments within the Confederate lines were nearer the bridges than Branch's left wing. The Confederates had to cross the Trent River before the Union gunboats entered the Trent. Branch managed to do it. He sent couriers to Colonels Vance and Avery with orders to fall back. He halted at the intersection of the Beaufort road and the railroad to rally his regiments as they fell back. At the intersection Branch found the Twenty-eighth North Carolina, Lieutenant-Colonel Lowe, just arrived on a train of cars. He ordered Lowe to hold the enemy in check and cover the retreat. The Seventh North Carolina arrived in two groups and were hurried on to the Trent River highway bridge to hold it.[23]

Colonel Lee, commanding Branch's left wing, extracted the Twenty-seventh and Thirty-seventh North Carolina from their places in the line and sent them to the rear, and went himself to move out the garrison of Fort Thompson, after they had spiked the guns. There was no time to blow up the magazine as the enemy were advancing and only forty yards away. Lee did stop at the other batteries where he had the guns dismounted and the magazines blown before the gunners left. Lee directed his men across the railroad bridge. He reported: "All the men of the left wing were saved, and retreated over to New Bern in tolerable order."[24]

On Branch's right wing the Thirty-third and Twenty-sixth North Carolina were too closely involved in fighting to retreat to the bridges. Colonel Avery of the Thirty-third and his detachment were surrounded and forced to surrender or be slaughtered. Lieutenant-Colonel Hoke, finding the Trent River bridge on fire, led the greater part of the regiment off to the right through the swamp to Bryce Creek. He collected a few small boats and crossed the creek, although some of the men swam the creek, thereby losing their muskets. Colonel Vance carried the Twenty-sixth by the same method and route, though three of his men drowned in the creek. The two regiments united on the far bank of the creek and marched to Trenton. Learning that the others had retreated to Kinston, Vance and Hoke force-marched there to rejoin Branch.[25]

Captain W.B. Rodman, in a letter to his wife datelined 14 March, Kinston, at night, told her "We were in the battle today. I am safe but jaded and worn beyond measure…" He said, too, he had lost all his clothes but what he wore and some of his men were wounded, some prisoners.[26]

General Branch withdrew through New Bern just in time, as Federal gunboats were off the town's waterfront when the Confederate rearguard marched past. A part of the Thirty-fifth North Carolina under Colonel Sinclair served as rearguard in the town when a false alarm of enemy cavalry flew through the ranks. It was at that point, said Sinclair, that Lieutenant-Colonel Craton deserted the regiment and disappeared. The Seventh regiment's rearguard destroyed the draw of the Trent road bridge. Branch had prepared a flat laden with turpentine-drenched cotton bales, which the other rearguard jammed up against the railroad trestle and torched. The bridge caught fire and was destroyed. Commander Rowan thought the incendiary flat was a fire-raft prepared for use against his ships, but it was more useful as a bridge-burner. Three of Rowan's vessels were injured by iron capped stakes, but "fortunately the torpedoes failed to serve the enemy's purpose." Rowan did not say whether the torpedoes were defective, or whether the navy disarmed them. Possibly both Burnside and Rowan had learned from agents some details of the Confederate defenses. As soon as the ships cleared the obstructions, they steamed to the city, capturing two steamers and a schooner on the way. The navy immediately began to ferry Burnside's regiments across the Trent and land them in New Bern.[27]

Branch did not attempt to hold New Bern. He and his officers directed the troops through the town and out the other side, where they marched up the railroad to

Tuscarora, though some of them rode the last train out of New Bern. Here the regiments rallied until arrangements were made to continue to Kinston. Some fires broke out as the Confederates retreated through New Bern, not a planned deed, but rather individual acts of soldiers.

General Branch arrived in Kinston late on the night of March 14 and the regiments came in for the next several days. His troops were demoralized and "hungry enough to eat army mules." Vance's Twenty-sixth North Carolina though "muddy, motley, and weary" were in the best condition, for Colonel Vance had found a keg of brandy which "restored his soldiers courage and cheered their souls."[28] On the Sixteenth, in the midst of the confusion and reorganization, Sergeant von Eberstein steamed in to the Kinston depot with his cars of ordnance and ordnance stores. He reported to General Branch who welcomed him and directed him to the ordnance officer. This officer welcomed the stores, but did not have time to sign a receipt for them. Sergeant von Eberstein, a determined man with friend or foe, located Captain Rodman who went with him back to General Branch where he got his receipt. Von Eberstein returned to the Tenth North Carolina and later the Sixty-first North Carolina to give the Confederacy good service in three states and to receive two serious wounds in battle.[29]

Burnside sent his troops through the town, too, and established picket posts on the roads, while scouts trailed after the Confederates. The few fires were extinguished and some of the soldiers and sailors, along with the Negroes of the town, began to loot and pillage the vacant houses. Most of the white citizens had left before the invaders arrived. The plundering continued all night of March 14 and into the next day. Burnside soon restored order by installing a strong garrison in the town, and patrolling the streets. The provost marshall sent details to collect the stolen property. Burnside selected a large, recently vacated house for his headquarters and moved in. He ordered the churches in the town to hold services of Thanksgiving on Sunday, March 16. A military government was established.[30]

What was the result of the battle? What was gained, what was lost? The Confederates lost a great deal: 64 men killed, 101 wounded, and 413 captured or missing, all the artillery in the forts, and the field guns of Brem's and Latham's companies, plus a few other older guns from Fort Macon.[31] The South lost not only the important port of New Bern, second only to Wilmington in most of the pre-war years, but also control of all the sounds and the lower rivers. The remaining river ports and Beaufort would soon fall to Federal might.

There were some gains for the South, although they were probably not recognized at the time. The troops gained experience in a hard-fought battle and in the toughest trial for soldiers, a retreat under fire. The regiments, though with some disorder, all got away reasonably intact and retreated to Kinston where they were reorganized and rearmed. The Confederacy gained battle tried leaders: Branch himself, Colonels Lee, Campbell, Avery (after exchange), Haywood, Barbour, and Major Gilmer, plus scores of company officers worthy of promotion. Most especially, the worth of Colonel Zebulon B. Vance and Lieutenant-Colonel Robert F. Hoke was demonstrated. The Thirty-fifth North Carolina, whose performance was poor, after reorganization and under new leadership became a battle worthy regiment. Colonel Sinclair was defeated in a new election for colonel and Matthew W. Ransom took his place.[32] The chief gain for North Carolina was the attention of the Richmond government and the recognition of the dangers accruing from Burnside's invasion. New commanders and more troops came to the scene. General Gatlin was made the scapegoat for the disaster and Major-General T.H. Holmes was appointed to command in the state. Several new brigadiers were sent with additional troops. Branch was not blamed for the defeat and was retained in command of the Second Brigade. By March 31 there were 24,030 soldiers (aggregate present) and 142 pieces of artillery in the state, enough to have repelled the invasion, but now necessary to try to hold on to the rest of the sound shores.[33]

Burnside's losses were small, considering his gains. Surgeon William H. Church listed 90 killed, 380 wounded, and 1 captured, a total of 471.[34] Federal gains were immense. The United States now had not just a toehold nor a foothold on the coast but a secure base on the mainland and complete control of the sounds and lower rivers. Besides a city of about 5,500 population and a portion of the east-west rail connection with the coast, the other river ports and Beaufort on the sea could now be plucked like ripe fruit by combined strikes of the army and navy. Secretary of War Stanton tendered Burnside thanks and congratulations for his "brilliant service," and even nicer, his commission as Major-General.[35] Burnside appointed General Foster military governor of New Bern and ordered General Parke to start his Third Brigade toward the coast and Fort Macon. But first there came a naval interlude.

The CSS *Nashville* was the first vessel commissioned as a government, rather than a private, armed cruiser. She was a fast side-wheeler sailing out of Charleston, South Carolina before the war. She eluded the Federal blockaders in early 1862, captured a prize in the English channel, and was pursued by the USS *Tuscarora*, a well armed steam sloop. Escaping the Federal ship by diplomacy, guile, and speed, Lieutenant Robert B. Pegram recrossed the Atlantic to Bermuda, capturing another prize on the way. Here she picked up a pilot for Beaufort, again eluded Federal blockaders, and anchored in Beaufort harbor on February 28 under the protection of Fort Macon's guns. The Federal navy knew where she was, and determined the *Nashville* would not get away from them again. Lieutenant Pegram was ordered to turn the ship over to a new owner at Beaufort. Pegram was transferred and Lieutenant William C. Whittle assumed command. The new owners did not arrive, but General Burnside did. Beaufort was no longer a safe haven and the Federal navy was sending more ships to blockade the inlet. Just after dark on March 17 the *Nashville* steamed out at full speed, evaded the two Union vessels close in and got away to Wilmington.[36] The sailing bark USS *Gemsbok* fired twenty shots, the USS *Cambridge* fired four times, but none of them hit. The two captains had to report failure. Assistant Secretary of the Navy G.V. Fox called the escape "a terrible blow to our naval prestige.... It is a Bull Run to the Navy."[37] It was not really such an important event, but the U.S. Navy was feeling very sensitive since the appearance of the CSS *Virginia* (*Merrimac*) in Chesapeake Bay.

Burnside turned his attention to Fort Macon. Brigadier-General Parke embarked with two regiments, the Fourth Rhode Island and the Eighth Connecticut, steamed downriver to Slocum's Creek, their original landing place, where they landed again. The troops marched inland to Havelock Station, where they were joined by the Fifth Rhode Island Battalion, which had marched down the railroad. An artillery force from the First United States Artillery joined Parke along with two mortar batteries under Lieutenant D.W. Flagler, his ordnance officer. The generals intended to haul the siege train on the railroad from Slocum's Creek, even though they had no engines and few cars. Branch had sent all the engines and most of the cars to Kinston, leaving but a few hand propelled cars with the boxcars. This plan was frustrated when Parke's men discovered that a detachment of Confederates from Fort Macon had burned the railroad bridge over the Newport River. Parke immediately secured the road bridge and marched on to Carolina City, leaving the Fifth Rhode Island Battalion to rebuild the railroad bridge.[38]

General Burnside soon had other distractions. The navy was nervous over the possibility of the Confederates sending ironclad ships down through the canals to attack in North Carolina waters. This was certainly a case of how a small seed of fact may grow into a magnificent blossom of rumor. The facts were that the Southerners were building shallow-draft gunboats in Norfolk, one of them possibly ironclad. Two ironclads were laid down in Wilmington and others were planned.[39] Naval Constructor Porter had submitted a model of a flat-bottomed, light-draft ironclad to the department as early as June of 1861.[40] The Confederate Government had, in fact, just let a contract for the construction of one of the shallow-draft ironclads on the Roanoke River. On April 16, 1862, the Secretary of the Navy signed the contract with the firm of Martin and Elliott. This was to be the famous *Albemarle*. On September 17, 1862 the same firm agreed to build a second ironclad at Tarboro on the Tar River.[41] A third vessel of the same class was contracted on October 17, 1862 by the shipbuilding firm of Howard and Ellis. This one was built at White Hall on the Neuse River and would become CSS *Neuse*.[42] But at the time of the battle for New Bern and the sounds, none of the ships were nearly ready. Nevertheless, the rumor grew. General Wool at Fortress Monroe first heard it, and passed it on to Flag Officer Goldsborough, who passed it to Commander Rowan.[43] Rowan and Burnside had to act, so a joint expedition steamed to Elizabeth City to bar the door. The flagship *Philadelphia* and the transports *Northerner* and *Guide* carried General Reno with the Twenty-first Massachusetts and the Fifty-first Pennsylvania. Burnside ordered Colonel Rush Hawkins on Roanoke Island to join Reno with elements of the Ninth New York, the Eighty-ninth New York, the Sixth New Hampshire, and a part of the Marine Artillery.[44] Hawkins, in his own account, expressed surprise at Reno's appearance, as he expected to command the expedition himself, because, as he claimed, he and Commander Rowan had planned it all.

Reno and staff landed about midnight of April 19 three miles below Elizabeth City on the road to South Mills. Hawkins and his regiments landed a few hours later. As Reno's two regiments had not arrived — the transports were aground — he ordered Hawkins to proceed toward South Mills and to demonstrate if he sighted the enemy.

Reno would catch up as quickly as he could. As soon as his troops arrived at daylight, Reno marched and was surprised to meet Hawkins only twelve miles up the road, instead of far ahead. Hawkins had been lost and had marched thirty miles to meet Reno. Hawkins blamed the mishap on using a "light mulatto man for a guide." Hawkins took his customary direct action: "When it was discovered that the guide had led my brigade ten miles out of the way, he was quietly taken to a wood out of sight of the troops and shot."[45]

All the regiments suffered much from the heat, but the joint force marched four miles further, to within a few miles of South Mills where they were halted by a Confederate line volleying musketry and artillery at them. This was not another green regiment nor militia. It was Colonel "Ranse" Wright and the Third Georgia, Hawkins's old foes from Hatteras. Wright had four guns of Captain McComas' artillery and two companies of militia. Wright formed his men in a lane fronted with a ditch and embankment along the edge of cleared land. Three hundred yards in his front was another ditch, a rail fence, and several buildings. The Confederates fired the houses, piled the fence rails in the adjacent ditch and fired them, so that the ditch would be too hot to occupy. Wright's map referred to this feature as "the roasted ditch." The guns were posted on one flank. It was a strong position.[46]

Reno posted his four guns, two of the Marine Artillery, and two that Hawkins' regiment had brought, and placed his regiments in line. He ordered the Fifty-first Pennsylvania and the Twenty-first Massachusetts to the right of the road to turn the enemy's flank, with the Ninth and Eighty-ninth New York in support. The Sixth New Hampshire filed to the left to support the guns. The men were worn out, Reno noted, and slow to move in position, but the two regiments on the right opened a brisk fire at last. At this point, Hawkins decided to win the battle at once. He ordered the Ninth to charge. They met blasts of canister, grape, and musketry and were stopped in their tracks. Casualties were heavy and the survivors were pinned down. Reno affirmed: "It was a most gallant charge, but they were exposed to a most deadly fire." Reno did not write it in this report, but it was also a most foolhardy charge. The Zouaves managed to rally on the Eighty-ninth New York. All of Reno's regiments were in the firing line and lapping round Wright's flank. Captain McComas was killed and the Confederate artillery started to withdraw, but Wright rallied them until their ammunition was all fired. The artillery withdrew, followed by the infantry, not to Norfolk as Reno hoped, but to a new line two miles in the rear. Wright fell back in good order to a prepared position across Joy's Creek, still guarding South Mills, and ready for the next attack.[47] Reno did not pursue. The troops rested until 10 P.M., then marched back to the transports, carrying ten or fifteen prisoners with them and leaving sixteen wounded on the field in care of a surgeon. The expedition returned to New Bern and Roanoke Island. Union losses were 13 killed, 101 wounded, and 13 prisoners, plus 20 stragglers captured the next day. Colonel Hawkins was wounded in the arm. Confederate losses were 6 killed, 19 wounded, and 3 prisoners, according to Wright's early report. Wright's men scavenged arms, accoutrements, and a quantity of powder from the battlefield.[48] The canal lock was not reached, much less destroyed. Reno could report that they had successfully demonstrated toward Norfolk. Although it was a Confederate victory, no ironclads came through the canal, because there were none. They would not appear until much later in the war in North Carolina.

A paper battle commenced when the reports of South Mills were filed. Hawkins sent his report directly to Burnside, ignoring Reno, and violating military procedure. His report magnified the actions of Hawkins's brigade, and implied that any failures were due to others. Burnside's adjutant sent it to Reno, causing Reno to file a new report verbally lacerating Hawkins. Hawkins wrote a new report for Reno, little changed from his original one. At this Reno reopened fire at Hawkins in a more personal letter to General Burnside. He referred to Hawkins as "that infernal scoundrel" and "the rascal Hawkins." He accused Hawkins of bad conduct on the field and of lying.[49]

Burnside must have been happy to forget Hawkins and resume the campaign against Fort Macon, where General Parke was making progress. Parke and his first two regiments arrived in Carolina City on March 22, and, one day later, demanded the surrender of Fort Macon, "In order to save the unnecessary effusion of blood," in the polite talk of the times. Colonel M.J. White declined. Parke sent troops to occupy Morehead City and Beaufort and to seize all boats and cut communications with the fort. Using a ship's launch carrying a boat howitzer, a detachment landed on Bogue Banks at Hoop Pole Creek opposite Carolina City, cutting land communications. Parke located his permanent camp and supply depot here, about four miles from the fort.[50]

Back in Newport the Fifth Rhode Island's men chopped trees and manhandled timbers, as they sweated to complete the railroad bridge. The battalion received a number of visitors, who followed their noses to Surgeon Potter's mess, for the surgeon's cook, "Doctor" Frank Diggs, had moved with the battalion from Roanoke Island. One visitor recorded: "One of the most popular attaches of this battalion is Dr. Frank Diggs, cook and caterer for Dr. Potter's mess." Another unexpected guest was a reporter for a New York paper, Henry M. Stanley, who later found Dr. David Livingstone in the African jungle.[51]

The new bridge was completed on March 29 and the battalion marched to join Parke in early April. The long stretch of railroad was the target of raids by Confederate cavalry, one of which captured nine prisoners from the Ninth New Jersey. Burnside repeatedly asked the War Department for a regiment of cavalry, field guns, and locomotives and cars to haul the vast amount of supplies and ordnance required for the siege of the fort. "The engines, cars, and wagons are absolutely necessary to us here."[52]

The regiments in New Bern were not idle. Foster kept the spade going building forts and entrenchments around the perimeter of the town, and constructing batteries and small forts guarding road junctions and bridges further out. He set crews to work rebuilding the Trent River bridges. Burnside reorganized his troops into three divisions and appointed his three brigadiers Acting Major-Generals, hoping the War Department would soon make the promotions official.

Acting Major-General Parke concentrated on getting his men and ordnance across Bogue Sound and on Bogue Banks. He could ferry his men over in small boats, but he needed steamers and flats to haul his siege guns. A 10-inch mortar weighed about four thousand pounds and a 30-pounder Parrott rifle 4,200 pounds. He asked for the *Union/Wheelbarrow* to come to him through Core Sound, but she was not available. The navy did send him the stern-wheeler *Old North State* and several smaller vessels. The *Old North State* drew too much water to land troops directly on the Banks, so Parke still depended on small boats, flats and rafts. The ships had to stay out of range of the fort's guns. He asked Burnside for contrabands or Negroes for additional labor to haul supplies. Until the bridge at Newport was finished, rations were scarce, but Parke reported they could supply themselves with "fish &c." That should have been no hardship. The town of Beaufort was in range, so that Union activity on the waterfront vexed the citizens who feared retaliation from the fort's guns. Parke stated there were rabid secessionists about and asked about taking oaths of allegiance and neutrality from the Union sympathizers. A delegation of citizens called on Parke, who was also Military Governor, to ask what he intended doing. Parke merely said he would let them know in due time, and concentrated on military affairs.[53]

Fort Macon had been built for coast defense, to guard Topsail Inlet and Beaufort harbor against enemy ships. It was not intended to fight enemy land forces, for the nation's coastal forts were supposed to be guarded on their landward sides by friendly troops. Fort Macon, in April of 1862, faced enemy ships at sea, an overwhelming force of enemy troops in the rear at New Bern, and strong enemy troops on the flank on Bogue Banks, beside enemy ships in the sounds. Its isolation was complete.

The fort was armed with fifty-four guns: two 10-inch columbiads, five 8-inch columbiads, four 32-pounder rifles, one 24-pounder rifle, eighteen 24-pounder smoothbores, eighteen 32-pounder smoothbores, and six 32-pounder carronades. The fort had 35,000 pounds of powder, not enough for a long siege, too few shells, but did have a six-months supply of food for the garrison.[53]

Colonel Moses J. White, an intelligent and able twenty-seven year old West Pointer not in the best of health, commanded the fort, though he was perhaps too strict and inflexible with volunteer citizen soldiers. He commanded 22 officers and 419 men organized in five heavy artillery companies. When General Branch gathered his troops to defend New Bern, he directed Colonel White to select the five companies to garrison the fort. White chose from the Tenth North Carolina Artillery:

Company B, Guion's Battery, was part of the original garrison.

Company F, Andrew's Battery, was part of the original garrison.

Company G, the Beaufort Harbor Guards, or Pender's Battery, was part of the original garrison.

Company H, the Topsail Rifles, which occupied Fort Macon during those first weeks, was transferred to Virginia where it served as infantry, then returned to Fort Macon and was designated heavy artillery.

Company F of the Fortieth Regiment was organized in New Bern. It was called Lawrence's Company, then Blount's Battery. First ordered to Fort Macon, then transferred to Harker's Island, it was transferred back to Fort Macon in March, 1862.

Companies G and H were raised locally and the men were concerned for their families safety in the impending battle, though it had but slight effect on their conduct.

During the brief time left, White set the men to strengthening the fort with sandbags, preparing cartridges, and practicing gun drill.[54]

Between March 29 when the first Union soldiers crossed to the Banks and April 10 Parke reported: "every hour of night and day available was spent in transporting men, siege train, and supplies." The Fourth Rhode Island, the Eighth Connecticut, the Fifth Rhode Island Battalion all crossed over along with Company C of the First United States Artillery and Company I of the Third New York Artillery. A signal officer went aboard the flagship of the fleet to establish army-navy communication. On April 11, Parke with three staff officers; Captain Williamson of the Topographical Engineers, Captain Morris of the artillery, and Lieutenant Flagler of ordnance, reconnoitered to within a mile of the fort, whereupon the fort opened fire. Parke and his men took cover behind the sand hills while the three staff officers selected sites for the batteries and entrenchments for the infantry. The blockading fleet shelled the fort and beach to help extract Parke and his escort. The next day the soldiers commenced digging the approach trenches. A skirmish developed between Confederate pickets under Captain Pool and the lead companies of the Eighth Connecticut. Pool's men retreated to the fort, yelling defiance as they went. The digging continued. The first line of earthworks was about two thousand yards from the fort.[55]

A siege was the most inexorable of nineteenth century military operations, proceeding with almost mathematical certainty from one stage to the next. It was conducted by infantrymen digging, and artillerymen emplacing guns, with no foolish bayonet charges. The terrain aided General Parke's besiegers, for the series of sand dunes, formed in ridges, which lay between the fort and Hoop Pole Creek, afforded cover and concealment for the Federal's operations. Only the road along the beach was visible to lookouts in the fort and a target for the fort's guns. Hence, artillery and supplies had to be hauled forward only at night. The guns of the fort kept up a desultory fire on the road and against what they could see of the parties working behind the dunes.[56]

Parke pushed the entrenching parties steadily forward, each regiment taking its turn in front. A soldier of the Fifth Rhode Island described it.

> When our turn came to take our tour of duty in the trenches, we would proceed along the beach, and when we had approached within range of the guns of the fort, the rebels would send us their compliments in the form of shot and shell ... one man was stationed on lookout duty near the top of the rifle-pit, while the others would remain below. When the lookout saw the flash of rebel guns he would sing out "Down!" the men taking to the rifle-pit like a woodchuck to its hole.[57]

Communications between the fort and mainland were almost completely choked off. Nine men, all from Carteret County, did manage to desert and cross over to the mainland. Concern for their families was probably their primary reason, combined with complaints about the bread ration. Colonel White detailed two officers and a boat's crew to attempt to break through and communicate with the Confederate command in the state via Wilmington. Lieutenant Thaddeus Coleman of Guion's company and Lieutenant Cicero Primrose of Cogdell's company led the detail on April 9, which eluded Federal blockaders and reached friendly lines. The officers carried reports and letters, including a request that Confederate troops break the siege. General Holmes had no relief force to send, but he did send Lieutenant Primrose with letters to General Robert E. Lee in Richmond. Primrose gave General Lee, at the time President Davis' military adviser, a personal account of conditions in the fort, including the affair of the bread ration. Lee was much concerned about "discontent and insubordination" among the troops in the fort and authorized General Holmes to withdraw the garrison if he thought it was advisable. It was too late to withdraw the garrison, and unnecessary, for the bread affair had been settled by the time Primrose arrived in Richmond.[58]

The bread unpleasantness should have been a minor incident, but it was magnified by nervousness of the soldiers, officers, and commander alike at being shut in and surrounded. It began with an order of Colonel White that company cooks would cease to draw flour rations, but would draw loaves of bread baked for all by a former baker in the ranks of one of the companies. It sounded like a more efficient operation than company baking, so the baker and his helper commenced work with the fort's large oven. The soldiers off duty watched with interest. The first batch of loaves were inedible. The spectators laughed, jeered, and shouted "try it again." The second batch was even worse—black and hard as ballast rocks. Somebody suggested the loaves could be used as solid shot. The alleged baker kept trying, the results were no better. The surgeon carried several loaves to the colonel and certified them not fit to eat. The company officers asked the colonel to resume issuing flour. The colonel was adamant and refused to modify his order. The matter became serious when men and officers together notified the colonel they were prepared to go to the commissary and take their issue of flour. Colonel White thought his officers did not support him properly, but he finally ordered the commissary officer to issue flour again and the ill feeling died away in a few days.[59] The men could concentrate on fighting the enemy who dug ever closer.

On the other side, work on emplacements continued. Nearest the fort was a front line trench, perpendicular to the sea beach, stretching inland, and manned by infantry. Directly in front of the trench stood the Eliason house and outbuildings, which were all burned to clear a field of fire. Behind the front line and 1280 yards from the fort, Parke emplaced the 8-inch mortar battery behind a sand hill and near the ocean. This battery was commanded by First Lieutenant M.F. Prouty of the Twenty-fifth Massachusetts Infantry, assisted by Lieutenants Thomas and Kelser of the Third New York Artillery. Echeloned inland behind them he placed Captain Morris' 30-pounder Parrott rifles 1,480 yards from the fort, and in back and slightly inland was Lieutenant Flagler's 10-inch mortar battery. More than digging was necessary on the artillery emplacements. The men built sandbag walls to hold the loose sand in place and constructed gun platforms of heavy timbers. The mortar positions were behind sand hills and invisible to the Confederates. The 30-pounder Parrots, flat trajectory, direct fire weapons, had to be placed near the top of the dunes with their muzzles pointing through embrasures and visible from the fort. They were a target, though a small one, for the fort's gunners. The embrasures were not cut through the hill until the last minute when all batteries were ready to fire. Colonel White, limited in his supply of powder and shell, could not order a full bombardment to stop the Federal working parties. Instead his gunners tried sniping with their cannon, trying for a direct hit on the front of the batteries or cutting the fuses on their shells exactly right so the shell would burst just beyond the sand hill and over the gun crew. The fort had no mortars for indirect fire that could drop shells on top of the gun positions.

White did all he could. He shifted his six old carronades, obsolete weapons of short range, and tried to make mortars of them. He built new gun platforms for them on the lower terreplein facing the enemy. He rigged high angle mountings for them with adjustments for elevation, and produced a clumsy but workable mortar substitute, lacking only proper observation to direct their fire.[60] The Federal mortars were regular siege mortars, squat, heavy barreled pieces, mounted on high-angle carriages. Their crews varied the range by both the angle of elevation and the size of the powder charge. The mortars lobbed their shells high in the air, over sand hills or fort walls, to fall almost straight down on the enemy. With a forward observer who could spot the fall of the shells and signal corrections to the batteries, the gunners could "walk" their shots onto the target. Colonel White had no observer outside the fort, but General Burnside had signal officers to assist Parke's gunners.

Burnside and staff inspected Parke's operations on April 18, and made several suggestions. The Confederates noted that something was going on, and saluted the general with several shots which did no damage. Burnside returned to New Bern well pleased. That night Colonel White sent two companies on a sortie to try to damage the Federal works. Parke's men drove them back in at a cost of two wounded. That same night, Parke's men, carrying out one of Burnside's suggestions, dug an advanced trench near the site of the burnt Eliason house, about five hundred yards from the fort. This was too close. The fort responded with a blast of grapeshot that wounded two men of the Eighth Connecticut and caused the permanent abandonment of the position. Confederate guns continued with a full bombardment of the Federal lines in the dark. No further Federal losses occurred, while the citizens of Beaufort and Morehead City were provided with a grand spectacle of the sights and sounds of battle.[61]

Burnside readied two vessels of the Marine Artillery mounting four 30-pounder Parrott rifles and one 12-pounder Wiard rifle to aid in the bombardment. The little barges were "armored" with wet bales of hay and cotton. On April 23, Burnside, in the *Alice Price*, towed them down and anchored about four miles from the fort. One of the fort's rifled 32-pounders, named "Maggie McRae" by her crew, greeted the general with two shells which flew extremely close. It was good shooting at that range. *Alice Price* quickly moved back and the general proceeded to his main purpose in coming to the scene, to give the Confederates another chance to surrender. Burnside sent Captain Herman Biggs of his staff, under a flag of truce, to deliver a note to Colonel White.

Biggs and White were old friends, but White nevertheless declined the offer. Colonel White did agree to meet General Burnside the next day. The two commanders landed on the beach of Shackleford Bank and held a courteous meeting at which White again declined to surrender. They agreed on two other items: White promised not to fire on the town of Beaufort, and Burnside gave permission for a load of mail from the fort be delivered to Beaufort under a flag of truce.[62] The commanders departed.

Burnside was ready to open the bombardment, but Parke wanted one more day to make ready. During the night Captain Morris' men dug out the embrasures and unmasked the Parrott rifles. At 5:30 A.M. on the twenty-fifth, Morris' Parrots fired the first shot, a hit on the parapet. The mortar batteries joined in, all firing rapidly. The fort returned the fire with spirit. The fort first answered with a 24-pounder of Manney's battery which hit near Morris' battery, then Captain Pool's carronade-mortars began to fire. Blount's 32-pounders and Guion's big columbiads roared. Both sides fired rapid salvoes, creating dense clouds of smoke carried by the wind back over the fort, and hindering the Federal gunners' aim. Prouty's 8-inch mortars nearest the sea retained some visibility, so he could correct his gunner's aim.[63]

The navy had received no notice that the bombardment would begin that morning, but hearing and seeing it were sufficient notice for Commander Samuel Lockwood in the flagship to signal his squadron to get underway. His ships were

> *Daylight*, screw steamer of 682 tons, Commander Samuel Lockwood, 4 long 32-pounders.
> *Chippewa*, screw steamer of 507 tons, Lieutenant commanding A. Bryson, 1 11-inch Dahlgren, 1 20-pounder Parrott rifle, 2 24-pounder Dahlgrens.
> *State of Georgia*, side-wheel steamer of 1,200 tons, Commander James F. Armstrong, 6 8-inch smoothbores, 2 32-pounders, 1 30-pounder Parrott rifle.
> *Gemsbok*, sailing bark of 622 tons, Acting Lieutenant E. Cavendy, 4 8-inch smoothbores, 2 32-pounders.

At 8 A.M. the ships closed the fort to within a mile and a half, or as close as the shoals would allow. The wind was fresh from the southwest, with a heavy sea running. The steamers moved in line in an elliptical course following the flagship. The *Gemsbok* anchored. All of the vessels rolled deeply, making accurate firing difficult. *Chippewa's* big 11-inch Dahlgren almost dipped water on the downward roll. *State of Georgia* scraped the shoal, but got off without injury. The fort returned the fire before the first round was completed. Pool's men left the carronades, ran to the southeast face with guns bearing on the ocean. The gun crews of the water battery and Guion's men on the upper tier manning the Columbiads and rifled 32-pounders laid their guns and fired furiously. This was the sort of battle the fort was intended to fight, and the targets were plainly visible. Water spouts rose all around the ships. Commander Lockwood reported that the fire of the enemy was excellent. The *Daylight* was hit by an 8-inch solid shot that smashed through the width of the ship, missing her machinery by inches and wounding one engineer. The *State of Georgia* was shot through the American ensign at her masthead, while the *Gemsbok* had her rigging cut up. The *Chippewa* reported no damage. All captains agreed with Commander Armstrong who stated, "The fire of the enemy was well directed, their shot and shell falling thick and fast around us." An hour and a quarter was enough of it for Commander Lockwood, especially as the rough sea prevented accurate shooting and most of the ship's fifteen-second fused shells had been expended. The squadron sailed back out the inlet, hoping to return if the sea moderated. The Confederate gunners cheered and jeered. The gunboat *Ellis* and the two armed barges lay across the inlet off Shackleford Banks out of range, so did not join the battle, though the *Grenade* fired her Parrott rifles.[64]

With the naval interlude ended, the Confederate gunners rushed back across the fort to the land face, where the Federal fire had increased in intensity if not in accuracy. The bombardment continued into the morning. As the hours passed, the Confederate gunners began to tire. Colonel White reported 263 men on duty, with a long sick list. Even though most of the sick were able to man their guns, there were not enough men for relief crews. The Federal artillerymen were just as tired, but were able to call on the infantry regiments for assistance. Both sides kept up the volume of fire. At midmorning Federal accuracy began to improve.

Second Lieutenant W.S. Andrews, of the Ninth New York, was on loan to General Parke as Acting Signal Officer. On Parke's orders he established a signal post on the third floor piazza of the Atlantic Hotel in Beaufort, with a clear view of the fort and the Federal batteries. Andrews' work initially was sending messages from the mainland to the troops on Bogue Banks during the day when fire from the fort prevented boat traffic. On the day of the great bombardment Andrews and his assistant, Lieutenant Marvin Watt, could see how the shots were missing the target. On his own initiative Andrews managed to establish communication directly with the batteries. Andrews reported after the action:

> My station was at very nearly a right angle with the line of fire, so that I was able to judge with accuracy the distance over or short that the shot fell. The 10-inch shell were falling almost without exception more than 300 yards beyond the fort.... The 8-inch shell were falling short.... The same was the case with the battery of Parrott guns, which were much elevated.... *After 12m. every shot fired from our batteries fell in or on the fort.*[65]

Captain Morris' Parrotts had a dual mission for their flat trajectory fire. First, to destroy or dismount the enemy guns visible on the parapets. The second was to breach the fort's walls, and in particular, to smash through the inner walls of the southwest angle protecting the magazine. General Foster had served in the Engineers in pre-war years, and had inspected Fort Macon. He prepared a drawing for the gunners showing the location of magazines and shell rooms. With his aim corrected, Morris' Parrotts just skimmed over the outer wall and bored into the magazine's wall. The Parrotts' fire also began to dismount guns in the fort. One spectacular shot that afternoon hit and rebounded, disabled three guns, including "Maggie McRae," killed three gunners, and wounded four. Confederate projectiles from the fort flew in the embrasures of Morris's battery, damaging one gun which stayed in action. Most of the parapet of Flagler's mortar battery was blown away, so that the men had to shovel sand to rebuild it as the shelling allowed. More damage to the mortar batteries came from concussion of firing and the heavy downward recoil of the mortars. The thick timber platforms began to break up, so that each mortar in turn had to cease firing while the men shored up the beds.

This damage was negligible compared to what was happening in the fort when every shot fired began to hit. The mortars began to rain hell-fire from heaven and kept it up. The Federal batteries fired 1,150 shots during the day, of which more than five hundred fell on or within the fort. Confederate fire dwindled as more guns were damaged and men had to seek shelter from the shell fragments. A total of nineteen of the fort's guns were disabled by enemy fire. The parade ground was cratered by shells and thousands of shell fragments were scattered over the fort. Colonel White, realizing he could not hold the fort much longer under such a fire, ordered a white flag raised about 4:30 P.M. The batteries ceased fire. A group emerged from the fort carrying the white flag. Captains Pool and Guion, with an unarmed detachment of soldiers marched down the beach. Captain Pell with Lieutenants Hill and Prouty from the batteries met them. The two parties, both rumpled and grimed from combat, greeted each other formally. The Confederates asked for terms of surrender in White's name, and General Parke was summoned to answer. As Parke could offer no terms other than unconditional surrender those present agreed on a cease fire until Burnside could arrive next morning.[66]

General Burnside came early in the *Alice Price*, sent two staff officers ashore to see Colonel White, and received White and Captain Guion who returned with them. White agreed to the terms, which were the surrender of the fort and all its contents to the forces of the United States, and secondly, the parole of honor of all the officers and men who would be released along with their personal possessions and returned to their homes. They could not take up arms again until properly exchanged. Burnside still did not want prisoners cluttering up his army. After the signatures were put on the document, they all sat down to breakfast. The *Alice Price*, meanwhile, steamed to the fort's wharf where they all marched ashore to assemble their respective troops for the final ceremony.[67]

Burnside, Parke, and staff strolled down the beach to the first entrenchments where the Fifth Rhode Island Artillery held the line. Major Wright formed the battalion on the beach with its brand new battle flag in front, the generals turned around, and the procession marched back up the beach and formed by the sally port into the fort where the Stars and Bars still flew. Colonel White had paraded his garrison to stack arms and had dismissed them to gather their personal possessions. The Fifth Rhode Island, the generals, and the growing cohort of correspondents, staff officers, and off duty men filed in. The Rhode Islanders took station around the fort as the officers gathered at the fort's flag pole. A detail lowered the Confederate flag, but they had no large United States garrison flag. With the help of a Confederate officer one was found in the fort. As the new color guard hoisted it, bugler Joe Greene of the

Fourth Rhode Island played The Star Spangled Banner "as if his very soul was in each martial note."[68]

The Confederate prisoners started for home as soon as their paroles were made out and signed. The Beaufort men crossed over that same day, Captain Guion's company started for New Bern on April 27 and the rest sailed for Wilmington in the *Chippewa* on the April 28. Two men, too dangerously wounded to move, were left in the fort in care of a nurse. The casualties on both sides were astonishingly low considering the volume of artillery fire that drenched both sides. Confederate losses reported by Colonel White were seven killed and eighteen wounded plus one dead of sickness. General Parke reported one killed and three wounded in the battle. Colonel Rodman, Fourth Rhode Island, also reported six deaths by disease during the time on the coast.[69]

Federal gains were again immense, the base in North Carolina was secure from all points. New Bern's supplies were assured with a good harbor and a reasonable inlet connected to the town by a good railroad. The damaged fort could be repaired to guard a needed haven for the navy and supply ships would no longer depend solely on stormy Hatteras Inlet.

The Fifth Rhode Island and the Second United States Artillery Company garrisoned the fort, the other regiments crossed to the mainland. Joint army-navy expeditions sailed from New Bern to the other major unoccupied river ports. Washington had been visited on March 20 and occupied on May 2 by the Twenty-fourth Massachusetts. Plymouth was next. Visited twice by the navy in May, the town was occupied in mid–June by a company of the Ninth New York. Gunboats took up position off both towns.

In New Bern, the troops settled down to occupation duties, though with frequent raids and marches into the countryside. Occupation was less hazardous than active campaigning, but there were other problems inherent in it, such as renewed emphasis on the military formalities of garrison duty. One soldier of the Twenty-third Massachusetts was assigned to guard the city dock during a drenching rain. He solved the problem of his comfort in a manner possibly acceptable in the field or in the batteries. He "found" an umbrella, and by breaking off the crook in the handle, fitted it in his musket barrel. He then walked his post, his musket at the carry, sheltered from the downpour. He marched around the corner of a building and was confronted by General Burnside and staff. He immediately snapped to and presented arms and umbrella. The general frowned, probably to mask a grin, and asked him, "Does that look soldierlike?" The astonished private could only stammer, "No."[70]

Chapter Seven

Occupation 1862–1863

ENERAL BURNSIDE'S CONQUESTS resulted in Federal control of the North Carolina coast from the rivers and inlets of Onslow County north to Virginia, with the navy cruising outside the Banks and both army and navy gunboats steaming the sounds and rivers. Federal troops occupied the mainland from New Bern to the sea, and Federal enclaves formed around the occupied river ports. Soldiers aided by the labor of former slaves dug trenches and built forts and blockhouses to form a fortified line around each town. The river shores and the fringes of the sounds were Federal territory within range of the steamer's guns. Although the area was stable for the next two years, it was not static. The Union army's enclaves swelled or shrank as the opposing forces raided, attacked, or counter-attacked. The Sand Banks, "the precious stones set in a silver sea," to borrow from Shakespeare, were still occupied. Roanoke Island contained the largest garrison on the Banks, Hatteras had several artillery companies, Portsmouth had a small guard detachment, and Ocracoke a tiny one. The Portsmouth garrison increased as the Federal Medical Service began to use the facilities of the Marine Hospital.

Although Brigadier-General Foster was Military Governor of New Bern, Burnside, as commander of the Department of North Carolina, had his hands full with administrative matters in addition to his military duties. The Banks and the other towns all had Military Governors who looked to Burnside for instructions. New Bern swarmed with escaped slaves, many more than came to Roanoke Island, and sheltered many impoverished white civilians. To handle this problem, Burnside brought in Vincent Colyer from Roanoke Island and appointed him Superintendent of the Poor.[1]

By late March the *Newbern Daily Progress* was being published again, the plant and presses under new ownership. The first edition published lists of new city and county officials, an article on the battle of Hampton Roads, and the announcement, "Salutatory — The Progress makes its appearance today under new auspices, and altogether new management ... an earnest advocate of that glorious Union."[2] A later edition of the paper published the important news that General Burnside had just been presented a 175-pound green turtle by Adams Express Company, saying: "This chap was ordered, and will add materially to the rotundity of the general's corporation." There were items of genuine importance to report, for in late May another newcomer arrived, sent to assist the general in governing.

Though the military government was firmly set and functioning, President Abraham Lincoln believed the appointment of a civilian as governor, one who would work closely with the military authorities, was the best procedure. Lincoln believed such a governor would improve the chances of detaching North Carolina from the Confederacy. He looked carefully for the right man and he would certainly have to be a better choice than Marble Nash Taylor.

In early April, 1862, Edward Stanly, city and county attorney of San Francisco, received a telegram from Secretary of War Edwin N. Stanton appointing him military governor of North Carolina and inviting him to come to Washington at once to confirm the appointment. Stanly, a former Whig congressman from New Bern, embarked by steamer to Panama, thence by railroad and another steamer for New York and Washington. After consultations with Secretary Stanton and President Lincoln, he received his commission on May 19 and took ship for New Bern, where he arrived on May 26.[3]

The next day, Governor Stanly conferred with General Burnside. The general reported to Secretary Stanton that he had "consulted fully" with the governor and their views were "remarkably coincident." When Vincent Colyer called on the new governor, Stanly commended him on the good work he had done caring for the destitute, but pointed out that schools for Negroes were contrary to state laws and would harm the Union's cause in the state. Though it was not ordered, Colyer immediately closed the schools. Another cause of disagreement was the treatment of escaped slaves within Federal lines. Stanly's method was to allow the slave's owner, if he swore allegiance to the United States, to find his former slave and attempt to regain him by agreement. This did not please the Abolitionists. Colyer went howling North to complain to the officials in Washington.[4] After much verbal turmoil, the disagreements were patched over, if not settled, and Colyer returned to New Bern and reopened his schools, but resigned his post in July 1862.

Governor Stanly's program of restoring trade in the occupied areas was of greater economic importance than slavery to the dwellers on the Sand Banks. There were few farmers on the Banks, save for Roanoke Island, but many unemployed mariners. Stanly issued authorizations to ship owners to trade within the sounds and rivers, and to certain residents of Washington and New Bern for shipping timber and naval stores to the West Indies via Hatteras. The shippers were instructed to bring back salt, a necessity for preservation of meat and fish. The governor issued his permits not only to those who took the oath of allegiance, but to some who declined, but would sign an oath of neutrality. This novel instrument was invented by Governor Stanly.[5] The licenses given to shippers involved Stanly in disputes with Union naval officers and eventually with Rear-Admiral S.P. Lee, Commander of the North Atlantic Blockading Squadron. When the dispute was referred to Washington, D.C. for resolution, the authorities there backed Admiral Lee.[6] The trading permits also conflicted with the instructions given another Federal appointee recently arrived in the state.

The *Newbern Daily Progress* announced in early June that a new customs collector had been appointed for Beaufort and was expected soon. He was John Addison

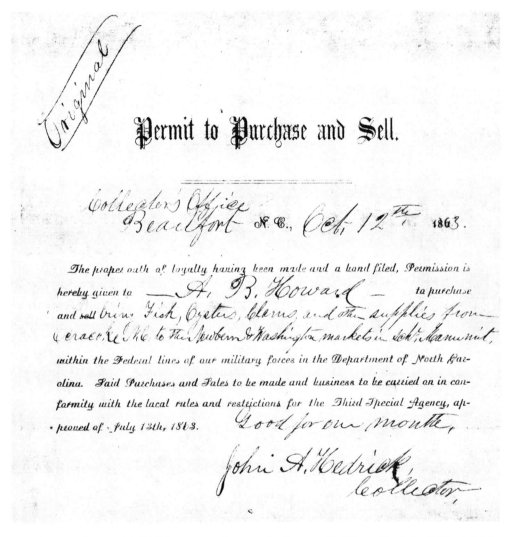

Permit to Purchase and Sell "fish, oysters, clams, and other supplies" issued by John A. Hendrick to A.B. Howard. (Treasury Agents Records, Myers House Papers, Brown Library, Washington, N.C.)

Hedrick, a Tar Heel and former resident of Salisbury. Hedrick announced his arrival in a letter dated June 10 to his brother in Washington, D.C. "I arrived here yesterday about noon. We had no bad luck though ran ashore in the sound and had considerable trouble getting ashore at Hatteras Inlet.... I expect to leave here tomorrow for Beaufort.... The cars between here and Beaufort have not commenced to run."[7]

The lack of locomotives prevented much use of the railroad even after the bridges were rebuilt. Not until June 24 was Burnside able to report that the trains were running between New Bern and Beaufort. Headquarters had finally shipped him four engines, of which two were lost in a gale at Hatteras Inlet, but two arrived safely.[8] Burnside had little opportunity to ride the train, for he received from President Lincoln an order on June 28: "I think you had better go, with any re-inforcements you can spare, to General McClellan." The order was amplified by Secretary Stanton on the same date. Burnside, with seven thousand men started for Norfolk on July 3, stopping at Roanoke Island to pick up part of the troops there. Here Rush Hawkins decided to interfere with the movement because he had heard a rumor that McClellan had captured Richmond. Hawkins queried General John A. Dix at Fort Monroe asking if the orders still held in view of this development. Stanton replied to Burnside to proceed with all speed to General McClellan, who had retreated, not advanced. The rumor was false. Burnside proceeded with eight thousand men and arrived with his advance party on July 7. Major-General John G. Foster was left in command of the Department of North Carolina and 9,434 men.[9]

Foster continued fortifying the towns and scouting and skirmishing in the country. Incidents of sniping by Southern irregulars occurred in some of the towns. A sentinel of the Twenty-third Massachusetts was wounded in New Bern by "one of the skulking, ruffianly miscreants" and the source of the shot was seen. Five men and one woman were taken from the house and jailed. Next morning the regiment marched to the scene, stacked arms, and shouldered axes and crowbars. They first moved all the furniture to the other side of the street, then demolished the fence, and cut down all the trees in the yard. Next came the house. Board by board, rafter, joist, and beam were pulled apart and piled in the yard. The chimney was the last thing wrecked. While the men were razing, the officers slashed down a field of corn behind the house with their sabres. For a finale, the regimental band played patriotic selections and the regiment marched away.[10]

In early August another newcomer to New Bern arrived, though he was previously at Hatteras. Down the gangplank of a steamer pranced Charles Henry Foster, former congressional hopeful. He wore a brand new blue uniform with captain's bars twinkling on his shoulders. He claimed President Lincoln had commissioned him and sent him to help recruit a loyal Union regiment in the state. "On August 5, 1862, Lincoln issued Foster a pass to New Bern. With orders from the Adjutant General's Office, General John G. Foster 'could not refuse [Charles Foster] the duty to which he was appointed.'"[11]

Recruiting soldiers for the Union in the state was a matter on which all agreed — Stanly, Generals Burnside and Foster, and the Lincoln Government. Burnside had authorized the organization of the first company of the First North Carolina Union Volunteers in Washington in early May, 1862. Captain Edward E. Potter, Foster's commissary officer, was to be Colonel and Mr. John A. Respess, Lieutenant-Colonel.[12] Mr. Respess, Mayor Isaiah Respess's son, resigned his position as soon as he realized what his friends and neighbors thought of him. In September, Governor Stanly was given authority to commission officers in the new regiment. President Lincoln authorized this to help pacify Stanly, who was concerned that the planned Emancipation Proclamation would hinder his efforts to reclaim the state for the Union.[13]

Recruiting for the new regiment had been slow, but Captain Charles Henry Foster commenced his new job with zeal and energy. By late summer he had selected several men to serve as recruiting sergeants and had begun to hold public meetings throughout the Union occupied counties. The *Newbern Daily Progress* of September 9 described Foster as "a persevering and energetic man" and announced that he would run for a seat in congress. Foster did not intend that his military career would interfere with any political possibilities. He did not bring his old friend Marble Nash Taylor along to help.

Some Southern editors were still having fun with "Governor" Taylor. The *Wilmington Journal* of July 24, 1862 published a proclamation purporting to come from "Governor Marble Nash Taylor, Captain-General,… Governor de facto and Minister Plenipotentiary to Hatteras." The document, said the *Journal*, was delivered by Underground Railroad and Shark Express. In the proclamation Taylor was quoted as saying: "A reasonable price will be paid for the carcass of Edward Stanly, if brought to me dead or crippled, at Hatteras; payment to be in fish or New York censation money."

Captain Foster's latest opportunity, the First Union, never formed as a regiment, nor marched in review behind banners, fifes, and drums. The companies formed were usually stationed in the towns of origin. Companies were raised in New Bern, Beaufort, Washington, Plymouth, Elizabeth City, Wingfield on the Chowan River, and on Hatteras Bank. These companies consisted of garrison troops, second-line troops, though some of the companies performed well in certain of the army's skirmishes and raids. No companies were organized at Portsmouth, Ocracoke, or Roanoke Islands, though detachments were sent to the islands for special duties. However, the Union Army did not leave Ocracoke Inlet entirely untenanted.

Major-General Foster (who was no kin to C.H. Foster) reported to Secretary Stanton on August 7, 1862:

> The health of the troops is as good as reported in my last. The hospital at Portsmouth is ready to receive patients, and some invalids are at present removed there, and in a short time I expect to have the greater part of my sick at the general hospitals at Beaufort and Portsmouth on the seaboard.[14]

Three other hospitals had been established in the area, as well. They were Foster General Hospital at New Bern, Hammond General Hospital at Beaufort and Mansfield General Hospital at Morehead City.[15]

The sea did not neglect the islands, but continued to take its toll of the limited number of trading ships. The *Newbern Daily Progress* of September 6, 1862 reported two shipwrecks. The schooner *Clifton* of New Bern carrying naval stores went ashore on the coast of Delaware and the schooner *Actor* of Washington went ashore on Bodie Island opposite Roanoke Island. The *Actor* was laden with liquor and onions. The paper learned that the liquor was destroyed, but the onions were saved. This seems an odd choice for soldiers or sailors to make.

Nor did the First Union's recruiters neglect the islands. The *Progress* reported that a large number of citizens of Portsmouth assembled in the church on the afternoon of September 19, 1862. The Reverend William C. Whitcombe, chaplain of the hospital, opened with a prayer. Following him was Mr. C.H. Foster who spoke at length on the hopelessness of the rebel cause and the sure success of the Union. The oration concluded with a resolution offered by Foster, that the people would cheerfully cooperate in the organization of the First Regiment of Union Volunteers. That night, the *Progress* continued, a similar gathering was held in the meeting house at Ocracoke, with at least a hundred men outside who were unable to obtain admission. Foster made the same speech and asked for the same pledge of support. The paper's reporter predicted that Portsmouth would furnish at least twenty Union volunteers.

The islanders may not have rallied to Foster's standard according to John Hedrick's next letter. Foster, Hedrick wrote, had gone to the Banks with his recruiting sergeant to get enlistments and did not return until Monday. He missed several other appointments in the Beaufort area. "He was so offended about something that he would not come to the hotel to get his dinner. I understand he was angry with the Secessionists, and was going to Newbern to get orders to punish them." Hedrick jeered at Foster's claim of having influence with President Lincoln and labeled his recruiting speeches as "more forerunners of his campaign harangues."[16]

The Marine Hospital at Portsmouth continued to expand its services. The *Newbern Daily Progress* of October 2, 1862 quoted: "Wm. C. Whitcombe, Chaplain of the U.S. Hospital at Portsmouth as announcing that 136 patients had been accommodated since August, representing ten different regiments. Not a death occurred among the military and only one among the islands four hundred inhabitants." Assuming the paper's figures were accurate, most of the Portsmouthers had returned home. In its October 7 issue, the *Progress* stated that the Reverend Mr. Whitcombe furnished more interesting statistics on the number of inmates, "which it may be best, for prudential reasons, not to publish to the world." If military censorship was applied, it lapsed on another page of the same paper, for it reported the arrival of the steamer *Allison* carrying thirty-five additional patients to the hospital under the care of Dr. Hall Curtis of Boston.

Medical and military personnel at Portsmouth made a growing United States presence. It was not so across the inlet at Ocracoke, for only sporadic visits by military or naval patrols were mentioned. The lighthouse was apparently unlit and unmanned as no mention of it appears in official reports until later in the war.

A few Confederate soldiers returned home to the Banks after the battle of New Bern. One such soldier was Robert Howard of Ocracoke, a youth of seventeen who had enlisted the previous October in Company F of the Thirty-third North Carolina. The regimental roster carries him as AWOL after March 14, 1862. Howard family history differs slightly. Private Howard, according to oral history, rejoined his company after the battle of New Bern and marched with the regiment in Branch's brigade to Virginia. After the battle of Chantilly he left the army and returned to Ocracoke. Shortly thereafter, he took ship at Springer's Point for Mexico. He came home after five years.[17] Springer's Point is located near Ocracoke Inlet and is adjacent to Teach's Hole Channel, a likely departure point for a foreign voyage. Howard's ship somehow passed through the inlet supposedly blocked by stone schooners.

Other information suggests that Ocracoke Inlet was again navigable. Commander H.K. Davenport, USN, senior officer in the sounds reported on October 1, 1862:

"The *Granite* has been employed in blockading Ocracoke Inlet and cruising Pamlico Sound."[18] The same report located thirteen other gunboats stationed at the various riverports or cruising the sounds. The sloop *Granite* kept station at Ocracoke, relieved periodically for re-supplying at New Bern and was transferred only when a crisis arose on the mainland.

Recruiting continued on the mainland for the First Union Volunteers. John Hedrick wrote his brother that an old man named Congleton, sixty-four years old, had been one of the first to enlist. Congleton was a strong abolitionist and had run for state office on the Free Suffrage ticket. He was also an admirer of Captain Foster. In this letter Hedrick referred to C.H. Foster as the "Humbug Foster," a title he used thereafter. Hedrick also explained the origin of the epithet Buffalo as applied to soldiers of the First Union.

> The men look first rate in their sky blue pants and dark blue coats and caps on. I believe that they make a better appearance than the Yankee soldiers do. Their uniforms make them appear so large that the people call them the "Buffaloes." I think they like to be called buffaloes. They go around in gangs like herds of buffaloes.[19]

Hedrick's next letter reported two local schooners had returned from the West Indies laden with molasses, sugar, and salt. These vessels sailed under his license from Beaufort as commercial shipping was not allowed to use other inlets. Hedrick reported nothing new on the Humbug Foster except that northern newspapers mentioned him as a political candidate in the state.[20]

The *Progress* of December 2, in an article on the ever-active Chaplain Whitcombe, reported: "He observed Thursday, Nov. 27, as a day of Thanksgiving and Praise" in a service held for soldiers and civilians in the church on Portsmouth. The *Progress* of December 20 continued with the chaplain's peregrinations. He held services on the Sabbath, December 14, on the long neglected island of Ocracoke. He addressed a mass of men, women and children who "thronging the ancient meeting house, listened attentively to the first sermon they had heard for more than a year and a half." The writer underestimated Ocracoke's population, giving it as about three hundred inhabitants.

The same issue of the *Progress* grandly proclaimed that for the first time in history, a stove was used on December 2 for warming the Portsmouth church. The stove had been placed there by Dr. Loren H. Pease for the use of both islanders and patients in the hospital. Despite the newspaper's claim, the use of stoves was not unknown on Portsmouth Island. Augustus Dudley, a merchant of Portsmouth later filed claims against the United States government for various goods and services rendered the Marine Hospital and others during the war. Among the items unpaid were "seventeen new four-damper stoves and three new six-damper cook stoves."[21] The *Progress* also noted the arrest and imprisonment of Robert Wallace of Portsmouth for threatening the lives of hospital officials, including John M. Spear, the Hospital Steward. The paper predicted it would "go hard with the prisoner" (Wallace) when he was tried.

Under a heading "New Light Houses", the paper announced that Captain Benjamin Lawrence, formerly of the Ordnance Department, was keeper of the light, which "is distinctly visible during the day at this Island, while its cheering light gleams with peculiar attraction during the darkness of the night. It is about six miles from Portsmouth." The lighthouse mentioned was probably that at Cape Lookout, though the distance is incorrect, because Ocracoke lighthouse was also described. "We are also blessed with another Light House, Ocracoke some five miles away, the prospect from the summit of which is the best in all this region." No keeper was identified for Ocracoke.

December 1862, was busy with both politics and recruiting in occupied North Carolina. Governor Stanly had ordered an election held on January 1, 1863, to select a representative for the Thirty-Seventh Congress from the old second district. Only four counties of the district were wholly or partially under Federal jurisdiction, with the remaining seven still in the Confederacy. Even so, both President Lincoln and Governor Stanly considered representation in Washington an important step in bringing the state back into the Union. Stanly had selected Jennings Pigott, a former Whig state representative, as his candidate. C.H. Foster was an unannounced candidate of the Free Labor Party. This was a local splinter party that opposed slavery and the Negroes alike. The party supported emancipation for the slaves and deportation of them as soon as they were freed. Foster finally declined the nomination as Free Labor candidate when he concluded an agreement with Federal authorities to raise a second North Carolina Union Regiment. If he was successful, he would be commissioned Lieutenant-Colonel of the regiment.[22] Foster's supporters, led by old Abraham Congleton, did not give up. After Jennings Pigott won the election, forty-five members of Company F of the First Union in Beaufort and thirty-six members of Company G in New Bern, petitioned Congress not to seat him. The two companies were partially successful in their role as political action committees. The House Elections Committee denied Pigott a seat and ignored Foster.[23] Humbug Foster intensified his recruiting efforts.

New Year's Day passed quietly along the Banks, as there was little to celebrate. The sea marked January 3, 1863, by casting up on the beach at Hatteras five blue-uniformed, sea-bleached bodies. The Hatterasers identified one of them. He had joined the Union navy and they had heard he was serving on a strange, new type of warship. They had not heard that the USS *Monitor* had foundered off Diamond Shoals on the last day of the old year. A detail from the 20th Indiana buried the bodies on a nearby sand ridge.[24]

The soldiers of the First Union made their presence felt throughout Carteret County and all along the Sand Banks, often in unpleasant ways. Harriet Ann Day Goodwin of Cedar Island was a young girl during the war. She told of bands of Buffalos crossing to Cedar Island from a camp on Core Banks. They raided gardens and stores of potatoes, preserved food, and barrels of salt fish. They carried off chickens, hogs, and cattle. After they stripped Cedar Island they raided Hog Island, too. When asked if the soldiers were black, she said they were not — they were white Buffaloes.[25]

James Warren Day, a young man from Cedar Island experienced the forceful recruiting of the First Union. Day and his nephew, Bosh (Abishia) Styron, carried Bosh's sick mother, Amelia Styron, to Portsmouth to the hospital. They shoved off for Portsmouth in Day's sprit-rigged sail skiff and entered Mrs. Styron in the Marine Hospital. While returning to their boat, they were captured by soldiers led by a Sergeant Styron — no kin! The sergeant told the young men he was sending them to Hatteras where they would enlist in a company of the First Union.

Bosh Styron and James Warren Day were sent in their own boat, under guard, to Hatteras. A sudden squall ripped the sail and broke the sprit, doing enough damage that they had to put back into Portsmouth, cold, wet, and miserable. Sergeant Styron met them at the landing and told them they were going to Hatteras next day, damage to the boat notwithstanding. That night the Cedar Islanders managed to repair the sail and sprit and escape from Portsmouth. James Warren Day, a guitar player and ballad singer, composed a song about their experience. It has been handed down by his descendants and begins thus:

> *Now gather round me men and boys,*
> *I'll have you all to know*
> *I won't be drug to Hatteras*
> *By no damn Buffalo.*

The last two lines, carried as a refrain in succeeding verses, expressed most Bankers' opinion of the Buffalos.[26]

Little noted at the time, but of importance to the state, was a project of the Confederate Navy Department. Naval Constructor Porter had developed plans and specifications for a shallow-draft ironclad ram. The Department sought bidders and signed contracts for three of the vessels in late 1862. One was for the Roanoke River, one for the Tar-Pamlico, and one for the Neuse River.[27]

A few trading vessels plied within Union-held waters under permits from Governor Stanly during 1862, and even fewer traded with the West Indies, licensed by Customs Collector Hedrick. There were plenty of schooners available, but few approved shippers. Hedrick's first letter noted "fifty or sixty [schooners], lying in harbor, apparently for no purpose." Even so, Hedrick reported on October 16 for the quarter ending September 30, collection of $327.90 in Duties on Imports and $66.40 in Fees for Clearances, etc.

With the new year, several changes occurred. On January 15, the disheartened Governor Stanly sent his resignation to Secretary Stanton, offering to stay until his successor arrived. The War Department answered on March 4 accepting his resignation as of March 1.[28] Stanly departed for California and the army resumed control. In March, also, the Secretary of the Treasury, by presidential proclamation, assumed all control of trade. Thirteen pages of regulations plus a nine page supplement were issued March 31, 1863, all titled "Regulations prescribed by the Secretary of the Treasury concerning INTERNAL AND COASTWISE INTERCOURSE." The new regulations, which canceled all previous ones, fixed the fees charged for trading permits

(5)

Affidavit on Application to Local Agent.

I R H Campbell of Beaufort County State of North Carolina make oath on the Holy Evangely of Almighty God that the memorandum of goods wares and merchandise hereto attached with their estimated value are required for my store in Washington N C in said County and if the permit is granted that the merchandise so permitted shall not nor shall any part thereof be disposed of by me or by my Authority Connivance or agent in violation of the terms of the permit and that neither the permit so granted nor the merchandise to be transported shall be so used or disposed of by me or by my Authority, Connivance or agent, as in any way to give aid, Comfort, information, or encouragement to persons in insurrection against the United States.

And Furthermore that I am in all respects loyal and true to the Government of the United States and that I have never voluntarily given aid to the rebels in arms, nor in any other way encouraged the Rebellion, and that I will at all times by my conduct and conversation, and by every other means I can properly use do all that should be expected of me as a loyal Citizen to Suppress the Rebellion and restore Obedience to the Constitution and Laws of the United States — and this without any mental reservation or evasion whatever

Sworn to and subscribed before me this 18ᵉ day of November 1863

R.W. Campbell

Affidavit on Application to Local Agent, submitted by R.W. Campbell to W.P. Ketcham, U.S. Treasury Agent, and showing the required Oath of Loyalty (Treasury Agents Records).

(twenty cents) with special higher fees for cotton or tobacco. Trade in naval stores was suspended until the navy filled its wants, except families in need could sell one barrel of turpentine or tar every two weeks. A fee of 5 percent of the sworn invoice value of goods shipped was imposed. Imports also were subject to a duty of 5 percent of value. Only the collector of customs at Beaufort could grant permits, though local special agents were appointed to assist him and stationed in New Bern, Plymouth, and Washington.

One exception from the import duty were sutlers supplying goods to Union regiments. Applicants for permits had to swear the Oath of Loyalty to the United States.[29] Under these restrictions, trade partly revived in the sounds and in coastwise intercourse.

Collector John Hedrick set sail for Portsmouth in early March 1863 to look after a vessel bound for Baltimore that had gone ashore on Ocracoke. He sailed in one of the two small cutters he kept for inspecting his district. He reported to Brother Benjamin on his return on March 13, that the cargo of sugar and molasses had been removed and sold, and the captain had gone north. One can imagine that a little of the short and long sweetening remained with the war-deprived Bankers as wages or tolls. As no mention was made of salvage, the ship must have been a loss. Hedrick determined the duty on the cargo would amount to about nine hundred dollars and reported same to the Secretary of the Treasury so the money could be collected from the registered owners. The department sent Hedrick two new Special Treasury Agents to assist him, Messers Carpenter and Wills. Carpenter, he noted, was taking in thirty or forty dollars per day for permits to fishermen. It was certainly a new departure for a coastal fisherman to buy a permit to set his nets — an expense to be avoided if at all possible.

Hedrick still reported on C.H. Foster and awarded him a new title, "The Swindler C.H.F." Humbug Swindler Foster had "stuck up posters calling for volunteers in this state," Hedrick wrote, and had intensified his recruiting methods. "The way deserters and refugees are treated is to put them in prison until they are willing to volunteer in the Union Army." Brother Benjamin apparently doubted what his brother had told him, for John, in a later letter, expanded his description of recruiting. He stated he "did not know how long the refugees were kept in prison, but he did know they were let out when they enlisted in the First Union." The army also paid them bounties for enlisting and agreed to care for their families. "When a refugee comes in," he said, "all the Buffaloes get after him, and before he knows what he is about, he has joined the regiment." John Hedrick reflected further: "It reminds me of my old Davidson College days when a new fresh comes."[30]

A perusal of the service records of the First and Second North Carolina Union Regiments yields an increasing number of soldiers sent to the Banks in 1863, indicating the growing strength of the two regiments as their companies filled up. The service records show approximately twenty-five soldiers of the regiments were hospitalized at Portsmouth during June, July, and August, 1863. Some were sent from the military hospitals in Beaufort and New Bern and some from the small company hospitals in other towns. Few fatalities were noted, suggesting that Portsmouth was generally used for convalescent patients.[31]

Even more Buffalo soldiers were detailed to the islands for guard and special duties. Though no companies were stationed on Ocracoke or Portsmouth, nearly seventy men were detached from their regular companies for special assignments. Most of them served on through 1863. Examples of those transferred were Sergeant Jas. Luton of Company H on Hatteras Bank and Corporal Benjamin Pendleton of Company D at Washington. Both men arrived in Portsmouth in September after being exchanged from Confederate captivity. Among those detached for specific duties were Privates

Andrew Robbins and T.J. Mason, both of Company B in Washington, who served at the Marine Hospital. Private Joseph O'Neal, Company H, was specifically assigned as guard at the Ocracoke lighthouse in June 1863. He was still doing guard duty at Ocracoke and Portsmouth in April, 1865. Private John B. O'Neal, Company H, joined Joseph on Ocracoke in May 1864, as a lighthouse guard.[32]

The increased presence of the First Union soldiers on the Outer Banks indicates that the Buffalo regiments were gradually replacing the department's regular Northern regiments as garrison troops. Some detachments of Northern regiments still remained along the coast and visited the islands at times. The oral history passed down through the generations at Ocracoke Island describes one such Union Army detail. Which regiment is unknown, but judging by their behavior, the men were probably regulars, not Buffaloes.

Captain Horatio Williams, formerly of the sunken schooner *Paragon*, had become farmer Horatio Williams. He cultivated truck crops, raised hogs, and ran cattle on the island's range. He supplied the local demand and was occasionally able to ship pork and beef across the sound for sale on the mainland. Williams was not neutral in the war — he was still a Southerner — so he did not deal with the occupying forces. He avoided Union soldiers as much as possible and had not been "drug to Hatteras by no damn Buffalo." The Federal soldier who caught Horatio Williams was a lieutenant sent to buy cattle, who brought with him a sergeant and a squad of men. The lieutenant's purpose was buying, not recruiting, so he informed Williams that the army needed some of his cattle.

Horatio Williams answered, "I don't sell to Yankees."

The lieutenant told Williams that he was authorized to buy cattle and pay a fair price. If the owner would not sell, the lieutenant said, he had authority to take the cattle.

Williams repeated, "I don't sell to Yankees!" Then, "If ye' git 'em, ye'll have to take 'em." He wheeled around and stalked off.

The lieutenant kept his temper as he directed his sergeant to have the men cut out and halter six of the best beeves. Mrs. Martha Williams, Horatio's wife had witnessed the confrontation. She addressed the Yankee, "You heard what the captain said. He won't sell to you. If you can pay, leave the money under that ballast rock by the porch." She pointed to it.

The lieutenant, a fair man, did leave the greenbacks under the rock. Mrs. Martha Williams, her patriotism tempered with pragmatism, waited until the Yankees left, picked up the money, and went into the house. When or whether she told the captain, oral history knows not.[33]

John Hedrick continued to report events to his brother. On October 3, 1863, he noted the arrival of C.C. Upham, a fleet paymaster, sent to buy naval stores. Upham indicated he could pay ten or twelve dollars per barrel for turpentine. Hedrick commented it was selling for thirty-five dollars in New York. The navy was not averse to a bargain, but as other sales were stopped until the navy obtained enough, the locals were caught in the price squeeze. Two days later, Hedrick reported collecting $830.58

on import duties during September and about $10,000 from coastal trade. He hoped he would get a commission on the latter, "which would make me a right nice business." In October he collected $9053.03 on Internal and Coastwise Intercourse and happily told his brother that he was allowed a 3 percent commission on collections. Trading around the sounds had indeed revived under the new regulations. Based upon the 5 percent duty collected, September's cargoes were worth $200,000. On December 27, 1863, Hedrick wrote that his December collections under Internal and Coastwise Intercourse would reach near $12,000, greater than any previous month. Included was the additional 1 percent tax added by General Butler.

A sample of the permits issued by the Special Treasury Agents includes a special license issued by G.H. Vanderhoel, treasury agent in Washington, to Benjamin F. Gautier for the schooner *Friends* for one month to make "a trip from Portsmouth and Hyde County … within our military lines for the purpose of procuring vegetables, poultry, eggs, fish, clams, fruit, chickens, mutton & c to Washington Markett for sale." Treasury agent W.P. Ketcham granted William T. Dixon a similar permit "to purchase apples, corn, and oysters in Hyde County and Portsmouth…." Ketcham also granted R.H. Campbell of the Sutler's Department of the 58th Regiment of Pennsylvania Volunteers a permit to transport a long list of fancy foodstuffs and supplies:[34]

1	Bbl Sour Kraut		2	Doz. qt Tin Cups
20	" Apples		2	Doz. Pt Tin Cups
1	" Almonds		3	Doz. Suspenders
50	Drums Figs		5	Bbls. Potatoes
2	Cases Imp'l Syrup		¼	m Needles
2	kegs nails		3	lbs. Blk Thread
3	Bbls Boston Crackers		1	Ream Sand Paper
3	" Soda di.		1	Doz Looking Glasses
3	" Ginger Cake		1	Gro. Tinpots (?)
1	Box A'd Candles		5	Bales Smoking Toba
2	Doz. Brooms		10	Tubs Butter
5	" Shoe Brushes		20	Cheese
5	Doz. Tin Plates		1	Bale Dates
5	Pocket Wallets		1	" Eng. Walnuts
3	" Post Monies (?)		10	Boxes Raisins
1	Gro. Pipes		1	Bbl Mackeral
3	Doz. Pocket Diaries for 1864		1	Bbl. Pickles
5	" Cott & Silk Hanks		100	lbs. Bologna Sausage
1	Box Toba		100	" Ham
500	Cigars		100	" Dd Beef
2	Gro Blacking		1	Doz U Shirts
10	Doz Winter Gloves		300	lbs. Codfish
¼	Ream Blotting Paper		10	Gross fine Cut Toba
100	lbs Ass. Candies		5	" Smoking di
10	Cases Sherry Wine		1	Bbl. Vinegar
1	Baskets Champagne		10	Cases Claret
2	Bbls. Onions		1	" Lobster
500	lbs. Best Wheat Flour		1	Doz Table Oil
2	Cases Peaches		1	" Sallat Dressing
15	Bbls. Cider			

The Sutler's stock was not subject to the 5 percent and 1 percent duties, so added nothing to Collector Hedrick's salary. Nevertheless, he did well on commissions, as all shipping during the years of Union occupation was from Beaufort. The NEWBECPO shipping comparisons on page 125 demonstrate the dramatic decline in 1861 with the outbreak of war, the war years, and a slow, slow revival of trade just beginning in 1865.

The opposing armies fought no major battles in the state after Burnside's New Bern campaign in 1862 and 1863. However, life was not peaceful for those Tar Heels living near Union lines on the mainland. Both Burnside and Foster after him were active commanders who engaged in continual skirmishes, raids, and expeditions, and the Confederates raided and counter attacked in return. One soldier of the Tenth Connecticut wrote home about one such raid:

> …the ruin devastation and utter abandonment of villages, plantations and farms, which but a short time ago was peopled fenced and stocked. Houses once comfortable that are now either burned or deserted, barns in ashes all along the roadside, fences destroyed for miles and over thousands of acres, no cows horses sheep or poultry to be seen…[35]

General Foster led an expedition through Martin County toward Tarborough in November 1862. According to Surgeon Potter of the Fifth Rhode Island Artillery, they spent the night of November 3 in Williamston, occupying some abandoned houses. He stayed in a doctor's house where his party helped themselves to the wife's preserves. Potter took a book, which he later threw away as too heavy to carry. One man marched off wearing the doctor's stovepipe hat, while another arrayed himself in a hoopskirt and parasol. This was only petty thievery, but it became more serious the next night in Hamilton. Some of the soldiers found applejack and after imbibing, not only looted, but ignited. A large part of the town burned.[36] Troops on the march were expected to help themselves to fresh meat from the enemy's supplies, but the mortality rate of pigs and poultry was extremely high on this march. General Foster later answered a complaint from the Confederate commander in the area saying it was done contrary to his orders and that the citizens should stay in their houses to protect them. Foster issued General Order Number 76 prohibiting pillaging and straying from the ranks, and adding "that no scenes of disgrace like those of Hamilton be permitted."[37] Foster tried, but with small success. One such raid, led by Brigadier-General Edward E. Potter in July, 1863, achieved a notable success, although its importance was not recognized at the time. Potter's men destroyed public property, robbed citizens, and drank dry the taverns from Greenville to Rocky Mount. While this raid may be remembered because of what was taken from the citizens, the raiders burned the railroad bridge and a mill at Rocky Mount before moving on to Tarboro. Here they destroyed two steamers, cotton, and other stores and most important of all, burned an iron-clad ram under construction.[38] Attacks and counter attacks continued.

Life was safer in the occupied towns than in the land between the lines, but no more pleasant. Citizens had to be very careful not to show too much Southern sympathy.

New Bern, Edenton, Washington, Beaufort, Elizabeth City-Camden, Plymouth, Ocracoke

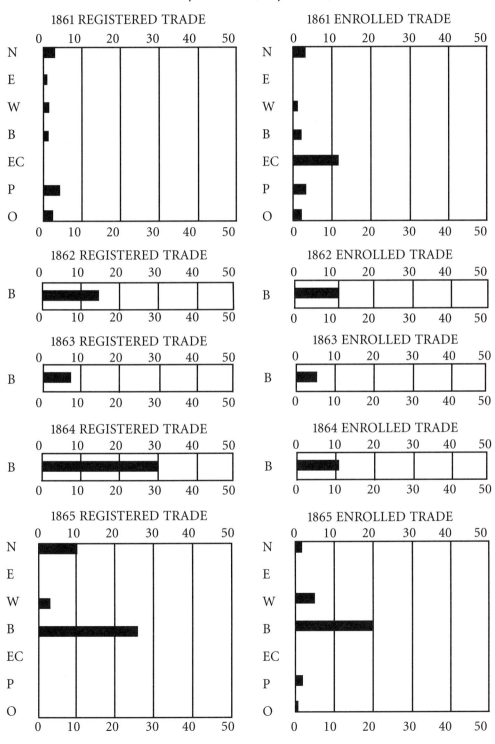

Mrs. Anne Blackwell Sparrow, wife of Captain Thomas Sparrow of the Washington Grays, and her two small children continued to live in her home in Washington. The Federal authorities in the town suspected her of secretly corresponding with her husband and sending him military information. They referred to her as "the Rebel mailbag" and ordered her out of town. A detachment of soldiers escorted Mrs. Sparrow and her children, with what luggage they could carry, through Federal lines and dumped them in the country. Friends helped them get to Tarboro.[39] John Rumley of Beaufort, former County Clerk, was also considered too Confederate. The Union headquarters dispatched a written order to Rumley saying "you and your family will be sent beyond the lines at 10 o'clock A.M. on Saturday, June 27, 1863."[40] There was no appeal.

Miss Emmeline J. Piggott, of Beaufort, described as "brilliant and beautiful," had a sweetheart in the Confederate army in the state. Miss Piggott was aware that some of the Union officers in Beaufort were carrying on an illegal traffic in cotton, buying it on their own account and shipping it north privately. They paid in goods scarce in the South and benefitted the Southerners as well as themselves. Miss Piggott may even have helped arrange these transactions. The sound shore of Carteret County is laced with creeks, coves, and hidden harbors that invite smugglers. Emmeline Piggott used her knowledge of this traffic to obtain permits to buy scarce items in Beaufort and permits to travel through the lines to Confederate country. She made two large pockets to tie around her waist underneath her hoopskirt. She filled these with needed commodities and crossed the lines. She became a blockade runner, aiding her friends in Dixie and the Confederate cause.[41]

The Federal commanding general, wanting to know just who and how many civilians of military age lived in the occupied posts, issued General Order Number 15 to conduct a military census of the Pamlico Military District. The census listed all white males of ages 18 through 35.

> Portsmouth had 35 men listed, compared to 85 in the regular 1860 census. Many young men had left the island. The rolls listed several newcomers and changed occupations for others. Augustus Dudley, for example, formerly a merchant, was listed as sutler. Samuel Tolson, previously listed as fisherman was now labeled shoemaker. The census taker was J.W.M. Davies, Assistant Surgeon in charge of the post. He also listed a physical description of each man.

> Ocracoke had 30 such men in 1863, compared to 57 in 1860. Captain Horatio Williams was shown as a mariner, not a farmer. The Captain had evidently aged quickly during the war, for he was listed as 35 years old, compared with 27 in 1860. J.W.M. Davies took the Ocracoke census and described the men as he had done on Portsmouth.

> Roanoke Island showed 36 men from 18 through 35. There were 5 seamen, 1 merchant, and 30 farmers. Captain Stephen D. Gardner, Co. A, 8th Mass. Regiment was the enrolling officer.

> Plymouth had 22 such men with occupations listed as farmers, merchants,

and one each editor and baker. The enrolling officer was Lieutenant-Colonel Stephen Moffitt.

The town of Washington, once a bustling port of about 1500 people, now had 31 in the military age group, including 4 foreign-born and several Northerners. The census taker included physical descriptions as well as remarks such as "mentally deranged" and "Reel-footed and Physically Imcompetent". The enrolling officer was Captain Chas. A. Lyon, Provost-Marshal.[42]

No data was unearthed for other posts.

Though increased maritime trade through the port of Beaufort provided income for a few ship owners and employment for a few more mariners, the lot of most citizens in the occupied areas was hard — no money, no job, no commerce.

For many, there were no ministers to offer the consolations of religion. The Ocracoke-Portsmouth Charge of the Methodist Church shared a minister before the war. The pre-war pastor, the Reverend A.R. Raven, fled from the island in 1861 "because of Civil War conditions that threatened his safety."[43] There is a paucity of church records of this period, understandable when one considers that storms have twice demolished the Ocracoke church building since the Civil War, and the Portsmouth church once, leaving memory as the only record.

Methodist Archives in Raleigh state Alexander Ravenscroft Raven left his first church by a routine transfer in December 1861. Far from fleeing the war, he was sent to the church in Morehead City where he met Burnside's soldiers head-on. After his church building was seized by the Union Army and many of its members moved away, Raven was assigned the church in Hillsboro in December 1862.

The First Baptist Church of Washington owned the only church building that survived the wartime fire in the town; hence its records survived. The Minutes Book of church conferences and councils noted on August 15, 1861: "The war came and no conference helt for three years." The record resumed in 1865 with the church listing only eleven members.

Carteret County had much the same problems. The Woodville Baptist Church records state that from 1861 to 1869 the church had "no pastor due to the Civil War." The Methodists of the area furnished so many regimental chaplains to the Confederate army that "these and other appointments left the New Bern District virtually stripped." A long list of churches without ministers followed. Those preachers remaining were urged to write patriotic sermons which were privately printed and widely circulated. When Federal troops occupied Morehead City, they also occupied the Methodist Church and established a bakery in the building. The structure burned at the end of the war and the Federal government paid a claim for it after the war.[44]

Perhaps the neatest solution of all for a wartime minister was that devised for St. Paul's Episcopal Church of Beaufort. The Reverend D.D. van Antwerp, who came to Beaufort as Chaplain at Fort Macon, helped establish St. Paul's Parish in 1857 and became the first minister. After Burnside's troops occupied Beaufort, van Antwerp was again appointed Chaplain, while he continued as Vicar of St. Paul's. One may assume that when Reverand van Antwerp recited in his service of Morning Prayer the part which asked for blessings for the President and all in Civil Authority that he prayed with equal fervor for Jefferson Davis and Abraham Lincoln, depending on which congregation it was.[45]

Further up the Banks, an Episcopal presence, All Saint's Church, had been re-established in 1849. During the war its building was demolished by Federal troops to provide material for building quarters for escaped slaves on Roanoke Island.[46] While they were but a small percentage of the slave population of the state, the numbers of Blacks escaping to Union lines became significant and caused problems for Union commanders.

John Hedrick's letter of July 5, 1863, relates an excursion he made to Shackleford Banks to witness a Negro picnic held to celebrate July 4. There were about four hundred people present "singing, speaking, promenading and cheering for the Union cause and groaning for the Confederates." There were three societies represented; the Atlantic, the Chapel Society, and the Sunday School Benevolent Society. They carried banners and some wore special scarves. They enjoyed themselves very well, Hedrick said. At least a few men were again rejoicing on the shore.

The Negroes within the Federal lines were generally referred to as contrabands at this time, although John Hedrick did not use the term. The name was originated by General B.F. Butler in May, 1861 when he commanded Fort Monroe. Butler interviewed three slaves who had escaped to Federal lines, and whose owner, Colonel Mallory of a Virginia regiment, asked for the return of his personal property. Federal policy at the time prohibited confiscation of private property, but Butler did not want to return them. Butler, though an inept general, was a shrewd politician, and an original thinker. He reasoned that as the slaves had been employed in building Confederate fortifications and he could use them to build Union fortifications, then they could be classed as Contraband of War. This gave him a semi-legal reason to keep them. The practice became general.[47] Federal congressional legislation later formalized the matter.

The term contraband was not intended to be disparaging of the Negroes, but was simply a convenient synonym for "escaped slaves who have come into our lines and whom we intend to keep." The numbers of contrabands, beginning at Hatteras, swelled at Roanoke Island, and grew by hundreds after the capture of New Bern. "Contrabands were something more than slaves but far short of being free men and women."[48] After Vincent Colyer's resignation as Superintendent of the Poor, Burnside appointed another New England chaplain to the job, the Reverend Mr. James Means. Chaplain Horace James of the Twenty-fifth Massachusetts assisted Mr. Means, and after Means's death from typhoid fever in April, 1863, James assumed the work.

Horace James was in charge of all of the Blacks within Union lines in North Carolina. About 15,000 in mid–1863 spread from Beaufort to Roanoke Island. By January 1864 there were

New Bern and vicinity	8,591
Beaufort and vicinity	2,426

Washington and vicinity	2,741
Roanoke Island	2,712
Plymouth	860
Hatteras Bank	89
Total	17,419[49]

The first planned settlement for Blacks was Roanoke Island, where Chaplain James was ordered by General Foster in May, 1863. James, assisted by Sergeant George O. Sanderson, late of the Forty-third Massachusetts, laid out avenues and streets in the unsettled northern portion of the island. Each section was divided into one acre lots which were given to each family, priority going to those who had enlisted in one of the Negro regiments being formed by Brigadier-General Edward A. Wild and to those Blacks employed by the government. James hurried North to solicit funds and material for his new colony. He returned in July, 1863, with money, clothing, a steam saw mill, and several female school teachers. James regretted that the island was not large enough to give his charges farms instead of one acre lots. He claimed the first company of Black troops in North Carolina, and probably in the country, was raised by General Wild at Roanoke Island in June 1863.

James wanted the Negro settlements to be self-governing under his supervision , and appointed a council of fifteen members to run the colony. The experiment was not successful, as the councilors were unable to keep written records or to agree on proper action. James realized: "To fit these people for republican self-government, education is the prime necessity. The sword to set them free, letters to make them citizens."[50]

The settlements near New Bern expanded greatly, especially after the Confederate attacks on the town in early 1864. Here the contrabands lived in three settlements clustered on the outskirts of New Bern. After Pickett's attack, Major-General John L. Peck, the new departmental commander, ordered all three settlements moved across the Trent River and consolidated. Streets were laid out and 50-by-60 foot lots surveyed, all within Union lines. The Negroes first lived in tents until they could build their own cabins with material furnished by the government. They planted gardens with the seeds and gardening tools supplied by James's organization. "The gardens, though small, were wonderfully productive, and furnished for the cultivators thousands of bushels of green vegetables."[51] The new settlement is still called James City today.

Many of the Blacks were employed by the military or other government agencies and some were self-employed in various trades and handicrafts. Of the 2,798 inhabitants across the Trent, 1,226 received help from the government as dependents. Their numbers swelled in 1864. Both the dependent and the unemployed Negroes drew government rations "a trifle smaller than the soldiers ration..." A ration consisted of:

10 oz. pork or bacon, or 1 lb. fresh or salt beef daily.
1 lb. corn meal, five times a week.
1 lb. flour or soft bread, or 12 oz. hard bread twice a week.

10 lbs. beans, peas, or hominy, 8 lbs. sugar, 2 quarts vinegar, 8 oz. candles, 2 lbs. soap, 2 lbs. salt, 15 lbs. potatoes, when practicable to every 100 rations. And for women and children, 10 lbs. coffee (rye) or 15 oz. tea, to every 100 rations.[52]

Not only the Negroes, but destitute white civilians were helped by Horace James's department. About four hundred civilians remained on Roanoke Island after the Federal occupation, most of whom took the oath of allegiance, though not all were loyal. There were others within the Federal lines in the occupied towns. James was fond of claiming that his Negroes worked much harder than the white natives. Various government departments employed civilian labor in the state. Vincent Colyer had set the rate: "work was offered to both the whites at the rate of $12.00 the month, to blacks at the rate of $8.00 the month." Colonel Rush Hawkins later raised the pay scale for contrabands on Roanoke Island to $10.00 per month.

The government could not furnish some necessities to the Negroes, chiefly clothing. The army had no civilian clothing and certainly nothing suitable for women and children. The need became critical during the smallpox epidemic of 1864, when all the clothing of the victims had to be burned. The freedmen's aid societies James had contacted in the North furnished many thousands of garments for him to sell cheaply or to distribute free, as he chose. "While the societies did not always get along amicably with one another, they cooperated admirably on getting clothing to North Carolina as needed." Each society resented another's intrusion into its territory. The three most prominent groups were the American Missionary Association (AMA), the New England Freedman's Aid Society (NEFAS), and the New York National Freedman's Relief Association (NFRA). The AMA became the strongest and longest lasting of the groups.[53]

Horace James continued his useful work for the Negroes through the sometimes frightful year of 1864 and on into 1865 and the end of the war. Then his task was assumed by the new Freedmen's Bureau. Even after the war, he remained in the state to rent two plantations on the Tar River to prove they could be operated at a profit with hired free labor.

There was another group of people in the state, some of whom became wards of the United States, some who were Union allies, and even more who were unsuccessful neutrals. These were the civilian Buffaloes, who now outnumbered the military Buffaloes in the First Union regiment; the term Buffalo becoming a generic name for those who avoided Confederate service and Civilian Buffaloes can be divided into two classes. The first — and worst — were those who refused military service on either side, hid out in the woods and swamps, and preyed on the inhabitants of isolated farms and homesteads. They were bushwhackers, thieves, and scoundrels who enjoyed living wild. The second and larger class were the non-violent fiscal Buffaloes. They traded between the lines under Union permits, or sold their services to the Northerners after Federal troops occupied parts of the state. Needless to say, Buffaloes were despised by other Southerners. Buffalo was not synonymous with Unionist. There were many Unionists in the state before secession, enough to defeat the referendum for the Secession Convention in 1860. Unionists, in the Tar Heel view, were misguided people who supported the Union too long, but Buffaloes were turncoats. The Hedrick brothers were Unionists, not Buffaloes, though they ran with Buffaloes. They had long been pro–Union and anti-slavery. Benjamin S. Hedrick had lost his chair as professor of Chemistry at the University of North Carolina when he began to publish his abolitionist beliefs.[54] Ulysses H. Ritch, on the other hand, was a prime example of a non-violent, fiscal Buffalo. He was a shipbuilder in Washington when Union forces captured the town. After the Federals destroyed the gunboat Ritch was building for the Confederate Navy, he re-assessed his allegiance. Helped by John Hedrick, Ritch got the job of Special Treasury Agent and came back to Washington to lord it over his former neighbors.[55]

Neither North Carolina nor the Confederacy had enough troops to hold all of the sections of the eastern counties not occupied by the Union. Hyde County was unoccupied, but several Union incursions were resisted by an active militia home guard using guerrilla tactics. The southern side of Albemarle Sound, from Plymouth to Roanoke Island also was bare of soldiers. The only post on the north side of the sound and east of the Chowan River was Wingfield sited between the river and the Sand Banks. Edenton, Elizabeth City, and Hertford had no permanent Union garrisons, but were sometimes visited by the Union Army. The Federal Navy patrolled the rivers and sounds and visited the towns more frequently. War, like nature abhors a vacuum, so into this stretch of ungarrisoned territory came the Buffaloes. Wingfield, originally a post of the First Union Regiment, had degenerated in its isolation from the rest of the army. It became a center of "fugitive negroes, lawless white men, traitors and deserters from the Confederate army." Their leader, Captain Jack Fairless, a deserter, and his men "pillaged, plundered, burned, and decoyed off slaves in their forays into Chowan, … Bertie, Perquimans, Hertford, and Gates Counties."[56]

The Federal Navy investigated reports of misconduct at Wingfield. Lieutenant Thomas J. Woodward in USS *Shawsheen* checked on the post.

> [O]n my arrival there on the 18th of September[1862] I found out of sixty-three recruits only twenty present; the others had gone to their homes or elsewhere as they chose. The captain was in a state of intoxication,… He has no control over his men, and [by] the manner in which he conducts himself he is doing much injury to the cause of the U.S. Government … what remaining arms there were I took on board for safekeeping.[57]

The problem was solved for Federal authorities when Fairless was shot dead by one of his men in a drunken brawl. Lieutenant Joseph W. Ethridge of Roanoke Island, a new recruit, assumed command and managed to repel a Confederate attack on Wingfield. Captain Ned Small with about twenty Confederate soldiers and a number of local partisans failed to destroy the Buffaloes, but did find the Buffaloes' weaknesses. Ethridge and his men, with many Negro, laborers built a strong keep of earth and logs which they armed with an antique cannon stolen from Edenton.[58]

The Confederacy scraped up enough regular soldiers to clear out the Buffaloes.

In January 1863 the Forty-second North Carolina moved into the state from Virginia. Under orders from General D.H. Hill, Companies B, E, and F marched to the Chowan under command of Lieutenant-Colonel J.E. Brown. From his new headquarters at Merry Hill, Brown posted pickets and crossed the Chowan at night to avoid Federal gunboats. His force of 150 men hid in the woods, intending to attack at night. An alert Buffalo spotted them and gave the alarm, at which the nearby gunboat shelled the woods. Brown recrossed the river safely that night. Three weeks later he returned to surprise and capture the fort. All but fifty of his men withdrew to the Bertie shore before the gunboat woke up and landed about 450 troops. By rapid firing, loud screeching of the "Rebel Yell" and bluff, the last fifty crossed by midnight, aided by the soldiers on the other side.[59] The vacuum was filled again by Southerners, the Home Guard or Partisan Rangers as the Northerners called them.

General B.F. Butler, the new commander of the Federal Department of Virginia and North Carolina, heeded the complaints of Unionists and Buffaloes in the area. He ordered in Brigadier-General Edward A. Wild and his newly formed regiments of Negro troops. On December 5, 1863, General Wild started from Norfolk by the Dismal Swamp Canal road to Elizabeth City with 1,850 men as follows:

> First U.S. Colored Troops, Colonel Holman
> Second North Carolina Colored Volunteers, Lieutenant-Colonel Pratt and
>   Colonel Draper
> Fifth U.S. Colored Troops, Colonel Conine
> Detachments from the First North Carolina Colored Volunteers, the Fifty-fifth
>   Massachusetts, plus two companies of Pennsylvania Cavalry and one section
>   of New York artillery.[60]

General Wild, who held a medical degree, was an experienced soldier who had twice been seriously wounded. He had served with Garibaldi and with the Turks in the Crimean War. He was a fighter, but he was not a good leader nor a popular one. His friends admitted he was eccentric. What his enemies said can be imagined.[61]

Wild's force reached South Mills, Virginia on the third day to find that his supply steamers had traveled by the wrong canal. Wild sent orders to the ships to meet him at Elizabeth City and began to live off the country "judiciously discriminating in favor of the worst rebels." He graced Elizabeth City with his presence for a week, while he sent out detachments foraging, recruiting, and collecting contrabands. He set the Elizabethans in a state of "perpetual panic" with his black troops. The white citizens named him a "monster of humanity" and "a cousin of Beelzebub."[62]

When his steamers arrived, Wild set out by land and by sea to clear the country of guerrillas. He sent detachments by ship to Powell's Point and Knott's Island. Others marched to Camden, Shiloh, and Currituck Court House. He was "pestered by guerrillas" who fired on his columns and his camp fires. They were men of the Sixty-eighth North Carolina Militia Regiment, the Home Guard. Pursuit was useless and in vain, Wild reported, but he captured two of their camps and destroyed their supplies. Wild's orders to his men were to shoot any guerrillas they captured and to burn their houses. He took a few prisoners, tried them by drumhead court-martial, and hanged one, Daniel Bright, a private of the 63rd Georgia Cavalry. Wild took three women and one old man as hostages for the proper treatment of his men taken prisoner. "Finding ordinary measures of little avail, I adopted a more rigorous style of warfare; burned their houses, ate up their livestock, and took hostage their families."[63]

Wild scorned the guerrillas' organization as loose and improper. While verbally slaying his enemies, Wild was better equipped than Samson the Israelite warrior. Wild did not need to borrow the jawbone of an ass. "They are virtually bandits, armed and hired by Governor Vance.... They can only harass us by stealing, murdering, and burning."[64]

While at Knott's Island, Colonel Draper of the Second North Carolina Colored Volunteers had burned the house of William H. White, a suspected guerrilla. He took as hostage White's young daughter Nancy and hauled her back to Virginia as a prisoner. At the outpost of the Ninety-eighth New York regiment on the North River, Draper met Lieutenant-Colonel Wead. Wead was so incensed at Draper's actions at Knott's Island and at his treatment of young Nancy White — all in violation of the laws of war — that battle was almost joined between the two regiments. Wead pressed charges against Draper on nine counts of violations of military law.[65]

General Wild began to withdraw on December 21, 1863. He included with his report a list of Union citizens of Elizabeth City and environs. He boasted of sending twenty-five hundred Negroes to Roanoke Island, as well as inflicting casualties and damage on the enemy. Wild appeared to be well pleased with himself and his men. Even General B.F. Butler thought Wild might have exceeded himself. Wild did his work, Butler said, with great thoroughness, but "perhaps too much stringency." At a public meeting in Elizabeth City, 523 citizens of the county signed a petition asking the state government and Governor Vance to withdraw the Partisan Rangers so that Butler would not send Wild back.[66]

Neither happened and the region returned to its pro–Confederate status. "It is doubtful whether Wild's methods were as effective as he thought. It has been said that their harshness galvanized Southern sentiment in the state, and as a result, 'we have heard no more of the peace movement in the Old North State.'"[67]

Chaplain James admitted that "at one time, during the winter of 1863-4, there was a degree of suffering on the island [Roanoke] from insufficient shelter." This was after the influx of contrabands sent by General Wild, and was probably the time that the Nags Head church was razed for building material.

There was a greater degree of suffering in the New Bern-Beaufort area that fall and winter by both races and both sides. Smallpox broke out in New Bern. John Hedrick was told by Doctor Page that there were 250 cases in the smallpox camp. The disease, he said, was especially prevalent among the Negroes.

Thus passed two dreary years of occupation. The outlaw Buffaloes were quelled, the fiscal Buffaloes slid along, and the military Buffaloes shouldered their way around their garrison posts. Federal troops controlled the towns. At sea naval vessels steamed past the Sand Banks blockading and patrolling. Inside, smaller vessels entered Hatteras or Beaufort Inlets to make for the inland ports. Gunboats guarded the inlets and islands. There were more small ships, gunboats, and supply ships than ever before in the war years in the sounds, all busily steaming here and there. An observer high aloft might have been reminded of water-bugs skittering across the surface of a pond.

In Virginia the battle fronts were quiet, a condition that could soon affect eastern North Carolina.

Chapter Eight

Occupation Threatened

O N JANUARY 2, 1864, General Robert E. Lee dispatched his first message of the new year directly to President Jefferson Davis.

> Mr. President: The time is at hand when, if an attempt can be made to capture the enemy's forces at New Bern, it should be done. I can now spare troops for the purpose, which will not be the case as spring approaches.... A large amount of provisions and other supplies are said to be at New Berne, which are much wanted for this army.... I have not heard what progress is making in the completion of the iron-clads [those on the Neuse and Roanoke Rivers] ... can they be had?[1]

With the president's approval, the attempt on New Bern was made. General Lee selected thirteen thousand men and recommended North Carolina's Brigadier-General Robert F. Hoke to command them, as such an attack had been suggested previously by Hoke. The Richmond officials modified Lee's plan by appointing Major-General George E. Pickett to lead, with General Hoke as second in command. As the ironclads were not quite ready, the Navy Department organized a boat expedition under John Taylor Wood, who held both naval and army rank — Commander and Colonel.

General Lee, on January 20, 1864, sent orders to Pickett at Petersburg, Virginia, notifying him that Hoke would give him further details. Pickett was to have Barton's, Kemper's, Corse's, and part of Ransom's Brigades, as well as Hoke's. A strong force of artillery under Major Dearing collected in Petersburg. Major-General W.H.C. Whiting in Wilmington readied Martin's Brigade for a march up the coast and an attack towards Morehead City. Lee stressed the need for coordination and secrecy. He directed that Whiting be notified of the day planned for the attack, as Martin's column had the longest approach march.[2]

The plan was complex, with five groups converging on the town. Four of the columns were close enough together to allow rapid communication with headquarters and each other. The fifth, Martin's force, was farther away, hence General Lee's special instructions. Pickett's troops outnumbered the Federal garrison in the town by about three to one, but the battle would not be easy. U.S. Brigadier-General I.N. Palmer occupied a strongly fortified position, with many guns and with reserves in Beaufort. He could call on the Federal Navy, too. The plan should have been successful if Pickett had exerted firm control. Pickett botched the attack by lack of coordination, so that each force operated as if on its own.

Major [Acting-Colonel] James Dearing's force on the north bank of the Neuse River consisted of the Fifteenth and Seventeenth Virginia Regiments, several batteries of artillery, and Colonel John N. Whitford's Sixty-seventh North Carolina. Dearing's orders were to capture Fort Anderson, a strong work on the north bank, if practicable. The fort was too well fortified for Dearing to take, but he did draw the enemy's attention to his threat.[3]

Commander Wood's expedition had more success. Wood gathered about 250 officers and men, mostly sailors, with some Confederate Marines, from the naval detachments around Richmond, from Wilmington, and from Charleston, S.C. The men, together with Wood's light cutters and launches, were shipped by rail to Kinston and put in the water at 2:00 A.M. on January 31. The men, well armed with rifles, cutlasses, pistols, and axes boarded the boats to row down the river in two divisions. They arrived off New Bern at 4:00 A.M. on February 1. In the dense fog they were not able to locate any Union vessels on the river. They withdrew to Batchelder's Creek before dawn, still retaining surprise. After a daylight reconnaissance on February 2, Wood attacked after sunset. This time Wood's men found the USS *Underwriter* anchored between two of the batteries in the town. The Confederates boarded her, fore and aft, and captured her after a short, hot fight. Wood planned to move the ship upstream and use her guns against the Union forts. *Underwriter*'s fires were banked and steam pressure was low, so she could not be moved quickly. When the Federal batteries woke up, they poured such a hot fire on the vessel that Wood had to burn her and withdraw his men. The Confederates lost five killed and about fifteen wounded, the Federals about the same. Wood was commended for his "brilliant exploit."[4] The captain of the *Underwriter*, Acting Master Westervelt, was mortally wounded defending his ship. He was the pilot who had so upset Flag Officer Goldsborough by giving him accurate advice on the possibility of closing inlets.

Brigadier-General Hoke's part in the attack was successful as long as the battle lasted. Hoke marched down the Dover road from Kinston with his own brigade, a part of Corse's and two regiments of Clingman's Brigade. He had the Fifty-sixth North Carolina Regiment of Ransom's Brigade and an artillery force of eight rifled guns and four Napoleons with their gunners.

On Monday morning, February 1, at 1:00 A.M. Hoke moved in to capture all the outposts on his front. He found the Federal troops guarding the crossing of Batchelder's Creek. Alarmed by the firing of the pickets on the outpost, the Federals had taken up the bridge. Hoke felled trees across the creek away from the bridge site and crossed two regiments to take the fortifications from flank and rear. This was done while Hoke repaired the bridge and crossed with the rest of his men. Federal reinforcements arrived and were routed. Meantime a troop train with more Federal troops started to cross the creek headed for the Confederate's rear. Hoke anticipated this move and sent a force pounding for the railroad in the Federal rear. The troop train reversed just in time, so the Confederates missed capturing the train by five minutes. Hoke had hoped to ride an assault force into New Bern on the train. Hoke moved within a mile of the town to await the sound of General Barton's guns as he attacked across the Trent River. Hoke was surprised to see two more trains arrive in town from Morehead City, showing that Barton's men had not cut the railroad on that front. After waiting all day Tuesday, Hoke heard from Barton that it was impossible for him to get across Brice's Creek. On Wednesday, February 3, Pickett ordered Hoke to withdraw across Batchelder's Creek and retire toward Kinston.[5]

Brigadier-General S.M. Barton led the flanking force attacking from the southeast. He led his own brigade, Kemper's Brigade, Ransom's Brigade, and guns with artillerymen. He also had a sizable cavalry force: Colonel John A. Baker with seven companies of his Third North Carolina Cavalry and Lieutenant-Colonel Kennedy with five companies of his Sixty-second Georgia Cavalry. Barton sent Kennedy ahead to picket the roads between the Neuse and Trent Rivers, and Baker to swing wide, cross the Trent and cut the railroad and telegraph wires at Croatan. Barton followed, heading for the old battleground of March 1862. At 8:00 A.M. on February 1, he came in sight of the Federal lines. Here Barton halted, talked to local citizens, sent out reconnaissance patrols, and surveyed the field and Brice's Creek. He did not like what he saw. There were more Union forts and batteries than he had expected and Brice's Creek was both deeper and wider than he had been told. He reported all this to General Pickett by couriers on February 2. Barton's formal report dated February 21 said, "I was therefore unprepared to encounter obstacles so serious, and was forced to the conviction that they were insurmountable by the means at my disposal." Barton's artillery dueled with the Federal batteries, his cavalry skirmished with the enemy and failed to cut the railroad, but nothing more was accomplished. Barton withdrew on the night of February 2 to join Pickett near Hoke's lines. He received orders on February 3 to march back to Kinston.[6]

General Martin's column, after its long march, was even more successful than Hoke. Martin's Brigade consisted of the Seventeenth and Forty-second Regiments of North Carolina troops, and in addition he had Captain Harlan's company of cavalry and Captain Andrew B. Paris's battery of artillery. He left Wilmington on Thursday, January 28. Previously, Martin had traveled to Goldsboro to talk to General Hoke about the details of the attack and the duties of the Wilmington column. Pickett was still in Petersburg. Evidently Pickett assigned the task of coordinating with Martin to General Barton.

Martin marched up the coast, communicating by courier as he traveled. His first message was headed "thirty-four miles from Wilmington." Subsequently he sent: "will be at Jacksonville … about noon tomorrow" and from White Oak Creek "my artillery is now crossing the bridge" and "forty miles hence to Sheppardsville, … please keep me informed," this last dated February 1. His next dispatch, dated February 2 was from Newport Barracks reporting to General Whiting his success, with a similar message to General Barton or "General Commanding around New Berne." Barton logged several dispatches to Martin, the first on January 31 told Martin he was behind schedule, then several reported success in New Bern, and lastly, two on February 3 ordered "Fall back. All troops are withdrawn." Martin received only those dated February 3.[7]

General Martin advanced toward Newport on Monday, February 1. He picked up a deserter from the enemy and gained valuable information. On Tuesday, February 2 the advance guard of the cavalry, two guns, and two companies of infantry captured or killed the Federal picket line, then charged and captured two blockhouses and one gun. Martin's main body came up and advanced on Newport Barracks. The regiments formed line with the guns well forward and charged the barracks. The enemy "broke and fled in disorder."

Martin's Confederates captured Newport Barracks, store-houses, stables, horses, and much booty. The road bridge and railroad bridge were destroyed, first ignited by the retreating Federals, then completely burned by the Confederates. Captain Leith of the Seventeen North Carolina, one of the captains who had abandoned Beacon Island, more than compensated for his mistakes in that early battle. He was killed leading his company against Newport Barracks. Martin sent his cavalry, followed by an infantry force toward Morehead City, but recalled them when he received Barton's message to fall back. Martin's Confederates destroyed barracks, bridges, ordnance, and stores, including a thousand barrels of U.S. Navy turpentine. The men helped themselves to clothing, blankets, and rations. Martin's casualties were light, the captured guns and material useful. He counter-marched to Wilmington, having accomplished his mission and a large part of Barton's.[8]

Major-General George E. Pickett called off the attack and returned to Petersburg with a part of his troops. He reported losses of about forty-five killed and wounded against about one hundred casualties for the enemy. His force captured thirteen officers and 284 privates plus mules, wagons, arms and supplies. He asked that Barton's want of cooperation be investigated. Barton asked for the investigation, too.

There were several side effects to the attack on New Bern. One was the capture of men from the North Carolina Second Union Regiment. In Kinston some of them were recognized as Confederate deserters and tried by court-martial as traitors. Twenty-two were convicted and hanged.[9] The second, and greater, side effect was caused by General Martin's attack on Beaufort and Morehead City. It was panic.

Events in the coastal towns were noted by Customs Collector John Hedrick. "We have just passed through one of the greatest panics that has happened during the war." He reported that the Ninth Vermont Regiment and a company of cavalry at Newport were both "completely routed" and made a "gallant defence." That night, Tuesday, February 2, a soldier brought him an order to report to headquarters. Hedrick seemed to have been reasonably calm and un-panicked himself, by his own words.

> Upon arriving at Front St. House, which is used for barracks and quarters, I was halted by a little sentinel on the steps, who informed me that I could not pass in. I then inquired for the officer of the day and was informed that he was away on duty. I then asked for the Commandant of the Post, Capt. Fuller, and was told that he was around at the Market house attending to putting up a barricade across the street. I asked for the Sergeant in charge, who was brought forth. He was unacquainted with me, but he managed to get a person inside who did know me, and I was then admitted. I was informed that Captain Fuller would be in shortly ... he made his appearance, a low pussy, thick set fellow about my height and weighing

about 200 lbs., with a nose that looked as if one might wring the whiskey out of it. Dr. Ainsworth, surgeon in charge of the Hospital here, another toper, was present.

After listening to Captain Fuller and the doctor exchange views on the situation, Hedrick managed to introduce himself and ask what the captain wanted of him. Hedrick had to explain what the collector and the customs office did in Beaufort whereupon the captain told him if the Rebs attacked, Hedrick would have to occupy the Customs House. "He was expecting the Rebs in town every minute and so I remained in my office all that night.... Morning came and brought no Rebs.... Wednesday night I remained at home."

Rumors of Confederate troops advancing spread. On Thursday merchants began to load their goods aboard vessels in the harbor to send them to safety. Colonel Jourdan, commanding at Morehead City, came to Beaufort and announced that he would confiscate any further goods sent away; the streets of Beaufort were blocked with hogsheads filled with sand and the troops erected board and cordwood barricades around buildings, "forming a kind of bull pen," said Hedrick, "Fort Folly."

By Saturday, February 6, a hand car came in from New Bern bringing accurate news and the panic died. Further communication was established by trains meeting on each side of the Newport River until the bridge could be rebuilt.[10]

After Pickett's departure, General Hoke and most of the troops were left in the state. Hoke filled up his ranks with recruits, while managing to comb out ninety-five carpenters and mechanics and fifty laborers to work on the two ironclad gunboats. Hoke could visualize their usefulness. General Palmer, in New Bern, discharged the civilians, both black and white, that he had armed during the emergency.

In Beaufort, Hedrick reported on revived shipping and collections and on the weather. Three inches of snow fell on the coast. On February 26 he noted that "old Mrs. Foster" was visiting the Humbug Foster. Hedrick ordered his spring garden seed. Normalcy had returned.

In Virginia, Lieutenant-General U.S. Grant, newly appointed commander of all U.S. armies, joined Major-General George Mead's Army of the Potomac and initiated his long, bloody march from the Wilderness to the Rapidan and James Rivers. Federal commanders in North Carolina rearmed and entrenched. Their chief concern was the two Confederate ironclads. The commanders in New Bern and Plymouth blocked the rivers upstream from their towns with sunken hulks and pilings. The Plymouth garrison added a 200-pounder Parrot rifle to a riverside battery. General Peck, commanding the military district had asked General Butler for reinforcements and additional gunboats to repel the ironclad on the Roanoke. Butler replied with good advice. "I believe Plymouth is as safe as Fortress Monroe, provided you keep from being surprised." He consoled Peck further, "I don't believe in the iron-clad arrangement, and if you cannot deal with her from the point we visited together with your 200-pounder Parrott I shall be very much surprised."

Federal troops had fortified Plymouth with a series of strong redoubts well equipped with artillery. A line of trenches with deep ditches and chevaux-de-frise encircled two thirds of the town. On the lower side several forts and redoubts guarded the Columbia road and the bridge crossing swampy Conaby Creek. Welch's Creek emptied into the Roanoke on the up-river side, very close to the edge of town and the redoubts and trench line. Fort Grey, on the river bank above town and near the obstructions mounted one 100-pounder Parrott rifle and two 32-pounder Parrotts. The heaviest guns were in the water batteries. On the western edge of town, on the river shore, loomed Battery Worth with the 200-pounder Parrott, the monster 8-inch rifle especially mounted to perforate the *Albemarle*. Fort Wessells, sometimes called the Eighty-fifth Redoubt, was sited about two thousand feet outside the trench line, and covered the Jamesville and Washington roads. It mounted one 32-pounder and two light field guns. In the center of the trench line, on the edge of town was Fort Williams with six guns. On the eastern environs stood Fort Comfort with three guns and the Conaby Redoubt, number of guns not listed.[12]

Brigadier-General H.W. Wessells commanded the post of Plymouth, with a garrison of 2,843 officers and men. They were

> Sixteenth Connecticut Regiment, Colonel Francis Beach
> Eighty-fifth New York Regiment, Colonel E. Fardella
> One Hundred and First Pennsylvania Regiment, Lt. Colonel A.W. Taylor
> One Hundred and Third Pennsylvania Regiment, Colonel T.F. Lehman
> Twenty-fourth New York Battery (six guns), Captain Cady
> Twelfth New York Cavalry, detachments from Companies A and F, Captain
>   Roche
> Second Massachusetts Heavy Artillery, two companies, Captain Sampson
> Second North Carolina Union Regiment, two companies, Captains Johnson and
>   Haggard.[13]

The Union ships stationed in Plymouth were commanded by Lieutenant-Commander Charles A. Flusser. They were

> *Miami*, Flagship, Five 9-inch Dahlgrens, one 100-pounder. Parrott, one 12-
>   pounder.
> *Southfield*, similar armament, Lieutenant C.A. French
> *Whitehead*, One 100-pounder Parrott, three 24-pounders, Ensign G.W. Barrett
> *Ceres*, two 20-pounder Parrotts, Act. Master H.H. Foster.

The armed transport *Bombshell* accompanied the squadron.

Brigadier-General R.F. Hoke was still near Kinston in early April. General Lee notified General Pickett that the new plan for Hoke's force was a good one and he had delayed recalling Hoke to Virginia until the last moment. He inquired about the gunboats. Again on April 14 Lee wrote General Braxton Bragg that Pickett should join Longstreet, but Hoke could remain. He hoped any action in North Carolina could be

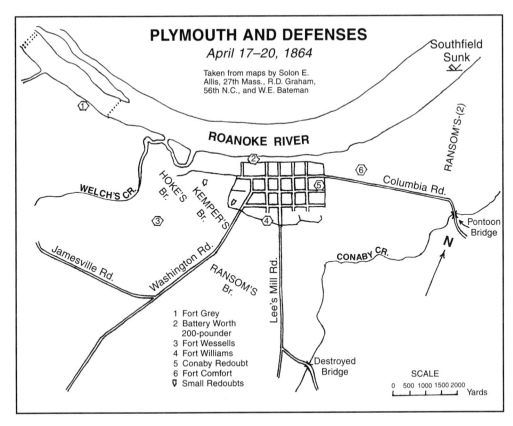

PLYMOUTH AND DEFENSES

April 17–20, 1864

Taken from maps by Solon E.
Allis, 27th Mass., R.D. Graham,
56th N.C., and W.E. Bateman

ROANOKE RIVER

Southfield
Sunk

WELCH'S CR.

HOKE'S Br.

KEMPER'S Br.

Jamesville Rd.

Washington Rd.

RANSOM'S Br.

Lee's Mill Rd.

CONABY CR.

Columbia Rd.

RANSOM'S-(2)

Pontoon
Bridge

N

Destroyed
Bridge

1 Fort Grey
2 Battery Worth
   200-pounder
3 Fort Wessells
4 Fort Williams
5 Conaby Redoubt
6 Fort Comfort
◊ Small Redoubts

SCALE

0   500 1000 1500 2000
                    Yards

Plymouth: Federal troops were well-secured for the battle on land but it was the battle on the water that won it for the Confederates. Sketched from J.W. Graham, "Capture of Plymouth," *Histories of The Several Regiments and Battalions from North Carolina in the Great War 1861–65*, editor Walter Clark (Goldsboro: Nash Brothers, 1901), vol. V.

done quickly.[13] General P.G.T. Beauregard came up from Charleston, South Carolina to Petersburg, Virginia to assume command of the Department of North Carolina.[15]

Hoke traveled to Hamilton on the Roanoke River to confer with Commander J.W. Cooke, the captain of the new ironclad *Albemarle*. Upon learning the details of Hoke's plan, Commander Cooke agreed to join in the attack on Plymouth. He would take his ship downriver on April 17, whether completed or not.[16] Hoke moved his troops by train to the nearest railhead, Tarboro, North Carolina. The march on Plymouth began. Hoke had with him:

Kemper's Virginia Brigade, Colonel Terry, consisting of the Seventh and
   Twenty-fourth Regiments
Hoke's own Brigade, Colonel Mercer, Senior Colonel
Twenty-first Georgia Regiment, Colonel Mercer
Sixth North Carolina, Lieutenant-Colonel S.M. Tate
Twenty-first North Carolina, Major Wm. J. Pfohl
Forty-third North Carolina, Lieutenant-Colonel Wm. G. Lewis

Ransom's Brigade, Brigadier-General Matt W. Ransom
Twenty-fourth North Carolina, Colonel Wm. John Clarke
Twenty-fifth North Carolina, Colonel H.M. Rutledge
Fifty-sixth North Carolina, Colonel Paul F. Faison
Eighth North Carolina, Colonel James M. Whitson
Thirty-fifth North Carolina, Colonel John G. Jones
Colonel Dearing's Cavalry detachment
Several batteries of artillery, Lieutenant-Colonel Branch
Tenth North Carolina Artillery detachments, parts of companies B, G, and H,
    the "Pontooneers," Colonel Pool.[17]

Hoke's column came pounding down the road from Tarboro, the cavalry jin-
gling ahead. Late in the afternoon of April 17 Confederate skirmishers drove in the
Federal pickets. A detachment of infantry and guns moved around to the west to
threaten the town and Fort Grey. Hoke's main column marched from the Jamesville
road to approach the town by the Washington road. During the night the Confederates
dug in, while the women, children, contrabands, and other noncombatants in the
town boarded transport vessels and steamed for Roanoke Island.

On Monday, February 18, the artillery on both sides fired a heavy bombardment,
with the Federal gunboats joining in. The transport USS *Bombshell* was sunk. Ransome's Brigade extended to the right of the Washington road. The artillery battle continued into the night. After several charges against fierce resistance, Hoke's Brigade
captured Fort Wessells. Hoke planned to use the fort as an artillery base against the
rest of the Union lines and particularly against Fort Williams, the strongest point in
the town's defenses. Hoke intended to take the town with artillery aided by the *Albemarle*, and to save his infantry as far as possible.[18]

The *Albemarle* was of the smallest class of Confederate ironclads, but built in a
similar pattern. She was 152 feet long, forty-five feet in beam, and drew eight feet of
water when loaded. She had a casemate shaped in an elongated octagon sixty feet long
and plated with two layers of iron, each two inches thick. With her slanted sides she
resembled the much larger *Virginia*, or *Merrimac*. The vessel was armed with two
Brooke 6.4-inch rifles. These were iron guns with heavy wrought iron bands shrunk
over their breeches for additional strength, They fired a 100-pound projectile, either
solid or explosive shell. The bow gun could fire ahead or to either side, the after gun,
with three ports also, could fire astern or to either side. The Brooke rifles were
mounted on pivot carriages which turned on heavy rollers and could be traversed
through 180 degrees.[19]

Commander Cooke left Hamilton as promised, with mechanics still bolting on
the last slabs of armor and operating a forge on the aft deck. A flat carrying more tools
and mechanics was towed astern. Several minor breakdowns were repaired and the flat
and extra men were cast off near Williamston. Shipbuilder Gilbert Elliott, an extra volunteer, rowed ahead in the launch to take soundings at the barricades in the river. He
reported back that a freshet, a rise in water caused by heavy rainfall upstream, had

raised the river's level enough so the ram could float over the obstructions. USS *Whitehead*, on guard in a side channel, escaped observation and sped downstream to report to Commander Flusser. It mattered little, for the ironclad was spotted by Fort Grey, which opened fire. The Fort Grey gunners hit the target. Elliott inside the iron shield, noted, "to those on board the noise made by the shot and shell as they struck the boat sounded no louder than pebbles thrown against an empty barrel." They did no more damage than pebbles.[20]

The *Albemarle* did not fire back, but Confederate army guns opened counter-battery fire on Fort Grey. In the pre-dawn dark and river mists, the ram gloomed against the far river bank, nearly invisible from the town as she passed. The 200-pounder rifle in Battery Worth was silent. Cooke ordered gun ports opened, and when ship's lights appeared ahead, he ordered the two Brooke rifles loaded. The small tender *Cotton Plant* dropped astern. As soon as Commander Cooke could see the enemy ships, about a mile below town, he ordered "all ahead, full" and charged.[21]

Both sides began firing. As the *Albemarle* closed the enemy, Cooke could see that the *Miami* and *Southfield* were loosely lashed together. Commander Flusser on the *Miami* had planned to trap the ram between his two ships while his big guns pounded her to pieces. This way the ironclad could not use her ram, but the Federal ships lost their maneuverability. Cooke headed for the gap between the Union vessels, turned slightly and crashed into the *Southfield's* starboard bow. The edge of *Albemarle's* armor, the knuckle, cut a gash in *Miami's* port bow. The iron ram smashed a huge hole in *Southfield's* side, penetrating as far as her fireroom. *Southfield* began to sink at once, dragging *Albemarle's* bow under until water began to pour in the forward gun port. The *Miami* continued to fire on the ram, with the brave but reckless Flusser firing her bow gun himself. On the third shot, which was a shell, the projectile rebounded from the ram's armor and exploded directly over Flusser's gun, killing him and wounding most of the gun crew. Many of the crew of the sinking ship scrambled aboard the *Miami*, while others swam ashore.

As the *Southfield* rolled over on the river's bottom, the ram's bow pulled free. *Albemarle* was ready to confront the *Miami*. Acting Master William Welles of the *Miami* wisely turned and retired down the river where he was joined by the *Whitehead* and *Ceres*. The three Union vessels fired defiant parting shots and left the Confederates in control of the river. Cooke anchored to inspect his ship and to communicate with General Hoke. The ram had suffered one man killed, and nine iron plates cracked. The ram's small boat had escaped damage, and was engaged in rescuing crewmen of the *Southfield*. Gilbert Elliott volunteered to seek Hoke. He "took Pilot Hopkins with a boats crew and proceeded down to the mouth of the river and up a creek [probably Conaby's Creek] in the rear of Plymouth.... He communicated with General Hoke and sent me dispatches."[22]

The artillery of both sides battled all day on Tuesday, February 19, with the *Albemarle* joining the field artillery and the guns of the Union forts returning fire. Confederate infantry skirmished, feeling out the Federal lines. That night Ransom's Brigade moved around to Hoke's right, forming on both sides of the Columbia Road. The

Federal left, behind Conaby Creek was less strongly fortified than the rest of Wessell's lines, depending on the creek and its swampy banks for protection. The "Pontooneers" of the Tenth Artillery forded several companies of infantry across in their boats, then build a pontoon bridge for the remaining regiments to cross.[23]

At dawn on Wednesday, April 20, the infantry, closely followed by several batteries of artillery, fought their way along the Columbia Road and into the town on Second Street. The Thirty-fifth North Carolina captured Fort Comfort after a hard fight and the Eighth North Carolina took the Conaby Redoubt, likewise a sharp fight. The performance of these regiments was very different from their conduct in early 1862. New leaders and months of on-the-job training had achieved much. The Confederates advanced on through the town against slackening resistance to capture Battery Worth, site of the 200-pounder and to surround Fort Williams, Wessells's strongest position. Here the Eighth Regiment, in the heat of combat, recklessly charged on the fort. They were repulsed with heavy losses. This was not a part of Hoke's plan and he sharply notified his colonels of his disapproval. Artillery could finish the job.[24]

General Hoke requested a personal interview with General Wessells, which was granted. According to Wessells, Hoke courteously pointed out that Wessells's men had made a brave fight, but their position was now hopeless. He demanded a surrender. Wessells refused. Within an hour all the Confederate artillery opened fire on Fort Williams. "This terrible fire had to be endured without reply, as no man could live at the guns." With no hope of relief, Wessells hoisted a white flag at 10 A.M.[25]

Hoke captured about 2,500 men, 28 guns, 500 horses, 5,000 stand of small arms, 700 barrels of flour, besides immense commissary, quartermaster, and ordnance stores.[26] Many of the men of the Second North Carolina Union Regiment escaped down river in canoes and were picked up by Federal ships. The Buffaloes were not sure how the Confederates would treat them. Some of the Buffaloes and many contrabands escaped into the swamps. Confederate troopers hunted them out and shot those who would not surrender. Just how many were killed has never been determined and estimates varied widely. General Wessells estimated his casualties as not exceeding 150, and believed the enemy's were at least 850.[27] Major Graham's count, taken from newspapers, lists eighty-two Confederate dead and 372 wounded from the North Carolina regiments. He had no list of killed from the Virginia regiments, but did list twenty wounded plus one killed from Bradford's Mississippi Battery. Graham's casualty count is probably too low, as others give the Eighth North Carolina Regiment's killed and wounded at 154, almost one third of its strength. After marching off his prisoners and leaving an occupation force, Hoke marched south to Washington.

As a stone dropped in a quiet pond sends concentric waves in all directions, so acted the battle of Plymouth. It was a very big rock dropped in the relatively quiet waters of eastern North Carolina. Roanoke Island and Washington first felt the effects of the shock waves. The repercussions broke full force on Beaufort and New Bern. The shock waves traveled on, reaching the Chesapeake Bay and were felt as far north as Richmond on the James and that other Washington on the Potomac.

Reinforcements from New Bern intended for Plymouth were diverted to

Roanoke Island and the sub-district headquarters, formerly in Plymouth, was re-established on the island. Commander H.K. Davenport, the Senior Naval Officer in the sounds, dispatched ships intended for Plymouth to Roanoke Island saying: "It is absolutely necessary that we protect Roanoke Island at all hazards." Admiral Lee, from his flagship off Newport News, dispatched more ships and advice to Davenport.[28]

A fast response came from Assistant Secretary of the Navy G.V. Fox. He telegraphed John Ericsson asking: "Can you have camels made to lift the *Tecumseh* so she will go over a bar with only 8 feet of water on it?"[29] Camels were pontoons tightly lashed to a ship to raise her partly out of the water. *Tecumseh* was one of the new monitors which drew fourteen feet of water. Ericsson's answer is not on record, but Fox's idea was impractical, for the sounds were too shallow for monitors to navigate. The decisive reaction came from Lieutenant-General U.S. Grant at his headquarters in Virginia. He telegraphed Butler: "It would be better to evacuate Washington and Plymouth than to have your whole force neutralized defending them." Grant sent a similar wire to Major-General Halleck, the Chief of Staff and the word filtered down the chain of command.[30]

Hoke, on the march to Washington, learned that the town was being evacuated, so did not hurry to attack it. When Hoke's leading regiments arrived they found the Federal troops gone and half the town burned. Brigadier-General Palmer sent Brigadier-General Edward Harland orders to evacuate on April 26. "A very delicate duty," Palmer called it. He ordered the evacuation to be quiet and orderly, with all supplies saved, and refugees, both white and black brought away. Palmer reported he was sending every steamer and schooner he could to assist the movement. Two regiments, the Fifty-eighth Pennsylvania and the Twenty-first Connecticut, took ship for Fort Monroe, as General Grant, like General Lee, needed more men in Virginia. Palmer also wanted the men of the First Union Regiment sent immediately to New Bern.[31] Palmer was the new district commander since General Peck had been relieved on the day Plymouth fell. The evacuation was anything but delicate, quiet, and orderly. J.A. Judson, Palmer's Adjutant-General, served on the Board of Investigation that was later convened. He commented:

> While the troops of this command … may take just pride in their many victories … yet a portion of them have within a few days been guilty of an outrage against humanity, which brings the blush of shame to the cheek of every true man and soldier … wantonly rendering houseless and homeless hundreds of poor women and children … bursting open the doors of the Masonic and Odd Fellows' Lodges, pillaged them both, and hawked about the streets the regalia and jewels….[32]

Adjutant Judson reported that the fires were caused by torchings in some recently emptied stables and from the river bridge which was fired by the navy. Fires were also deliberately set by drunken looters. Martha Matilda Fowle, the Portsmouth diarist, helped her father save their warehouse by pouring buckets of water on the roof. A few old men, black and white, helped them. Except for a few other heavy masonry buildings, the entire center of town burned.

Mrs. Josephus Daniels was one of the unlucky. Her house was in the path of the fire. Her son, Josephus, Jr., later editor of the *News and Observer* and Woodrow Wilson's Secretary of the Navy, remembered it. His father, Joseph Daniels, although a Unionist, had worked in the Confederate shipyard in Wilmington for two years. He then returned to the New Bern-Washington area to enter the mercantile business, associating himself with fiscal Buffaloes. He owned a house in Washington and had rented a house at Ocracoke. He was away when the town burned. Mrs. Daniels carried her children to safety before she tried to save her possessions. She was in the flaming house, removing her good mahogany table, when she caught a plundering Union soldier stealing her last ham. "She followed the thief amid the lurid flames and compelled its return." Left homeless, young Josephus, his younger brother Frank, and Mrs. Daniels crossed the sound in company with their friends the McDaniel family and "quite a number of Washington families."[33] There were undoubtedly many others who sought refuge on the Banks, but no records of refugees were kept during those trying times. To avoid the fighting, Unionists went east, while Confederates traveled west.

The refugees from Plymouth fled to Roanoke Island, but those from Washington sped to Beaufort and New Bern. There was a horde of them — soldiers, dependents, Buffaloes, and contrabands. Little of note occurred in the Beaufort area in early April before the battle of Plymouth. Hedrick's letters of April 7 and April 16, besides office news, mention only the Confederate attempt to destroy the Cape Lookout lighthouse. A party of Confederate raiders exploded two kegs of powder in the tower, wrecking the stairs and shattering the lenses. The structure, though bulged, was intact. The attempt brought an immediate complaint from Admiral Lee with a demand for better guards.[34]

Hedrick's letter of April 25 was filled with "stirring News" and conflicting rumors about Plymouth and the terrible ram. He noted with approval that many ladies had gone north and said that officers' wives should stay home anyway. It was a "general skidaddling."

General Palmer, from New Bern, reported to Butler's headquarters at Fortress Monroe that all the troop movements ordered in the district had been pushed as rapidly as possible. General Harland, in Washington, reported the enemy in sight toward Plymouth on April 28. Palmer stated that towed schooners were bringing in the contrabands. He noted further: "The First North Carolina Regiment is here. They have with them some 300 women and children. I shall make the best use of them I can, but these Carolina regiments are a great drag upon us at such a time as this." He planned to use the hospital buildings at Beaufort or Morehead to shelter them at present. "I hope you will make my peace with the medical director for this." Palmer expected three thousand contrabands from Washington. "I wish very much that Captain James could be here to provide for them."[35]

In many of the companies of the First and Second Union, the dependents far outnumbered the soldiers. A roster of B Company dated June 6, 1863, when the company was forming in Washington, listed forty-three soldiers and 105 dependents.[36] Palmer notified Colonel John Jourdan, commanding at Beaufort, that he would get the

First Union Regiment plus other troops very soon. He emphasized to Jourdan, "Don't let your people get stampeded!"[37] Nevertheless, a stampede developed among the Buffaloes, both civil and military.

John Hedrick reported on the events of Beaufort. He wrote there was so much news stirring that he hardly knew where to begin. The rebels were expected at New Bern soon, and unless they were diverted by events in Virginia, "I cannot see how we will be able to hold out much longer." The town was crowded with women and children from Washington and New Bern and three flat loads of Buffalo wives were brought over from Morehead City. We have enough of women and children," he grumbled; "The N.C. troops have been brought down from Washington and it seems that everyone of them has a wife and about a half-dozen children." He went on to report that rebel cavalry was reported near Newport. "I never thought soldiers could be so easily frightened as our troops have been. They seem to be more panic stricken than even the citizens, and seem to be ready to run at the first approach of the enemy." His only happy note was that the garden peas were blooming. As the transfer of the First Union regiment continued, Hedrick made a statement more appropriate for the British Raj than a North Carolina customs office: "So you see we are guarded by native troops."[38]

Meanwhile, Hoke's force marched through the embers and ashes of Washington. A second fire broke out after the Confederates arrived and burned a part of the east end of the town. Hoke left the Sixth North Carolina as a garrison, while the rest of his regiments marched toward New Bern. Hoke himself rode to Greenville and then Kinston. Further planning and coordinating was necessary — again the navy would help him. The navy's plan was to clear the sound of Union vessels and join Hoke before New Bern. The *Albemarle* was to have assistance in this task, for her sister ship, CSS *Neuse*, would steam down the river to give battle. *Neuse* was even further behind schedule than *Albemarle*. Only one layer of her two-inch armor was completed, not enough iron had been delivered to finish the second course. So, on orders from the Navy Department she left Kinston and started downstream on April 22 even though her gun crews needed more practice.

The water level in the river had been falling. When the *Neuse* struck a sand bar a half mile below the town there she stuck, her bow four feet out of water and her stern afloat. She remained on the sand bar until mid–May when the river rose and she could return to Kinston.[39]

Cooke in the *Albemarle*, followed by the captured *Bombshell* and the *Cotton Plant*, left Plymouth on May 5 at noon. The *Bombshell*, just raised from the bottom of the river, was armed with two small rifles, but was intended chiefly as a supply vessel for the ram. She carried extra coal and general supplies. The *Cotton Plant*, another tender, was unarmed and described as "rifle screened." This meant she was shielded from musketry, possibly with light iron sheets, but more likely with bales of hay or cotton. The three Confederate vessels entered the sound about 1:30 P.M. and sighted four Union ships which retreated down the sound. The Union ships were the *Miami* and the *Ceres*, previous opponents of the ram, along with the *Commodore Hull* and the transport *Trumpeter*. *Commodore Hull*, a converted ferry boat of 376 tons, mounted two 30-pounder Parrott rifles and four 24-pounder smoothbores. Lieutenant French in the *Miami*, the senior officer, sent the *Trumpeter* racing ahead to warn the rest of the fleet. French's three ships stayed in sight of the ironclad as they retreated.[40]

Commander Cooke reported essentially the same as Lieutenant French.

> As soon as we reached the mouth of the Roanoke River we discovered six of the enemy's gunboats in the sound, about 10 miles distant. They immediately got underway and stood down the sound E.N.E., until we had run about 16 miles, when three more gunboats, double-enders, of a much more formidable class, carrying from ten to twelve guns each, made their appearance.[41]

These Federal ships were much more formidable. The *Mattabesett*, the flagship led. She was a 974-ton, 14-knot, double-ender, with a heavy armament. She mounted two 100-pounder Parrott rifles, four 9-inch Dahlgren smoothbores, two 24-pounders and one 12-pounder plus one 12-pounder rifle. The *Sassacus* and the *Wyalusing* were sister ships with the same big guns and similar smaller smoothbores and rifles. The three big double-enders had been sent into the sounds especially to fight the *Albemarle*. The *Whitehead*, of 139-tons, was comparable to the Federal *Ceres*, except she carried one big 100-pounder Parrott.[42] Commanding the entire Federal flotilla was a newcomer to the North Carolina sounds, Captain Melancton Smith. He had been hastily removed from command of the big, new monitor *Onondaga*, and sent to the sounds to take command and make plans for destroying the ironclad.[43]

On sighting the Federal flotilla rushing to meet him, Cooke signaled to the *Cotton Plant* and *Bombshell* to head back up the Roanoke River. *Cotton Plant* obeyed, but *Bombshell* delayed leaving until too late. *Albemarle* alone steamed toward the enemy, two guns against twenty-six big guns and thirty-four 30-pounders and smaller.

Fighting against great odds was nothing new for the Confederate Navy, especially in North Carolina waters. The decision of the Confederate Navy Department to concentrate on a few superior ironclad ships was proven correct. The Union Navy had no suitable ironclads to fight the *Albemarle*. A class of shallow-draft monitors ordered by the Department of the Navy were behind schedule in construction and had defects in design that were to make them unserviceable when completed.[44] Commander Cooke steamed straight for the enemy, relying on the strength of his ship, the toughness of her armor, and the spirit of his crew. The *Albemarle* had weak points, as Cooke knew, but he was needed at New Bern to help Hoke's soldiers as he had done at Plymouth.

Captain Smith formed his vessels in two columns, a half-mile apart, and led one of them in *Mattabesett*. The Federal ships had practiced various maneuvers, but Smith had made no rigid plan for each ship other than the initial approach. The two columns were to pass on either side of the ironclad, each ship firing when she came abreast of the ram. The battle opened at about 4:40 P.M. Commander Cooke did not dance to Captain Smith's quadrille by continuing down the lane between the two lines. He ordered a wide turn to starboard, firing as he turned and disrupting Smith's columns.

The Confederate ironclad ram *Albemarle*. From Richard Rush et al., eds., *Official Records of the Union and Confederate Navies in the War of the Rebellion*, Series II, Vol. 1.

Albemarle fired first, hitting *Mattabesett* twice, with little damage done. The Federal ships fired as fast as they could, whenever their guns bore on the target. One of the early guns fired made a direct hit on the muzzle of *Albemarle*'s after gun, breaking off twenty inches of the underside of the muzzle. The Brooke rifle continued to fire. The little *Bombshell* joined in the firing and took a hit from *Mattabesett*'s smaller guns. *Bombshell* dodged away, but Lieutenant Albert Hudgins still did not order a retreat while he could. The *Bombshell* began hitting the *Sassacus*, which answered with broadsides from her heavy guns. Hit three times in her hull, *Bombshell* hauled down her flag and surrendered.

The *Albemarle* was surrounded by the Federal ships, all firing rapidly. The smoke of many guns blending with black coal smoke from the stacks cut visibility, especially in the ram's enclosed gun deck. The Federal gunners almost smothered *Albemarle* with fire, solid shot, and shells. Everything above the armor was hit, but no shot penetrated the iron. *Sassacus* charged in full speed and rammed the ironclad just at the after end of the casemate. Her bow rode up on the *Albemarle*'s deck, cracking a few plates and tilting the ram enough that a gunport momentarily shipped water. *Sassacus*'s bow was damaged, but worse was to come. *Albemarle* fired back at point-blank range, flame scorching her foe. One of her shots, smashing through several compartments, penetrated the boiler, filling *Sassacus*'s engine room with scalding steam. The ram broke loose from *Sassacus*'s bow and steamed on. *Sassacus* limped away, out of the fight.

USS *Miami* carried a spar torpedo on her bow, but Lieutenant French, her captain, could not maneuver his unwieldy ship fast enough to make a bow-on charge. The *Commodore Hull* tried her special tactic next. She dragged a heavy net across *Albemarle*'s path, hoping to tangle it in the ram's screws. It did not work. The battle had lasted three hours when the *Albemarle*'s speed dropped and she turned away. She fired a parting shot and slowly steamed a crooked course toward the Roanoke River. The Union ships did not pursue.[45]

Albemarle slowed because the steam pressure in her boilers dropped. She had run out of coal, but that was not the major problem. A hot fire under the boilers depended on a good draft to pull air into the firebox and a good draft depended on the height of the smokestack. Practically speaking, the ship had no stack left above the casemate. The exterior part of the stack was so ripped and tattered by shot and shell that the fires no longer drew in air. The firemen threw cabin furniture and bulkheads into the furnaces, anything that would burn with a low draft, but it was not enough. Someone had a better idea. The ship had a full larder, if empty coal bunkers. She stocked a large quantity of lard, butter, and bacon, fuel that would burn with a negligible draft. The fires flared up with the new fuel, steam pressure rose. The ship's speed increased, though she still steered poorly due to a hanging section of armor plate that counteracted the rudder.[46] *Albemarle* steamed up the river, wafting the odor of frying bacon behind her. Surely, no naval battle has ever smelled better.

Commander Cooke realized he could not join Hoke before New Bern until repairs had been made. He began them at once. Meanwhile, General Hoke had not waited idly.

Hoke established his headquarters in Kinston and moved his brigades into position along the Trent road. He knew the ground well from previous battles, studied it again, and determined to attack New Bern from the south, the route taken by General Barton during his unsuccessful January attack. General P.G.T. Beauregard came down from Petersburg to Kinston on May 2 to confer with Hoke and approved his plans.[47] Union headquarters had no idea of Hoke's plans or his exact position. Colonel P.J. Claassen, commanding the Union line at Batchelder's Creek on May 3 wrote: "I have satisfactory proof that no force of the enemy are now menacing New Berne, either by land or water."[48] Claassen was correct on his front only.

Brigadier-General Palmer in New Bern had been regrouping his troops since the battle of Plymouth. Palmer ordered Colonel Henry T. Sisson, of the Fifth Rhode Island Artillery, to detach two companies for service on the Banks, where the attack of the dreadful *Albemarle* was feared. Companies D and I boarded the transport *Pawtuxent* on April 21 for Hatteras. Here the artillerymen occupied the fort on the inlet, which was garrisoned by two companies of the First Union regiment. The Rhode Islanders moved a 100-pounder Parrott to a better position, repaired gun platforms, and rebuilt the carriage of the fort's 11-inch Dahlgren. Next they reported to the commander at Roanoke Island on May 2. The companies manned two of the batteries there, Fort Foster and Fort Parke, to await the ram.[49]

Hoke's leading regiments, south of the Trent River, on May 5, crossed Bryce's Creek, which General Barton had said was impossible. They captured the blockhouse guarding a mill dam, which Barton had judged too strong to assault, and prepared for a full-scale attack on New Bern.[50]

On the same day, a detachment of cavalry and infantry force-marched to

Croatan, halfway to Newport, to cut the railroad. A small fort there was garrisoned by Company A of the Fifth Rhode Island, an experienced regiment. Hoke's soldiers surrounded the fort and after a fire-fight of one and a half hours, compelled its surrender. The Federal loss was one man wounded. The prisoners, including the regimental chaplain, were allowed to take with them what spare clothes and rations they could carry, while Hoke's men took the rest. The chaplain thought this was very hard. They marched to Kinston.[51]

At this point the Confederates had gained moral ascendancy over the enemy in North Carolina. There was no lack of courage on the Northern side, but rather a lack of confidence in victory. The Union Navy expected the *Albemarle* to appear anywhere and they did not know what to expect from the *Neuse*. The Union Army was just as nervous as the navy, manning the forts while remembering Plymouth. The First Union regiment was now worthless. General Palmer, Captain Melancton Smith, and a few subordinates retained their confidence. This was the day Palmer advised his subordinates, "Don't get stampeded."

On this day, too, General Hoke received an order he did not want. May 5, 1864, was eventful.

General P.G.T. Beauregard, back in Petersburg, Virginia, telegraphed General Hoke to break off his fight, whatever the stage of his attack, and start at once for Virginia. Beauregard was charged with the protection of Petersburg and the railroad connections with North Carolina, vital to the Army of Northern Virginia. A strong force under Major-General B.F. Butler was advancing on Beauregard's lines, hence his orders to Hoke. It is not certain whether the order originated with Beauregard or General Braxton Bragg in Richmond, but the wire was sent over Beauregard's name. Thus ended the campaign to restore the eastern counties to the Confederacy. Hoke started marching to Kinston on May 6 and arrived to board the trains on the night of May 7.[52] The threat to Petersburg was not quite so desperate as Beauregard thought. After all, B.F. Butler was commanding the Federal advance.

When Brigadier-General Hoke arrived in Virginia he learned he had been promoted to Major-General. Commander Cooke was promoted to Captain. Both officers received the thanks of Congress for their splendid service at Plymouth.

Although the danger to Union-held North Carolina was no longer acute, the effects of Hoke's and Cooke's successes lingered. General Palmer reported to the Secretary of War directly on May 15, as he was not able to communicate with General Butler:

> The North Carolina troops I considered useless unless they were placed at some point where they could consider themselves secure from capture, as the execution of the Carolina troops at Kinston had very much demoralized the whole of them. They would have been useless to General Butler, and I have placed them all in the Sub-District of Beaufort, where, as they feel secure, they will, I hope become reliable.[53]

The navy continued to evacuate civilians from threatened areas. Lieutenant Henry Eaton, commanding USS *Louisiana*, reported to Commander Davenport on

June 5 that he had on board nineteen men and women and twenty-two children destined for New Bern and Portsmouth Island.[54] John Hedrick's letters after the crisis said that business was very dull, but his garden peas, lettuce, and radishes were abundant. Subsequent letters commented on the weather and the crowds of refugees filling the hospitals and the Baptist and Colored churches. About a dozen refugee children had died of measles in a week. The Negroes were also dying, but not so fast as previously noted. Hedrick's friend, Mr. Norcum "lost two last week, or rather two died which had formerly belonged to him." Hedrick explained some local terminology in vogue for different classes of the population.

> All who came down with the Union Army are called "Yankees." Those who lived here before the war and were opposed to secession and unwilling to join the rebel army are called Sawed-noons. The North Carolinians who have joined the Union Army are called Buffaloes, while those who are in favor of dissolution of the Union are called Secesh. Some call the negroes Rights because the rebs used to say that they were fighting for their rights, whereas they were fighting for their negroes.[55]

The terms "Sawed-noons" and "Rights" evidently never spread far beyond the environs of Beaufort.

After the alarms of Hoke's campaign died away, General Palmer made a careful survey of his district, with particular attention paid to the Banks. He reported his findings both to the Adjutant-General and to General B.F. Butler on May 31. Beach erosion, he said, had partially destroyed Fort Clark and he recommended that it be abandoned and its guns be removed to the fort at Portsmouth or the Fort on Beacon Island. He requested the War Department's approval to garrison the new fort with men from Hatteras, leaving only Fort Hatteras to protect that inlet. He asked that Ocracoke light be established and the inlet channel be buoyed as had been done at Hatteras. "Ocracoke Inlet has now become quite as good if not better than Hatteras Inlet," and the harbor at Ocracoke is "infinitely better."[56] No mention was made of wrecks in the inlet.

The navy also was concerned with Ocracoke Inlet. Captain Melancton Smith reported to Admiral S.P. Lee that USS *Miami* would be useful at Ocracoke Inlet since the *Granite* was again at Hatteras. Captain Smith received orders to resume command of the *Onondaga*, but just before leaving he sent a memorandum dated June 27, 1864 to his replacement in the sounds. He advised Commander W.H. Macomb: "A vessel ought to be stationed at Ocracoke Inlet, as there is nearly as much water on that bar as at Hatteras. The commanding general intends placing a force there also."[57]

Neither the Adjutant-General nor General Butler made any immediate reply to Palmer's request for approval of his plan. The Navy had sufficient vessels in the sounds to approve Commander Macomb's recommendations. The *Bombshell*, back in the Union Navy, took station at Ocracoke Inlet, while the *Granite* guarded Hatteras Inlet. By July 20 the little *Bombshell*, once sunk and twice bombarded, was, not surprisingly, leaking so badly that she had to retire to New Bern for repairs.[58]

The Union Navy's chief concern in the sounds during the summer and fall of 1864 was "*Albemarle* Watching." Launches and picket boats scouted up the Roanoke River, gunboats patrolled Albemarle Sound. Patrols slogged through the swamp to peer at the ram from the opposite bank of the river. Naval officers interrogated Confederate deserters, refugees, and contrabands to gather intelligence of the ram. They learned some facts and collected an incredible number of rumors including the one about the new ironclad vessel which would be ready in three weeks.[59] The navy sowed torpedoes in the mouth of the Roanoke while the army planted them in the Neuse above New Bern.

The navy's secondary concern was an even more rigid control of trading vessels than heretofore. As maritime trade began to revive and both gunboats and schooners began skittering anew across the sounds, naval vessels questioned even the permits issued by Customs and Treasury Agents. Commander Macomb asked Secretary Welles, in a letter dated July 7, for guidance:

> I respectfully request the Department to inform me whether persons having permits from the special agents of the Treasury are to be allowed to trade without the military lines.
>
> I have reason to believe that many such persons are violating their permits. I have taken the liberty to forward this direct to the Department, so that the persons awaiting the decision may not lose time and money.

Secretary Welles replied with a generalization: "I know of no authority that transcends the law and regulations on this subject. Trade and free communications are inconsistent with blockade."[60]

The navy began hunting down anything afloat. In June gunboats captured five trading schooners in Pamlico Sound and carried them into port where they were held until their papers could be verified. In July the gunboat *Lockwood* raided up Pungo River where she captured three schooners, only one of which had sails and an anchor, six log canoes, besides a quantity of cedar shingles.[61] July brought another fine haul when USS *Shawsheen* captured five schooners at Cedar Island, namely the 14-ton *Sally* and *Helen Jane*, both of Portsmouth and owned by Cedar Islanders. Next came two 80-ton schooners, the *Elizabeth* and the *Dolphin* of Portsmouth with no one aboard. Finally the 10-ton *James Brice* of Portsmouth was taken. Acting-Master Henry Phelon reported the owners were said to be rebels.[56] In a display of the grandeur of sea power USS *Louisiana* landed in Hyde County up Pungo Creek. A landing party destroyed a bridge and captured a four-mule wagon loaded with cornmeal and flour. The driver escaped, but the traitorous mules were shot.[63]

Confederate actions also consisted of pin-pricks and hornet-stings. There were few troops left in North Carolina following Hoke's campaign and they were spread throughout the district guarding towns, rail lines and bridges. In all the Confederate Second Military District, headquartered in the Kinston-Goldsboro area, there were the Sixty-eighth North Carolina, Whitford's Regiment, Sixth North Carolina Cavalry, plus two companies of the North Carolina State Cavalry. There were three companies of heavy artillery and six companies of light artillery. Dearing's Cavalry Brigade mustered four small cavalry regiments, one battalion and one battery. The Kinston provost guard and five hundred men of the North Carolina Reserves completed the list. Beauregard's returns for his department list no count of troops in the abstract of June 10, 1864.[64]

There were also the *Albemarle* and *Neuse*. The *Albemarle*, repaired and refitted lay at her dock in Plymouth, subject to indecision of the War and Navy departments over her best use. Captain Cooke, due to bad health, was relieved from command and replaced by Commander J.N. Maffitt, a successful blockade runner. In Kinston mechanics continued to bolt the rest of the armor on *Neuse*.

Maffitt organized a party of his crew under command of Pilot James B. Hopkins to capture or destroy the Federal mail boat that regularly traveled the Dismal Swamp Canal. Hopkins's venture was successful. On the night of September 9 they captured the mail boat *Fawn*, her crew, passengers, and cargo and burned the vessel. Hopkins withdrew with twenty-nine prisoners, including a colonel and two majors. Seven men from the *Fawn* were killed or wounded by Federal accounts. Commander Macomb sent three gunboats carrying extra Marines in pursuit, too late to catch Hopkins's party. The gunboats proceeded to Elizabeth City where Lieutenant-Commander English arrested seven citizens whom he sent to Norfolk as hostages.[65] Later in the fall, Confederate raiders blew up the lighthouse at the entrance to Croatan Sound.[66] The small-scale war continued around the sounds. Elsewhere it was large scale.

By the late summer of 1864 war weariness was increasing in the North. It was brought about by the tremendous Federal casualties in Virginia and by the apparently static positions of both Meade's and Sherman's armies. In eastern North Carolina many people were surprisingly optimistic. The *Albemarle* was ready to give battle and somehow New Bern might even be captured. When Sherman took Atlanta on September 2, Northern spirits soared while Southerners' fell. In New Bern the forts fired a one hundred gun salute.[67]

John Hedrick in Beaufort had little to report during July and August other than the weather and new regulations promulgated by General Butler. In September he gloated over a newspaper article about C.H. Foster's dismissal and his (Foster's) demands for an investigation. General B.F. Butler had cashiered Foster for inefficiency and sent him out of the state. On September he noted that business was very good and he had taken in $2800.00 in one night. In spite of the cessation of trade during the Confederate offensive, 1864 showed the greatest number of ships trading through Beaufort in both registration and enrollment. Later in the month Hedrick mentioned an increase in sickness among the Merchant Marine, much more than usual. On September 12 he stated that "The sickness in Newbern continues unabated. The people are dying very fast. I heard Saturday that the Doctors had given it up as yellow fever."[68] By early October, an estimated one thousand people had died in New Bern of the fever. Hedrick listed friends, co-workers, officers, and surgeons who had died of the Black Vomit. The hospital in Beaufort housed between eighty and one hundred victims. He reported a heavy frost and cool weather in October, but the fever continued. By

October 22 the fever was abating, the weather was cold and clear, and there was no war news.[69]

In late October the Confederacy and the State suffered a shattering blow. Rear-Admiral David D. Porter, the new commander of the North Atlantic Squadron, sent an order to Commander Macomb on October 15: "On the arrival of Lieutenant W.B. Cushing you will supply him with all the men he will need in the performance of the duty assigned him." On the night of October 27, Cushing, with thirteen officers and men, ascended the Roanoke River in a steam launch equipped with a spar torpedo. In an act of unsurpassed bravery, Cushing exploded the torpedo under the *Albemarle's* bottom, sinking her in a few minutes. The launch was swamped. Several men drowned, most were captured, with only Cushing and one other man escaping separately down river, where they were rescued by Union gunboats.[70] Cushing was feted as a hero in the North, a well deserved tribute. In North Carolina, hopes for a Southern victory went down with the *Albemarle*. Plymouth was recaptured by Union forces on October 31. Washington was reoccupied soon thereafter. Admiral Porter ceased chiding his ship-captains with having "Ram Fever."

December 1864 brought false hope back to the state. A Federal attack on Fort Fisher at the mouth of the Cape Fear River failed. The navy subjected the fort to a bombardment of "stunning violence," but the army's land attack, commanded by B.F. Butler was repulsed. The battle was reported as a great victory throughout the Confederacy.[71] The resulting jubilation was short-lived.

Chapter Nine

The End and the Beginning: 1865

HE NEW YEAR BEGAN in North Carolina as the old one had ended, with a Federal attack on Fort Fisher, on January 13–15, 1865. The second attack was even more ferocious than the first and was successful. Beaufort harbor was the staging area for the warships and transports, and again, as John Hedrick had stated before, "the harbor is full of coal schooners and gunboats and monitors." The two main battlefronts closed in on the state. The Federal army in Virginia continued its bloody assault on the Army of Northern Virginia, while Major-General W.T. Sherman's "bummers" ravaged their way into South Carolina. Little time was left for the Confederacy, though no immediate change was apparent in the eastern counties.

Rear-Admiral Porter dispersed his ships after the battle of Fort Fisher, sending more vessels into the sounds. Lieutenant-Commander J.S. Thornton received orders to proceed through Hatteras Inlet and report to Commander Macomb, Senior Officer in the North Carolina sounds. His ship, USS *Iosco*, one of the useful double-enders, was newly armed with an 11-inch Dahlgren in addition to her four 9-inch and four smaller howitzers. The 11-inch Dahlgren was considered the best gun to fight ironclads by many naval officers, as it was faster firing than the ponderous 15-inchers used in some of the monitors. Porter also notified Macomb that three more double-enders, *Agawam*, *Chicopee*, and *Tacony* were coming to him, plus the smaller *Hunchback*, *Henry Brinker*, and *Martin*, all equipped with spar torpedoes. Admiral Porter added, "If, with a torpedo on the bows of all these, you cannot destroy one ram, I do not know how it can be done."[1] There were seventeen Union warships in the sounds by February 25, a strong reception committee for the lonesome CSS *Neuse*.[2] There was another ironclad under construction up the Roanoke River, an improved *Albemarle*, but she was far from ready.[3]

General Palmer in New Bern continued his re-shuffling of his regiments. On February 28 he ordered all of the First Union Regiment, which had absorbed the men enrolled by C.H. Foster in the Second Union, to concentrate at Beaufort and Morehead City. Company H from Hatteras was ordered up to rejoin the rest of the regiment.[4] Company H, which had been stationed at Hatteras since the first enlistments in 1861, was but a skeleton formation in early 1865 due to special transfers. Individual service records of the soldiers show approximately forty-five additional men were detached for "special guard duty" at Portsmouth and Ocracoke. Most of the detached men remained on guard around Ocracoke Inlet until June when they were brought to Beaufort and mustered out.[5] No reason was recorded for this increased guard detail, nor do the transfers appear in any general orders from headquarters. General Palmer, apparently, managed to reinforce the two islands as he had suggested to General Butler in 1864.

With the seventeen steam gunboats cruising the sounds and with only the *Neuse* flying the Confederate flag, the Union Navy felt secure enough to relax trade regulations. Admiral Porter directed Commander Macomb to allow loyal persons to take out farm products whenever they wished.[6] The easing of the requirements for trading permits was welcome around the sounds, though there were few schooners available for increased trade. Most of the vessels that had escaped capture had been laid up in creeks and upper rivers for several years. Time and capital would be required to fit them out again. The *C.A. Johnson* was an example. This fine, big schooner was owned by Augustus Dudley of Portsmouth. In the first weeks of the war he sent his schooner up the Pamlico River for safekeeping. He placed her at the shipyard of Ulysses Ritch. When shipbuilder Ritch left for more lucrative wartime work, the *C.A. Johnson* lay at his dock. A party of Federal troops, ordered to find a flagpole for their headquarters, decided to take a spar from Dudley's schooner. By unskillful rigging, the soldiers managed to drop the spar and punch holes through the deck and side of the vessel. The soldiers wrenched the spar loose and carried off their flagpole. At the next extra low tide, the *C.A. Johnson* settled on the bottom, rolled over on her side, and filled with water when the tide surged in. Much labor and money would be necessary to fit her out again.[7]

Any farm products shipped under the new regulations had to be hauled by small sloops, canoes, and even old perriaugers. Most of the special trade permits issued during this period specified dugouts and canoes, which included perriaugers.[8] These last were large dugouts, improved Indian canoes, made from two or three logs. Maritime historian Gordon Watts has called the perriauger the "pickup truck of the eighteenth century."

John Hedrick's letter of March 10 spoke of troop movements toward Goldsboro and few soldiers left around Beaufort. He also said "The young lady arrested for blockade running is Miss Emeline Piggott of Calico Creek near Morehead … Miss Pigott is still in jail." Cousin Levi Piggott continued the story.

Miss Piggott, accompanied by her brother-in-law Rufus Bell, drove out toward Bell's home in the country on January 10, 1865. Miss Piggott was wearing her freight-carrying hoopskirt. The two were arrested and carried to the Provost-Marshal's office, where Miss Piggott was confined in an upper room. The Marshal sent a black woman to undress and search her. Miss Piggott threatened to kill the woman with a burning brand she snatched from the fire. The Marshal sent a white woman who got the same treatment. Finally the Marshal announced he would send a file of soldiers to search her by force if she would not submit to the ladies. Miss Piggott agreed to undress herself and hand her garments to the white lady, who carried them downstairs. When the freight pockets were unloaded, the gathered Federal officers roared with laughter. They were stuffed with a razor, soap, hose, shirts, handkerchiefs, a suit of gray cloth, other small items, and a pair of cavalry boots. Also there were several letters with information on Union troop movements.

The Provost-Marshal seemed to know everything about her actions, so she knew someone had betrayed her, but she had no idea who. Cousin Levi Woodbury and his wife immediately went to see Emmeline. Cousin Levi said, "I have never seen nor do I ever expect to see as mad a woman again."

Levi's wife stayed with Emmeline in the Marshal's lockup and later accompanied her during the time she spent in the New Bern jail. The Federal officers who had helped her get permits did what they could, but the letters she carried made her crime a serious one. The officers were anxious that Emmeline not testify to their smuggling business, so they continued to work behind the scenes on her behalf. "I was agreeably surprised, and utterly astonished, when she obtained her release," wrote her cousin. Emmeline Piggott went home to her mother. She never married, but kept up her friendship with her old friends of the Confederate Army. She never considered herself a daughter of the Confederacy, but rather a Confederate veteran.[9]

Federal troops again flooded into North Carolina. General Sherman, approaching from South Carolina, had selected Goldsboro as his new supply base, a site with good rail connections with the coast. A Union force pushed up the Cape Fear River to capture Wilmington on February 22. Major-General J.B. Schofield, the new commander of the Department of North Carolina, found few wagons and little rolling stock in Wilmington. He shifted his coastal base to Beaufort-Morehead City which had an intact railroad to New Bern, with a fair supply of engines and freight cars. Much of the track between New Bern and Kinston had been removed to be rolled into armor plates for the two ironclads, hence General Palmer's efforts to repair the line as Federal troops advanced. Schofield decided General Palmer needed help, so sent Major-General J.D. Cox to take command.[10] Cox brought up more troops to fight his way to Goldsboro, while work gangs replaced the rails behind him.

Those two splendid fighters, Major-Generals D.H. Hill and R.F. Hoke commanded the outnumbered Confederates. In overall command was General Braxton Bragg, a good planner with President Davis's confidence, but a field commander almost as inept as B.F. Butler on the Union side. At this stage of the war, it made little difference. Hill and Hoke's men fought gallantly at Southwest Creek and Wise's Forks below Kinston, but were pushed back. Federal troops entered Kinston on March 12. The ironclad *Neuse* shelled the cavalry advance units. Then her Captain ordered her stores removed and set her on fire. She sank in the bend of the river at Kinston.[11]

There was one further warning of a Confederate ironclad ram. The Federal Navy Department received news from Europe that a large vessel built in France had been transferred to the rebels. This rumor proved to be true, for the seagoing ironclad ram *Stonewall* had bluffed and frightened a Federal squadron that was showing the flag in Spain and had started across the Atlantic Ocean. General Palmer, on May 8, passed on the warning to the Commandant at Fort Macon: "ammunition should be held in readiness and the guns continually manned."[12] The formidable vessel did not come.

Sherman's vanguard entered the state on March 3. The final battle was fought at

Bentonville, North Carolina before Major-General W.T. Sherman and General J.E. Johnston settled the terms of an armistice and surrender on April 17–18. Following suit, Major-General J.M. Schofield stated the terms of surrender for all Confederate troops in the eastern counties. The senior Confederate officer present, Colonel J.N. Whitford, accepted the terms and the fighting ended.[13]

The clangor of the muskets ceased, the roar of the guns stilled. The armies prepared to go home. Most of the Union soldiers in the state marched west, then north to entrain for the nation's capitol and a grand victory parade. The few regiments still guarding the coast settled down in their old quarters to wait for the transport steamers.

The Fifth Rhode Island Artillery, which had fought on the Banks early in the war and manned the forts around New Bern and Beaufort for nearly three years, was typical. The detached companies were brought in from Roanoke Island and Hatteras and united with the rest of the regiment. Then the artillerymen fretted in the forts waiting for the transport *Ellen S. Terry*, which at last arrived on June 30. The Fifth's regimental history described their last look at "the low, forest covered shores, now fading in the gloom," and the "mingled tenderness and sorrow for comrades whom no earthly reveille would ever awaken." Of the voyage up the coast, the history's author stated, "Hope, joy, hilarity even marked the demeanor of all," in spite of the snail-like steamer. "The reception of the Fifth was one continued ovation" as the regiment debarked in Providence.[14]

The First Union Regiment mustered for the last time on June 27, 1865, at New Bern. Here all companies, including the special detachments from Ocracoke and Portsmouth, were paid off and discharged.[15] The men and their dependents would be shipped to their homes or their posts of enlistment as steamers were available, or on vessels with other missions which had available carrying capacity.

There was that other army — the defeated army. Confederate soldiers came home too. They came in ones and twos, sometimes in scattered coveys, trudging the long miles from their last camps or prison. They brought with them only "the satisfaction that proceeds from the consciousness of duty faithfully performed."[16] Weeks and months elapsed before all the survivors returned. Some came home to ashes and desolation, some to abandoned farms, but many returned to intact homes and joyful families.

Charlie Bishop's return to his home in Washington was in many ways typical, though his enlistment differed from the usual. First, he had to slip through the Union lines and make his way west to join the Confederate army. Secondly, somehow young Charlie Bishop joined the Confederate States Marine Corps instead. Private Bishop served in Company B of the regiment of Marines. He was captured on April 6, 1865 at Farmville, Virginia, and sent to the prisoner of war camp at Point Lookout, Maryland. He was released after taking the Oath of Loyalty to the United States on June 24, 1865.[17] He began the long walk home.

The journey took long, long weeks. Sometimes he walked in company with other veterans, sometimes alone. He lived on handouts from the homesteads along the way. The people were kind to returning soldiers and shared what they had with them. He slept where he could, usually in barns or haystacks. He was one of the lucky ones, for his home was intact, and his mother, sisters, and stepfather were there to greet him. He was thin, worn, and dirty, but he was alive. His mother shrieked her joy at seeing him and began to hug and kiss her baby. She fingered a seam on his tattered jacket, then shrieked her dismay. Charlie Bishop was teeming with lice. His mother began to heat water, sisters Mary Ann and Adele fired up the big wash pot in the yard, and step-father Schirmer took Charlie to the woodshed. He brought the big tin bathtub, home-made yellow soap strong enough to clean an alligator, a towel, and clean clothes. He brought the buckets of hot water. While Charlie Bishop scrubbed, the sisters boiled his uniform, and Mr. Schirmer, an old soldier himself, tried to explain to his wife that lice are sometimes part of a soldier's burden. When Charlie Bishop was clean and dressed, the hugging and kissing resumed.[18]

The soldiers dwelling along the coast were more fortunate than some of those from the urban centers on the mainland that had been fought over or burned. The homes and families of the Bankers had survived, though were worn by four years of military occupation. War damage was minimal, but the islanders faced a future even more bleak than their compatriots across the sounds. Gone were the days when forty sail anchored inside the Ocracoke swash awaiting a fair wind, and gone were the years when fourteen hundred vessels exited the inlets. Even if civilian trade revived, the Albemarle and Chesapeake Canal would attract a huge share of it. Revived trade was of the greatest importance, but the immediate problems at war's end were putting food on the table and putting aside wartime hatreds.

One Union naval officer commented on the latter problem as he added to it. On May 3, 1865, Ensign James H. Kerens, commanding the gunboat *Henry Brinker*, reported on conditions in Washington, North Carolina:

> On my arrival there I found great animosity between the loyal inhabitants [Unionists] and those who had evacuated previous to the capture of the place by our forces in 1862, but have since returned, opening stores and trading under the guise of loyalty. I closed their stores and found great quantities of cotton stowed away belonging to unloyal people.[19]

Ensign Kerens further stated that one "strong secessionist" returned bringing his furniture and a load of cotton without permission. Kerens immediately seized the cotton. His high-handed actions undoubtedly fueled the animosity he observed.

There was some ill will on both sides, the natural result of a long and bloody war. Wishes for vengeance smoldered in the minds of some who had lost loved ones in the fighting, but such feelings were usually short-lived. The Bankers, because of their contacts through ships and mariners, were less insular than many mainlanders. Four years of Union occupation made the transition to peacetime easier. There was less hate, too, in the hearts of the soldiers than of the civilians, for the soldiers had formed a mutual respect for each other. Only a few years after the war, Union veterans began to visit former battlefields. Few ex–Confederates could afford such jaunts.

Two men of the Forty-fourth Massachusetts Regiment toured the battlegrounds

ALBEMARLE AND CHESAPEAKE CANAL TRAFFIC

Year	Steamers	Schooners	Sloops	Barges	Lighters	Boats	Rafts	Total
1860	116	393	29	67	248	136	10	999
1861	671	1,139	74	153	300	179	8	2,524
1862	453	192	88	69	275	188	—	1,265
1863	377	62	71	16	292	125	—	943
1864	953	24	15	124	96	174	5	1,391
1865	1,300	266	190	122	79	602	3	2,562
1866	1,062	739	302	256	338	921	18	3,636
1867	1,112	907	358	313	763	761	29	4,243
1868	1,093	944	442	381	778	1,066	26	4,730
1869	1,093	752	398	297	950	1,077	36	4,603
1870	1,487	859	437	167	911	486	35	4,382
1871	1,659	941	555	183	1,030	483	49	4,900
1872	1,667	1,070	523	158	752	553	85	4,808
1873	2,075	1,380	592	225	886	469	152	5,779
1874	2,214	1,607	654	338	937	411	122	6,283
1875	2,408	1,837	722	340	697	425	73	6,502
1876	2,463	1,719	720	292	639	260	113	6,206
1877	2,376	1,626	508	344	587	277	123	5,841
1878	2,627	1,759	640	226	661	243	171	6,327
1879	2,798	1,615	569	334	552	379	186	6,433
1880	3,209	1,537	392	496	570	362	288	6,854
Total	33,213	21,368	8,279	4,901	12,341	9,577	1,532	91,211

This table shows the rise in shipping traffic in the years after the war. From T.C. Purdy, "Report on the Canals of the United States," in *Report on the Agencies of Transportation in the United States* (Washington: Government Printing Office, 1883).

and graveyards of eastern North Carolina. On the train near Kinston they met a former captain of Confederate cavalry who said he was "right glad to see us," as he
pointed out features of the country. It was the same in all the places the two New Englanders visited:

> The visit was exceedingly interesting. Those who had been in the Southern
> Army were particularly cordial, and anxious to do all they could to make
> our trip agreeable. All were hospitable, and hoped that more of the boys
> who wore the blue in North Carolina would pay them a visit.[20]

The men of the Twenty-seventh Massachusetts Regiment marched and fought in
every campaign in eastern North Carolina, from the Outer Banks in 1862 to Plymouth
in 1864 and ended the war in Virginia. Some of the Twenty-seventh veterans visited
the battlefields and met some of their Confederate opponents at Drewry's Bluff. A regimental association was formed in 1872 at a subsequent meeting, Colonel Shurtleff of
the Forty-sixth Regiment, gave a "vigorously applauded" speech:

> He pointed out the fact that the Drewry's Bluff struggle was a gallant one
> on both sides, and remarked that the hearts of the soldiers on both sides
> reach out toward each other today, and those of the whole American peo-
> ple beat as one, if politicians and demagogues will only leave them alone.[21]

Continued animosity was an expensive emotion in the post-bellum South.
Times were too hard to waste energy on anything but working toward recovery. Any
residual animosity was soon to be directed toward carpetbaggers and Radical Republican officials. The feeling of former Confederates for Buffaloes was more of an antipathy and it was long lasting, reaching into succeeding generations. There were a few
government jobs to be filled immediately after the war and these naturally were
awarded to Unionists or Buffaloes, thereby extending the antipathy.

All through his correspondence with his brother, Customs Collector John
Hedrick expressed interest in filling vacant positions. Patronage was important to both
of them, for John Hedrick got his job through patronage. He was politically perfect,
when he came to Beaufort, to assume the office of Collector of Customs. According to
the 1860 census, Jas. E. Gibble was the Collector. Mr. Gibble was seventy-five years old
in 1860, and even if he wanted to continue in the office, he may well have disqualified
himself by serving as Confederate Customs Collector. A new customs officer for Ocracoke-Portsmouth was the first significant position to be filled after the war, and John
Hedrick wanted to select the new man. The appointment would be made in Washington, D.C., and the Hedrick brothers had the requisite influence. Benjamin Hedrick had
the attention of some Republican legislators and he did not hesitate to use his power.
His influence later began to wane when he advised moderation to some of the radicals
in congress.[22] All during his tenure at Beaufort, John Hedrick had recommended local
people for government appointments such as tax collectors, special treasury agents,
and assessors. He recommended his friend Ulysses Ritch for promotion after the
Buffalo stampede from Washington, N.C. in 1864.

In July 1865, John Hedrick heard that a J.S. Taylor had been appointed collector for Ocracoke Inlet, but could not find anybody who knew him. Some Ocracoke and Portsmouth people told him it was supposed to be Colonel Jas. H. Taylor. Neither Hedrick nor Ritch knew him. Hedrick wanted his former assistant, R.W. Chadwick, to have the job. In his next letter he mentioned Stephen F. Willis as an excellent choice, but still pushed for Chadwick. He had heard that Homer Styron of Hatteras Bank was recommended by Ritch. Hedrick saw nothing remarkable about Styron and further stated: "I have generally found those Hatteras people to be lazy, wrecking, lyeing no account fellows." A better choice than a Hatteraser, he said, would be old Dr. Dudley of Portsmouth, who could probably last a few years longer [23] In August Hedrick learned he had been successful and Chadwick had indeed been appointed, though he now thought Chadwick deserved something better. In late August he announced that Chadwick was moving his family to Portsmouth.

Hedrick's final news of the Portsmouth office was written in 1867, when he notified brother Benjamin that F.A. Hall, "the nephew of Mr. Creecy of the Treasury Department," had succeeded Chadwick as Deputy-Collector and Inspector. Hedrick said he had never met Hall, but thought he made a mistake in "bringing his mistress with him to his new field of labor."[24] Deputy-Collector Hall and his lady friend may have enjoyed their visit to the seashore, but their stay was short. Later in 1867 the customs offices were reorganized into districts and the Portsmouth office was abolished. The new Pamlico District had its office in New Bern.[25]

There were other offices to be filled around the sounds. Postmasters along the Sand Banks were generally part-time jobs. Wilson F. Piver, a forty-two year old pilot, was Portsmouth Postmaster from 1857 to 1865. He may have been politically suspect as he had been Confederate Postmaster for fifteen weeks. Piver was replaced by Jeremiah Abbot who came to the island from Maine according to the 1870 census. In 1868 the office was returned to a native Portsmouther, John W. Hill. The Ocracoke Post Office, like Portsmouth's, was established in 1840. Daniel Tolson served as Postmaster from 1855 to 1866, when Abner B. Howard, an Ocracoker, was appointed and served until 1869. Sidney E. Howard, another Ocracoker, was Postmaster until 1873. Research fails to reveal the political beliefs of either Howard. The Hatteras Post Office had similar changes.

Another Federal position on the Banks was Lighthouse Keeper, perhaps more prestigious than Postmaster. Lighthouses, lightboats, buoys, and beacons were controlled by the Lighthouse Board, a division of the Treasury Department. Although the chairman of the Lighthouse Board was usually a former naval officer, the Board had no connection with the navy nor the army. The Lighthouse Board marched to its own drummer. Its first requirement was professional competence to operate a lighthouse, with politics a secondary though noteworthy consideration. In 1860 the Board ordered a new lantern installed in Ocracoke Lighthouse to replace the "4th order Fresnel fixed light" that had been in service since 1854. The next report of the Board was in 1862 which stated the tower was standing, but the lens and lantern had been removed. With the island back in Union hands, the Board had the lighthouse "refitted and re-exhibited" in 1863.[26] The light evidently was not illuminated permanently at this time, as General Palmer requested that it be done in 1864 at the same time he asked to have the inlet reopened. Thomas Styron was keeper from 1853 to 1860, when William J. Gaskill was appointed to serve two years. When the Board resumed control of the lighthouse, Enoch Ellis Howard was named keeper at a salary of $560.00 per year. He remained keeper for thirty-five years. All three were Ocracokers.[27]

The Cape Hatteras lighthouse had been remodeled in 1853, the tower being elevated to a height of 150 feet and a new Fresnel first-order lamp installed.[28] The 1860 census shows William O'Neal, age 40, and Samuel Farrow, age 21, as Keepers of the Light.

One lighthouse furnished no job for Buffalo or native after the war. The Bodie Island light, a brick tower fifty-four feet tall was illuminated in 1848 by Keeper Samuel Tillett. When the Confederate troops retreated up the Banks in 1861, they blew up the tower. It was an ugly thing, said to resemble an upside down, truncated ice cream cone.[29]

The Cape Lookout lighthouse was new. Work on it started in 1857 and was completed in 1859. Its first-order Fresnel lens was 156 feet above the water.[30] John R. Royal was appointed keeper in 1854 for the old light and continued with the new one. Confederate raiders damaged the lens in 1861. When the damage was repaired and the light re-lit on February 24, 1863, a new keeper was appointed. He was G. Chadwick, very likely a Unionist of Beaufort. On May 25, 1864, John R. Royal took over again and served until 1868 when W.W. Mason was appointed.[31]

One northern man was rewarded with a lighthouse job according to a Confederate newspaper: "Mr. J. Sellers Poole of Wilmington, Delaware died at Portsmouth, N.C. Hospital of lock-jaw from accidental gun shot wound. Poole was on Light House Duty."[32] The account does not state where his brief service was. It could have been one of the lighthouses or aboard one of the several light boats in the sounds.

The Federal Navy continued to search avidly for Confederate vessels and particularly for cotton. Prize money was still being paid. On May 10 two steamers lying at Halifax, North Carolina were surrendered to the Colonel commanding the garrison at Plymouth, with the claim that they were private property and not subject to confiscation. A few days later a naval expedition landed at Halifax and seized everything at the site, all vessels and the contents of the shipyard. The matter became complicated with the army claiming the war was over and seizures illegal and the navy still taking prizes. The affair was bucked up to Generals Schofield and Grant who requested the Secretary of War to ask that naval commanders be sent orders to cease seizures. Secretary of the Navy Welles did order that naval expeditions and seizures cease. This was on June 23. A few days later Welles ordered the property in question be sent to the Prize Court in Philadelphia for adjudication. The vessels in question were the *Cotton Plant*, stern wheel, the *Fisher* and *Egypt Mills*, screw propellers, the *Halifax*, an unfinished gunboat; and a lighter loaded with iron—plus a quantity of cotton. Welles emphasized that property of the Confederate navy did belong to the victors.[33]

Meanwhile, Secretary Welles, on June 24, notified Acting Rear-Admiral William

Radford, new commander of the North Atlantic Squadron, that the sounds of North Carolina were to be abandoned as a naval station. Further, "Withdraw all naval vessels and all naval property from those waters… Keep at Beaufort, N.C., a steamer which can cross the bulkhead and proceed to New Berne, or elsewhere in the sounds in case of emergency."[34] The Navy admitted that the war was over.

The medical services in the Beaufort–New Bern area began to contract and consolidate their facilities as soon as the fighting ceased. Hospital ships carried patients fit to travel to hospitals in the north closer to the patients' homes. Foster General Hospital in New Bern was removed to the hospital buildings in Morehead City. Mansfield Hospital at Beaufort was closed on June 25, 1865.[35] The military hospital at Portsmouth was closed by that date, but probably before, as the First North Carolina personnel had been called to Beaufort for mustering-out. It was almost as sudden as slamming a door, and it left a great gap in the lives of the Portsmouthers. The large Marine Hospital building was vacant, never to open as a government hospital again. Some of the islanders had worked there, unloading supplies from schooners or helping to bring in new patients. The hospital director hired cleaning crews and carpenters for maintenance. Local fishermen sometimes sold their catch to the hospital kitchen. Many non-military jobs vanished with the close of the war.

Old Doctor Samuel Dudley was still practicing medicine on the island, as he had done since 1829. He used part of the building as a private clinic for a short time after the war, but most of the windows glared vacantly at the sea and sound.

One young Portsmouther had witnessed the soldiers come and go and had observed the convalescents and the Buffaloes who guarded them. He even had a brief mention in the navy's official records when he declined to take the job of sound pilot that was offered him back in 1861. He kept away from soldiers and sailors and Buffaloes and plied his trade. He fished and he repaired shoes. He had been a mariner, but few berths were available. He needed work after the war and that is why he sailed to Elizabeth City at exactly the wrong time, mid–April 1865.

Samuel Tolson may not have noticed the startled looks he drew from a group of Union officers as soon as he landed at Elizabeth City, but he did notice the squad of soldiers with fixed bayonets who seized him and threw him in jail. They searched him and measured him and locked him in a cell. The Provost-Marshal charged him with the assassination of President Abraham Lincoln, for Sam Tolson exactly fitted the description of John Wilkes Booth that had been sent to all army posts. He matched Booth in stature, in appearance, and even in hat and shoe size. The other islanders on the schooner tried in vain to convince those Yankees that he was Sam Tolson from Portsmouth. He was finally released when soldiers learned that the real assassin had been caught.

Uncle Sam Tolson lived to be ninety years old and fished all his life. He never went to Elizabeth City again.[36]

The war was done and peace begun. The problem was making a living in a near-ruined land. The so-called Reconstruction had begun.

The wartime regiments had gone home, but the state was under military government and a few soldiers were needed for occupation duties. Colonel J.F. Lehman, commanding the 103rd Regiment of Pennsylvania Veteran Volunteers, occupied Roanoke Island at the end of the war. Initially, 745 men and forty officers of the regiment constituted the occupation force, with 396 men absent on other duties. The number of soldiers in occupation rapidly decreased.

General Order Number 12 of the Second Military District established the strength of the occupation garrison in New Bern in April 1867.

> The Military Post of New Bern, to embrace the counties of Craven, Onslow, Carteret, (except Fort Macon), Jones, Beaufort, Pitt, and Hyde; to be commanded by Brevet Major J.J. Van Horn, Captain 8th Infantry . headquarters at New Bern, N.C. Garrison; Company F, 8th Infantry and Company C, 40th Infantry, the latter to remain at Fort Hatteras, N.C.[37]

Two companies were sufficient to administer the same territory that General Burnside had won with three big brigades in 1862. The other garrisons were similar in strength. The Hatteras company numbered eighty-five men through 1867. In 1868, Second-Lieutenant Robert W. Webb held Fort Hatteras with ten men and Ordnance Sergeant Harper of the Forty-first Infantry Regiment.[38]

Fort Macon's garrison in 1866 was Company L of the Thirty-seventh Regiment of U.S. Colored Troops. Lieutenant James H. Griggs's troop return noted that the fort housed two horses, six mules, and one wagon belonging to the Freedmen's Bureau. The garrison was changed several times, with companies from the Fortieth Infantry, the Fifth Artillery, the Thirty-third Infantry and the Eighth Infantry. In February, 1870, Major J.A. Stewart arrived by steamer with Companies K and L of the Fourth U.S. Artillery, the garrison listed in the 1870 census.[39]

Occupation duty for the soldiers was probably boring, certainly not bloody. There was little for the troops to do, and the civilians were busy with their own affairs. Most Tar Heels were scratching hard to recover from the war during the dreadful Reconstruction Era.

Chapter Ten

Reconstruction and Recovery

$\mathcal{T}$HE SEA, THE SOUND, and the wealth of fishes were the salvation of the coastal dwellers after the war. As long as people had lived on the Banks there had been fishermen among them. The coastal Indians fished from the islands and the earliest English colonists learned from them which local fish were best. In 1663 Peter Carteret, agent of the Proprietor, Sir John Colleton, found his best source of revenue was oil from cast up whales—not grapes, and not tobacco. Upon realizing what they had, the Lords Proprietors declared that "Whales, Sturgeons and all other Royal Fishes in the Sea, Bays, Islets and Rivers" belonged to them.[1]

Although the Bankers fished all through the years up to the Civil War, fishing was not their chief occupation. As historians have pointed out "the typical Banker was a man of many talents." He might have engaged in stock-raising, piloting, freight-hauling and fishing.[2] It was during the Civil War and after that the Bankers realized what Peter Carteret and the British knew. According to Outer Banks historian David Stick:

> The one certain thing is that full realization came to most Bankers at the time of the Civil War that the seafood in the nearby waters represented a vast source of potential income, with the result that the three-quarters of a century or so between then and World War II might be described as the great era of commercial fishing on the banks.[3]

Census figures for 1870 show a great increase in the number of fishermen on the Sand Banks over previous census years. For Portsmouth, the 1860 count of fishermen is far greater than that of 1850, showing that economic misfortune began earlier there than on the other islands. Portsmouthers listed as boatmen, mariners, or pilots had converted to fishermen. Many youths, too young to have an occupation in 1850, were classified fishermen in 1860.

The first venture in post-war fishing was the taking of a valuable fish that was not even good to eat, the menhaden. Tar Heels called them fatbacks. The fish were valuable for oil and fertilizer, and a menhaden industry was just developing in New England as the war broke out. The first North Carolina menhaden processing plant was established on Harker's Island in 1865 and operated until 1873. Northern capital was required to build processing plants and several firms became interested in the area. The Quinnipiac Fertilizer Company of New Haven, Connecticut sent a group of fishermen to investigate conditions at Roanoke Island. They spent the winter there, but were not welcomed by the local people, "whose jealousy of strange fishermen led them to tear up their weirs." The newcomers relocated to a spot near Cape Charles, Virginia.[4]

Another company, the Excelsior Oil and Guano Company established a processing plant at Portsmouth in 1866. This plant was evidently a large one, for the United States Fish Commissioner estimated its value at thirty thousand dollars. Excelsior's venture was abandoned in 1869 due in part to the scarcity of the fish in the sounds and the roughness of the ocean off the islands. The chief reason was the shallowness of the sound's waters. Purse seines, the best type for catching menhaden, do not work well in shoal water, nor do fish school as thickly in shallow water.[5]

Other investors continued to try to bring needed capital to the Banks. In 1870 Church Brothers of Rhode Island established a plant at Oregon Inlet that operated for two years. Difficulties in using the inlet to fish in the ocean caused the plant's closing. A Captain I. Kain tried sound fishing again at Roanoke Island, but soon abandoned his efforts. The Fish Commissioner valued these other plants at five thousand dollars. The only site of successful menhaden fisheries has been the Beaufort-Morehead City area, where an easier inlet allows purse nets to be used outside the shoals.[6] Menhaden boats still operate today out of Beaufort harbor.

There were other fish in the sea and the most important one for economic recovery of the Bankers was the mullet. One writer from Beaufort stated in 1871:

> This species is the most abundant of the locality and affords sustenance and employment to thousands of persons on the coast of North Carolina. From the month of May, when small sized individuals appear, fishing continues during the entire summer ... and frequently until November ... The numbers taken are simply enormous, sometimes as many as 500 barrels being secured at a single haul. It was estimated by competent observers that not less than 12,000 barrels of mullet were captured on the coast of North Carolina Friday, September 22, 1871.[7]

Mullet were truly lifesavers for the Bankers, for they were both savory and saleable. Mullet, like shad and herring, could be salted or smoked without losing their flavor, an important consideration in the days before refrigeration. The fish were gutted, split, and scored before salting and packing in barrels for shipment. In 1879 the state standardized the size of salt fish barrels, requiring them to be twenty-five inches stave length with a head diameter of thirteen inches. Later the law was amended to allow half-size kegs for salt fish. The standard fish barrel held one hundred pounds of fish which sold for $2.75 to $3.50 by 1880.[8] Both cooperage works and salt evaporating pans joined the list of recovering industries, though still only in a small way. The Banks fishing industry had a growing need for revived trade with the salt islands of the West Indies.

Many of the salt mullet were bartered with farmers across the sound. The fish were shipped via trading schooners whose captains got a share of the proceeds. As very few people had any money, the usual rate of exchange was five bushels of shelled corn for one barrel of mullet. A significant number of the mullet fishermen came from the mainland. They built temporary camps on the beaches and joined the Bankers in fishing as a way to add to their incomes.[9] No friction was reported between the islanders and the visitors, as there were mullet enough for all.

The shelled corn brought home by the mullet traders brought work for the millers and each community had a windmill. There were sixteen windmills operating on the Banks from Portsmouth Island to Currituck Beach during the nineteenth century, and twenty-four more along the sound shores of the mainland. The windmill at Portsmouth was probably the first one built.[10]

The mullet packed on the islands early gained a reputation for quality. "The reputation of 'Portsmouth' mullet was mostly a matter of tradition and was due in great part to the care the Portsmouth fishermen took in cleaning them for market.[11] Ocracoke "corned Mullet" were no less desirable in the mainland markets. They have been sold locally, though in dwindling supply, until recent years. According to one ancient fisherman, the secret of good flavor in a mullet, fresh or corned, was to "break the fishes' neck as ye' pull him out the net, and bleed him."[12] The Bankers knew the secret.

In the late 1860s and early 1870s the pound net was introduced into Albemarle and Pamlico Sounds. With the advent of this cheaper and more efficient means of catching fish, shad fishing became of primary economic importance.[13] Though herring were also caught in vast quantities, they brought a much lower price than mullet, while shad commanded the highest prices. Shad, like herring, must spawn in the fresh water of the upper rivers. They enter the inlets in the spring, pass across the sound, and ascend the rivers. The pound net shad fisheries eventually became so thickly set that they almost barred the passage of the fish to their spawning streams. Control by the state became necessary to maintain an open channel for the fish, and resulted in the Vann law of 1905.[14] Shad, like mullet filled many a net and many a poor Banker's pocket.

Various other kinds of fish were taken in the sounds. Graytrout, croakers, mackerel, and sometimes sturgeon added to the fisherman's catch. Fish were not the only harvest of the waters. That most ancient reptile, the turtle, commanded the highest price per pound of any of the sea creatures. Though sea turtles were saleable, the diamond-back terrapin became the gourmet's delight. These terrapins first came into prominence in 1849 when J.B. Etheridge of Bodie Island sold 4,150 of them for $750.00. They were marketed by local fishermen until World War I when the supply was depleted. Diamond-back terrapins were most plentiful in Pamlico and Roanoke Sounds and their favorite breeding grounds were the Roanoke Island marshes and those on the western shore of Pamlico Sound.[15] Turtle catchers from the Banks had the opportunity to repay the calls made upon them by mainland mullet fishermen.

Shellfish also added to the islander's income. Ocracoke was the center of commercial clam production. In 1877 a cannery was moved from Elizabeth City to Ocracoke and operated for several years until the shellfish supply dwindled. The plant employed fifty people in raking and packing clams and another fifty part-time clammers. A second clam factory was established in 1898 by J.H. Doxsee, who canned whole clams, clam chowder, and clam juice. Again the supply gave out after several years.[16]

Oysters have always been an important product of the Outer Banks fisheries. The extensive Indian shell mounds demonstrate the Native American's fondness for oysters. During the early years of the North Carolina's history, most of the sounds were covered with natural oyster beds which were first harvested by hand and then by tongs. Oyster tongs were long-handled scraper-grabbers similar in action to posthole diggers. Portsmouth became the hub of oystering during the 1880s. However, increased post-war oystering led to a decrease in the natural beds by the 1880s. The state again was forced to regulate the trade and passed a law in 1882 banning the use of heavy oyster dredges, leaving tonging as the legal method. Maryland and Virginia oystermen, having nearly depopulated the Chesapeake oyster beds with heavy dredging, invaded North Carolina in the 1890s. Another war between the states nearly resulted until North Carolina regulated the invaders.[17]

Neither crabs nor shrimp obtained any market during the years of recovery, but any other marine creature found on the land, in the sea, or in the air that could be sold was harvested. A considerable demand developed after the war for waterfowl. A small market developed on the eastern shore of Pamlico Sound about 1882 for plumage. Hunters shot terns, grebes, and especially egrets for their feathers which were used to decorate ladies' hats. Audubon Society game wardens stopped this practice by 1903.[18]

Market hunting for waterfowl became a leading occupation on Currituck Sound, for it was home to more waterfowl than any other part of the sounds. Two changes, again one natural and one man-made, promoted the harvest. When New Currituck Inlet closed in 1828 Currituck Banks became a peninsula, reaching down from Virginia to Oregon Inlet. The salinity of landlocked Currituck Sound decreased, oysters and saltwater fish departed, and fresh water seaweeds grew. Ducks, geese, swan, brant, all kinds of waterfowl, flocked in to Currituck. The other factor was the opening of the Albemarle and Chesapeake Canal, which offered a fast route to Norfolk and northern markets for perishable goods.[19]

Late in 1865 visitors from the North came to Currituck County, not the blue coated ones that came during the war, but civilians. They were members of the Currituck Shooting Club, organized in 1857 in New York. A committee of club members came to see about repairs to the clubhouse, check on their thirty-one hundred acres of woods and marsh, and get ready for the hunting season. The committee probably knew that another committee, this one local citizens, had confiscated the club's guns, ammunition, decoys, and boats in 1861 and sold them at the courthouse steps.[20] Very possibly some of the guns and ammunition helped arm the two North Carolina regiments on Roanoke Island in 1862. The decoys had little military utility unless Colonel Shaw fired them out of his Mexican cannon in lieu of proper 18-pounder shot. Other hunting clubs were attracted to the area after the war. These visitors created a few jobs and bought some supplies locally to help the economy, but market hunting by local people had a far greater effect in the years after the war, and until the peak years after 1900. The Migratory Bird Treaty Act of 1918 outlawed the sale of migratory waterfowl. There are no records of the number of birds killed during those years before the ban. A few statistics give some idea. In November 1905, St. Clair Lewark and three others shot twenty-three hundred ruddy ducks. In one day Russell and Vann Griggs killed 892 ruddy ducks. The highest prices were paid for canvasbacks and redheads. Swans, geese, and the smaller ducks were in less demand. In the early days, the birds were hung up to cool overnight, then shipped to Norfolk as fast as possible. Later, when ice became available, they were packed in barrels with ice for shipment north. In some cases, the hold of a sailing vessel was packed full of alternating layers of ice and birds.[21] Both market hunting and sport hunting spread southward along the Banks and on the main, but it was never so large a factor in recovery as it was in Currituck.

Trade flourished in the North immediately following the Civil War, shipping burgeoned along the coast, if not in the sounds. Wrecks along the coast proliferated. This was, according to David Stick, the result of a large number of war craft being hastily converted to commercial use. In the five years preceding the war, 1856–1860, twelve vessels were lost on the North Carolina coast. During the post-war years of 1866–1870, twenty-six vessels were wrecked.[22] These losses emphasized what mariners had been saying. The state's coast was poorly beaconed by lighthouses, made worse by wartime damage. In 1852 David D. Porter, then a lieutenant noted this about Cape Hatteras Lighthouse "The most important on our coast, and without doubt the worst light in the world." The Lighthouse Board made improvements, but the system needed much more work. This resulted in the first of many Federal building projects on the Sand Banks, projects that would offer jobs to the Bankers as well as safety to mariners.[23]

Before commencing with lighthouse construction, there were more than twenty-six wrecks on the shoals. One was of little economic significance, but was of great interest to the Hatterasers. The steamer *Flambeau* drove ashore on Hatteras Island near New Inlet about eight miles south of Oregon Inlet in March of 1867. No lives were lost, but the ship was totally destroyed.

The *Flambeau* burst asunder on the beach, her cargo floated out and washed ashore along miles of beach. She was laden with ten thousand stovepipe hats! They were beaver hats, no longer stylish, having been replaced by silk high hats, and they were practically unsaleable. Two promoters had bought up all they could find and shipped them to South America where they were still in fashion. Cape Hatteras wrecked their plans. The promoters were not willing to give up their sartorial coup, so turned to political influence. Every man, woman, and child on Hatteras had one or more of those hats until the officers of the Military Government began a house to house search on orders from Washington, D.C., intent on returning the hats to their rightful owners. One Hatteraser was quoted as saying that even the porpoises wore stovepipe hats that spring. The final accounting of the promoters' hat venture is not known.[24]

The great period of lighthouse construction began in March of 1867, when the Congress of the United States appropriated $75,000 to build a new lighthouse at Cape Hatteras. It was to be of the same design as the Cape Lookout lighthouse, but at 180 feet, considerably higher. The Lighthouse Board was determined to do it right: "quality is a much greater object than price … it is desirable to take every measure to secure the very best materials." Rather than contract the work, the Lighthouse Board hired

Dexter Stetson as Superintendent and built the tower itself. The Board contracted for one million "prime dark red brick" and other materials and parts. Much preliminary work was done. Dexter Stetson started with workers' quarters, mess hall, shops, derricks, and storage buildings. He built a wharf, a tram road, and scows. All projects needed labor, unskilled and skilled, making work for needy Bankers. Stetson dug in a massive timber and stone foundation and began to lay bricks. The structure was topped with a first-order flashing lens which was illuminated during the fall of 1870. Hatteras light flashes yet today.[25]

Bodie Island light came next. Dexter Stetson moved his equipment, materials, and workmen up the beach to a location about four hundred yards from the ruins of the old lighthouse. The new Bodie Island light was of the same design as Cape Hatteras Lighthouse, but only 150 feet tall. It was illuminated on October 1, 1870. To fill the gap between Bodie Island light and the light at Cape Henry, Virginia, another tower was needed on Currituck Beach. Another 150 foot lighthouse was built near Corolla. It was completed and lit on December 1, 1875. The Lighthouse Board ordered distinctive painting of the towers for easy daytime identification. Cape Hatteras was painted in spiral black and white bands, Bodie Island showed horizontal black and white bands, while Cape Lookout was to be black and white checkers. The painters installed the black checkered squares resting on a corner, giving the impression of diamond shapes. From this came the tale that the painters had mixed up Cape Hatteras and Diamond Shoals with Cape Lookout and Lookout Shoals. There was no confusion resulting from the Board's decision to leave Currituck Lighthouse its natural red brick color.[26] Ocracoke Lighthouse remained all white.

While restoring the lights and in the years following the Federal Government built lifesaving stations along the North Carolina coast. Seven were built from December 1873 to December 1874. They were "Jones's Hill [later Currituck Beach], Caffrey's Inlet, Kitty Hawk Beach, Nags Head, Bodie's Island [located just south of Oregon Inlet], Chicamacomico, and Little Kinnakeet." Initially the lifesavers' pay was low. The Keeper in charge was paid $200 per year, with six surfmen, employed for four months, December through March, for $40 per month. They were on call at other times, for which they received $3.00 per wreck. The government had trouble finding enough competent people. Conditions had improved by 1876 when the bark *Nuova Ottavia* went ashore on Currituck Beach. Experienced or not, the crew from Jones' Hill bravely launched their surfboat in the crashing waves and the entire station crew drowned when the surfboat capsized. Other wrecks resulted in great loss of life: the USS *Huron* at Nags Head on November 24, 1877, and the *Metropolis* on Currituck Beach on January 31, 1878. The Nags Head station was inactive at the time, and the Jones' Hill station was several miles away and was late in learning of the disaster. Congress then authorized eleven new stations: Deal's Island (Wash Woods), Old Currituck Inlet (Pennys Hill), Poyners Hill, Paul Gamiels Hill, Kill Devil Hills, Tommy's Hummock (Bodie Island), Pea Island, Cedar Hummock (Gull Shoal), Big Kinnakeet, Creeds Hill, and Hatteras (Durants). These were in operation in the winter of 1878–1879. By 1883 three more were added: New Inlet, Cape Hatteras, and Hatteras Inlet, with the station on the

Ocracoke side. After a few more years, stations were added at Ocracoke [village end], Portsmouth, Core Banks, Cape Lookout, Fort Macon, Bogue Inlet, and Oak Island. Counting the station at Cape Fear, this made twenty-nine Lifesaving Stations on the North Carolina coast.[27]

With all the government construction up and down the Banks, Portsmouth Island had only the Lifesaving Station. The old Marine Hospital building stayed vacant until a Weather Bureau station located there, and operated until 1885.[28] One of the last residents on Portsmouth remembered that the government operated a telegraph office in the hospital building at sometime after the hospital closed.[29] Another Portsmouther, the very last resident to leave the island, offered happier, though wistful recollections: "Jesse Babb played violin for the square dances. They danced at the hospital in the old days."[30]

Private reconstruction and rebuilding began on the northern Banks, initially in a small way. Nags Head had been the site of beach development long before the war.

> The small summer trickle of planters and merchants from the Albemarle to Nag's Head, a trend said to have been initiated by planter Francis Nixon of Perquimans County, soon increased to a freshet of the fashionable and development along the sound grew apace.... By 1838 a large hotel, complete with a grand ballroom and said to have accommodated 200 guests, had been built near the sound.[31]

An advertisement appeared in two North Carolina newspapers in May of 1841 for Thomas White's new hotel, The Ocean Retreat, at Nags Head. The ad promised "a fit vessel, commanded by a prudent and skilful person" would run twice a week to convey passengers to the hotel. The *North State Whig* of June 11, 1851 announced the opening of Riddick and Bateman's Nags Head Hotel. A railroad (with horse-drawn cars) would carry bathers from the hotel across the Bank to the ocean. Schedules of the steamer *Schultz* and several packet schooners were listed, to convey guests from mainland towns to Nags Head.[32] All these hotels and ferries were gone by 1865.

Some of the planters managed to hold on to their beach cottages and resumed their old summer visits. "There on the island, perhaps, the old order was resumed, in contrast to the changes sweeping the state during Reconstruction." Nags Head, said the *Norfolk Journal* in August, 1867, "has never been patronized more than during the past season."[33]

Dr. W.G. Pool of Elizabeth City was the first man to build a cottage on the ocean front. The doctor bought a tract of land north of the hotel property that ran from the sound to the sea. Pool's family felt lonesome there, so Dr. Pool divided his frontage into building lots, "and commenced to donate to his friends' wives, building lots which were about 130 feet wide with a 40-foot street between each lot, running from west to east to the ocean."[34]

Hotel construction at Nags Head began shortly after the war ended. A.E. Jacobs of Elizabeth City advertised in 1867 that his Alexina House was open with charges of $45.00 per month or $2.50 per day. "The table will be supplied with the best the country affords, and the bar stocked with the choicest of Wines and Liquors."[35]

Alexina House was buried by moving sand in the 1880s, its burial site a giant new sand dune named Hotel Hill.[36]

Other hotels followed. Davis and Jennings advertised their Atlantic Hotel, also in July, 1867, for the reception of "Gentlemen Boarders." Their hotel was built of all new timber, the bar well supplied, and board was moderate they claimed.

C.W. Hollowell and J.C. Perry advertised Nags Head would be opened on July 1, 1880, with "The fine Steamers *Harbinger* and *Mary E. Roberts* making regular trips during the season, touching all points between Edenton and Norfolk."[37] Edward Outlaw's book relates that C. Wilson Hollowell promoted a new hotel which was covered with shingles taken from the wreck of the *Frances E. Waters*, which came ashore bottom-side up. Perhaps Hollowell built more than one hotel at Nags Head, for the *Frances E. Waters* was wrecked on October 24, 1889, according to historian David Stick's list.[38] Or perhaps Hollowell's builders were exceedingly slow in finishing the job. In either case, the owners of the *Frances E. Waters* may be credited with promoting the use of shingles as a good-looking and practical finish for beach construction. Shingle siding came to be used on cottages, hotels, and lifesaving stations. The varying hues of the shingles, from rich red-brown to weathered silvery gray, indicate their age as clearly as the service stripes on a sergeant-major's sleeve show his length of service. Building continued as Nags Head prepared for the twentieth century.

The economic recovery of the Bankers depended not only on their own efforts as fishermen and lighthouse builders, but in large part on the recovery of the mainlanders. Jobs for mariners would come from revived shipping, and shipping would come from growth on the mainland. As the Bankers first turned to the sea, the mainland people turned to the forests.

During the first years of peace there were no exports reported from the river ports of Washington and New Bern. For the period December 1867 to July 1868, the new Pamlico District exported the pitiful total of twenty barrels of tar and six bushels of apples.[39] A general statement of the exports of the Pamlico District for five years shows, besides the eight dollars' worth of apples:

900 bushels of Indian corn	$900
23 barrels of rosin & turpentine	50
358 barrels of tar and pitch	685
1,025 gallons of spirits of turpentine	564
lot iron and steel products	45
5,300 pounds of lard	704
320,000 board feet lumber and scantlings	5,262
3,255 M. Shingles	10,309
Shooks, staves and headings	4,940[40]

These totals for what had been consistently active ports in pre-war years show that the export trade was slow to revive. The most significant figures in the list are the totals for lumber, shingles, and barrel parts. That's where the money was.

The domestic market was quicker to revive. The forests of the eastern counties were extensive and the demand in the North for forest products was strong. Shingles had been a staple product before the war as a home industry and as a factory product. Shingle makers started work immediately after peace came. If a farmer had a few acres of woods, especially swamp land with cypress or juniper trees, and some handiness with tools, he could become a shingle maker. An empty belly promoted fast learning. He needed only a crosscut saw, an axe, a froe, and a draw knife. The specialized work bench needed, called a shaving horse, he could have hewn out himself. If he managed to hire a helper he could more than double his output. Shingles became a cash crop for many during the winter months or in times of bad weather.

Former Confederate Major W.B. Rodman, owner of vast farms and forests, in a letter to his wife, discussed his venture into shingle making. Rodman wrote from the legislature in Raleigh in 1868: "From 250,000 shingles, I ought to clear at present prices about $1100 over all expenses. These undertakings must go on."[41]

In 1869 an excursion of business men touring by steamer from Norfolk, Virginia visited most of the towns around the sounds, touting Norfolk as the best port for export and coastwise shipping. In each town they visited businessmen, manufacturers, and shippers. In Washington the reporter with the group noted that they saw "two million perfect shingles" collected in Gallagher and Burton's yard. They also inspected 10,000 gallons of Scuppernong wine, probably the most pleasant path to recovery seen on the trip.[42]

Sawn lumber, unlike shingles, required a large investment in a steam powered mill and in timber land or timber leases. There was little investment capital left in the South, but a few energetic men managed to find it. One such man was a young Confederate veteran of Washington, North Carolina named Eugene M. Short. He scraped together seven hundred dollars to buy a small sawmill and turpentine distillery on the edge of town. Short's affairs prospered by hard work and good management through the decade of the 1870s when he began to ship lumber to northern markets, and on into the 1880s, good years for the timber trade. On December 10, 1894, the boiler in Short's mill exploded, killing Mr. Short and four employees and putting 250 men out of work. It was said that the explosion was the greatest shock in the town between the Civil War and World War I. Mrs. Bettie Lee Short and son Frank rebuilt the mill and continued to operate it until 1909.[43]

Another young man, Dennis Simmons of Williamston, North Carolina built a sawmill in 1866 on the Roanoke River at Astoria Landing near Jamesville. His venture prospered slowly, and by the end of the century he had mills on the Tar River at Avon in Pitt County and on the Chowan at Tunis in Hertford County. Other mills took root in other river ports as well.[44]

Northern capitalists had no intention of investing in the war torn South, with its worn out railroads, few ships, and over-cropped farms. The smart moneymen looked out West, where better prospects in land acquisition and railroad development beckoned. These men overlooked the southern forests.

Only a few people did look South, men ready to invest themselves and their money. Edward D. Springer of New Jersey served as an ensign in a Union gunboat in Pamlico Sound. He looked with great interest at the noble stands of timber along the creeks and rivers his gunboat cruised. He returned home in 1865, engaged the help of his brother Willdin and his father Samuel, and made plans for the family's future. All three came South and in 1866 formed the firm of Edward D. and Willdin Springer. They settled in the village of South Creek and built a sawmill.[45] The mill and the Springers prospered. There are page after page of listings in the Beaufort County deed books showing Springer land acquisitions through 1914. The Springers were not carpetbaggers, for if they brought a carpetbag it was full of their own money. They were investors and welcomed citizens.

The things Edward Springer saw from the deck of his gunboat, another Yankee recognized from the back of his horse. He was John L. Roper, who served in a Union cavalry regiment in eastern Virginia. In 1865 Roper brought his bride to Norfolk and settled there to see what he could do. He found a partner in Norfolk, Edward R. Baird, and built a sawmill at North Landing on the Albemarle and Chesapeake Canal. Initially the firm concentrated on cypress and juniper (also called white cedar) timber. Profits were invested in buying additional timberland. The partnership expanded into North Carolina and began to acquire pine timberland. North Carolina pine lumber was not preferred on the northern markets because of a blue discoloration — mildew — that often set in during the air drying of the cut lumber. All that changed after 1879 when the dry kiln was developed, which allowed the lumber to be cured, unstained, in a few days instead of months. Then North Carolina pine was accepted, even preferred, for its appearance, strength, and durability. During the 1880s, sawmills proliferated in the state.

After the pioneer mills perfected the process and developed the market for southern yellow pine, northern capital was attracted. Northern lumbermen swarmed south like ants to a picnic. New arrivals and natives alike built more sawmills.

The John L. Roper Lumber Company grew astronomically, with mills and timber holdings in every county around the sounds. Roper built three mills in Gilmerton, Virginia; two each in Roper, Belhaven, and Clubfoot Creek, North Carolina; and one each in Scranton, Winthrop, Oriental, New Bern, Pollocksville, Jacksonville, James City, all in North Carolina.[46] As sawmill historian Louis May stated, the dry kiln was as important to the lumber business as Whitney's gin was to cotton plantations and cotton spinning mills.

One last factor was necessary for economic recovery of both Bankers and mainland dwellers: shipping. Shipping was the key in building for recovery, in carrying farm and forest products to market, and in providing jobs for mariners. New Bern may well have been home port for more vessels than other towns, but all the river ports had shipowners and shipping firms. The problem was to refit the schooners and put them back in trade.

Samuel R. Fowle of Washington, the same shipowner whose schooner had transported the Washington Grays' detachment to Portsmouth in 1861, had a few schooners afloat at the conclusion of the war. He also had pre-war contacts in northern cities.

Three-masted lumber schooner, name unknown, passing through drawbridge at Washington, circa 1935. Photo by Clark Rodman (author's collection).

The firm of S.R. Fowle and Company was not necessarily the largest in the area, but it was the largest in Washington.

Samuel R. Fowle had a sharp eye for a staunch ship and a bargain. He saw both in the *C.A. Johnson*, which had been lying sunk at Ulysses Ritch's dock for two years. Fowle bought the wreck for $150.[47] He raised the schooner, re-rigged and repaired her, and put her in service carrying cotton and timber to New York. The *C.A. Johnson* made monthly voyages, almost as regularly as a steam packet, until she was wrecked on Hatteras Bar in July 1872. Fowle cleared approximately five thousand dollars each year from the *Johnson's* voyages, benefiting himself, local farm and forest owners, and mariners.[48]

Another schooner owner, Horatio Williams of Ocracoke, noted the demand for vessels had increased. He told himself the time was right for resurrection. He was probably tired of farming. Horatio Williams contacted his co-owner of the sunken *Paragon*—the schooner he sank on April 12, 1861—for approval and help. Williams's former partner Jobey Wahab had died and his son and heir, Henry, was running a cotton gin at Germantown across in Hyde County. Williams and Henry Wahab, with a few well-chosen helpers, sailed up the Roanoke River to the *Paragon's* underwater storage site. The captain's son, Horatio Williams, Jr., told of the raising in his later account.

> It was quite a job.... They had to pontoon her with barrels until her decks were above water. They pumped the water out of her with hand pumps. She wasn't damaged in the least.... So the *Paragon* wasn't hurt none. And

the heart of red cedar, of which she was built, won't rot. So she was just about as good as ever. And that canvas my father buried was still in good condition, too.... They sailed the *Paragon* right down the Roanoke and put her in trade again.[49]

She was first in trade under charter to the S.R. Fowle Company. Fowle dispatched the *Paragon* in August 1866 to New York laden with five hundred barrels of tar. David Gaskill, an Ocracoker according to the census, was her master.[50]

The *Paragon* and Captain Gaskill continued to sail out of Washington and often appeared in the "Ship Arrivals" column of the newspapers. She was noted in June 1867: "Schooner *Paragon*, Gaskill, from Wilmington with mds. to J.B. Willard."[51] About this time Williams and Wahab sold the *Paragon* to Tilmon Farrow of Ocracoke. Captain Horatio Williams again went to sea in the Ocracoke schooner *Annie Wahab*.

The Fowle firm began to run the steamer *Old North State* to Norfolk hauling cotton.[52] From New Bern the steamer *Louise Moore*, Wallace, Master, also plied a regular New York course carrying cotton, naval stores, and timber.[53]

Other shippers were dispatching their vessels to New York. The firm of Jos. Potts of Washington associated with Zophar Mills of New York advertised: "The schooner Mary Louisa, Captain Gaskill, is now on her way to New York and will continue to run regularly between this port and New York."[54] The same issue of the newspaper and subsequent ones advertised that the old Washington firm of John Myers and Sons had managed to recover their steamer *Cotton Plant*, which had been seized by the Union navy in 1865. Myers put her back on her pre-war schedule of thrice-weekly trips between Washington and Tarboro, hauling passengers and freight to the rail head. Other schooner owners on the Sand Banks added their vessels to the coasting trade. Typical was one "Marine News" column:

> Schooner *Friend*, Abbott, Master, from Portsmouth with fish.
> Schooner *Helen Jane*, Emery, Master, Cedar Island Oysters and Fish.[55]

The revival of trade continued into the next decade. New Bern advertised that the "Pioneer Transportation Co. will inaugurate a new line of steamers between New-Berne and Norfolk", on to various northern cities, and ending in Boston. Another firm, B.L. Perry, Agent, announced that the steamers *Jos. A. Gary*, *Hackensack*, and *Commerce* were forming a five day line to and from Baltimore.[56]

Elizabeth City, too, advertised steamship lines. Wm. H. Clark, agent of Frederic & Pratt of Baltimore notified the public that: "The new Steam Ship 'North Carolina' will take Freight from Baltimore to Elizabeth City, N.C., every other week sailing from Baltimore April 29th 1871."[57] In 1874 another newspaper grandly proclaimed: "That prince of Steamboat Captains, Thomas Southgate, of the 'Pamlico', is to make another excursion to Nag's Head and Washington, N.C., on September the 9th."[58] The same issue stated that citizens of Gates County were planning a "grand Jollification in celebration of their recent political success. Governor Vance was expected to be present, as well as a brass band. Other signs of recovery continued, other shipping lines were announced. C.W. Carson advertised that he had leased the town wharf in Edenton and built the finest warehouse in eastern North Carolina. He was agent for the "fine Steamers, *Louisa* and *Commerce*" with connections to Norfolk and Baltimore.[59] The Cashi Steam Navigation Co. began to run the steamer *Bertie* daily except Sunday between Windsor, Plymouth and Edenton, and making connection with all steamers running up the Roanoke River.[60]

In Washington, John Myers and Sons added to their river and sound shipping during the 1870s. The steamer *R.L. Myers*, Captain William Augustus Parvin, one of the Washington Grays at Portsmouth, plied the Tar River. She was joined by the *Edgecombe*, the *Beaufort*, and the *Annie Myers*.[61] S.R. Fowle added the large schooner *Nellie Potter* to the New York run along with the *C.A. Johnson*. In 1874–1875 the Fowle ships *Caroline*, Captain David Gaskill, and the *Nellie Potter*, captain Edward Farrow, were engaged in the lucrative West Indian trade. The two schooners freighted timber and shingles to Guadaloupe, St. Vincent, and in 1876, to Barbados.[62]

The revival of maritime trade can be shown more concisely by use of the NEW-BECPO bar graphs on pages 182–183. The Treasury Department reorganized the seven minor ports of the state into three customs districts in 1867, with offices in New Bern, Edenton, and Beaufort. However, the ports of Plymouth and Elizabeth City managed to cling to their customs offices for a few more years.

New Bern, Edenton, and Beaufort ports controlled maritime trade into the twentieth century. The graphs on page 184 show the vessels in trade up to 1900. Although the New Bern district peaked during the late 1880s and 1890s, the increase in schooner traffic is not sufficient to reflect the vastly increased lumber trade during those years. All of the graphs displayed show mostly schooners, the vessels in which the majority of the lumber cargo was carried. The few steamers and barges in the trade are also included.

Vessels from Chesapeake Bay freighted much of the increased lumber traffic and were registered or enrolled in their home ports. They might or might not have taken temporary enrollment in North Carolina ports. Shipbuilders on the Nanticoke River developed a large, heavy schooner especially for the lumber trade from the lower Chesapeake Bay and eastern North Carolina. These were three masted "baldheaded" schooners; that is, they carried no topsails and the masts were all the same height. They were up to 135 feet long, but with beams, initially, of just less than twenty-four feet in order to pass through the locks of the Chesapeake and Delaware Canal. They were usually called "rams", a strange name for a trading schooner. The name was given by a Marylander on his first sight of one of the big schooners shouldering her way through a flotilla of lesser schooners, all heading for the canal. "Look at that damn thing butting her way through the other schooners: she's acting just like a ram."[63] Along with the rams came many large barges and steam tugs. Rams and barges carried lumber through Carolina waters up to the 1930s.

Commercial fishing had increased, naval stores again found a market, the lumber trade boomed, and shipping had resumed. What changes had occurred among the people around the sounds? The census of 1870 best reflects changes in the population.

New Bern, Edenton, Washington, Beaufort,
Elizabeth City-Camden, Plymouth, Ocracoke

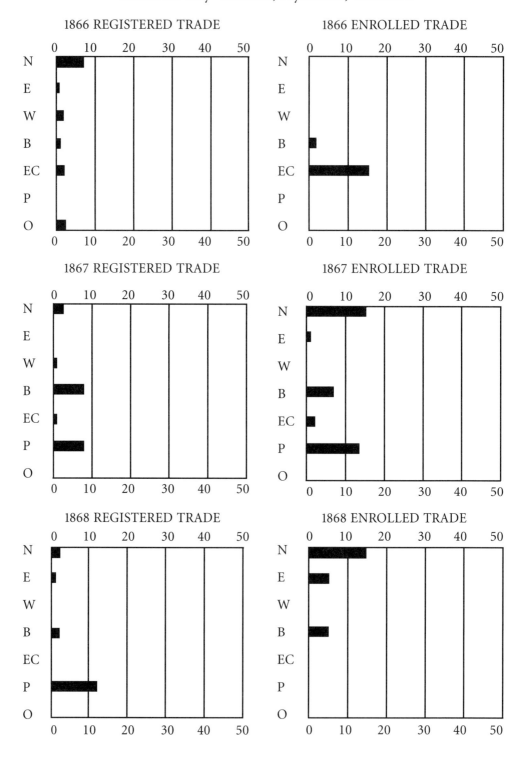

New Bern, Edenton, Washington, Beaufort, Elizabeth City-Camden, Plymouth, Ocracoke

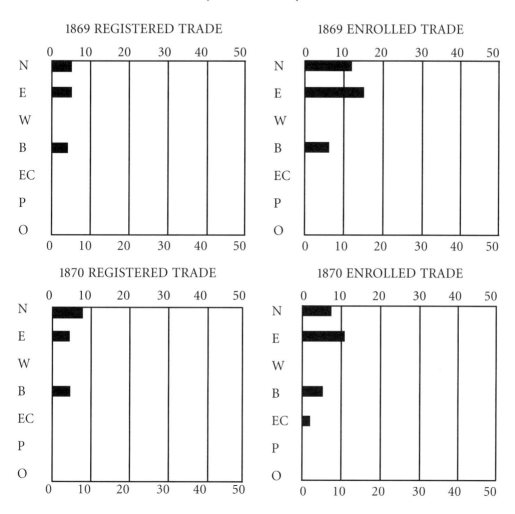

The censuses of the three outer Sand Banks were more exact than those of the main-land towns, and more accurate than those of 1860.

Beaufort, in 1870, showed much the same occupations as before the war, but with increased population. The new census listed Beaufort township, not solely the town of Beaufort, so exact comparisons are not practical. The pages list ninety-three seamen and mariners, sixteen ship carpenters, two sailmakers, and four smiths, all connected with maritime trade. There were more steam engineers and machinists, but still a har-ness maker. House carpenters numbered twenty-nine, with several brick masons and painters. There were many fishermen, with five coopers to supply them with barrels and kegs. All was not well, for seventy-seven men were listed without occupation.

Carteret County voters had apparently regained some political control of their local government, for John Rumley, banished from Beaufort in 1863 for being too

NEB Ports

Legend: ● New Bern   + Edenton   ★ Beaufort   ○ Multiple

NUMBER OF VESSELS IN REGISTERED TRADE 1870–1900

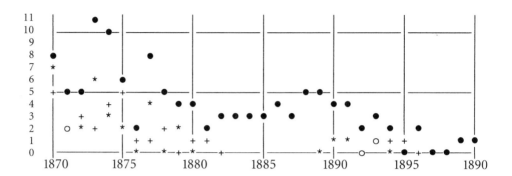

NUMBER OF VESSELS IN ENROLLED TRADE 1870–1900

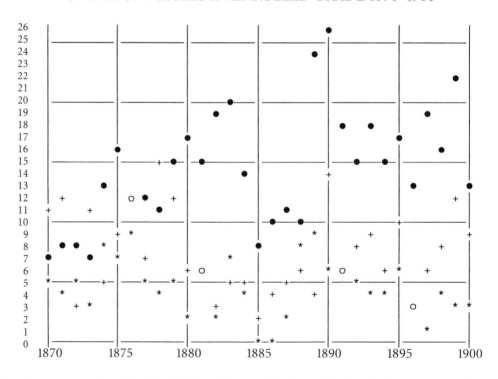

Confederate, was back in his old job of County Register. His brother James was again Clerk of Superior Court.

     A new section was included in the census of Carteret County, that of Fort Macon. The fort was commanded by Major Joseph Stewart, USA, assisted by four lieutenants, six sergeants, two corporals and a doctor. There were fifty enlisted men and one bugler.

1870 CENSUS

Occupations	Portsmouth	Ocracoke	Hatteras	Kinnakeet
Pilot	9	9	13	0
Mariner	37	56	29	29
Fisherman	38	38	124	147
Storekeeper	2	1	1	1
Teacher	2	1	1	
Ship Carpenter	1	1		
Carpenter	1	0	9	5
Merchant	1		4	1
Gardener	1			
Brick Mason	1			
Physician	1	0	1	
Minister		1	0	
Miller		2	0	
Lighthouse Keeper	2	1	2	2
Assistant Keeper	2	1	3	
Official	0	1 (State Legs.)	1 (Customs)	
House Keeper	57	73	134	127
Domestic Servant	10	2	19	17
Occupation, None, Male	2	1		
Occupation, None, Female	34			
Houses	60	71	140	116
Vacant Houses	4			
Total Population	341	368	599	603
White	335	361	569	603
Colored	6	7	30	0

Locked up in the casemates, now used as cells, were twenty-four convicts. Many of the soldiers had their families with them. The population of the fort was "Native whites 65, native Colored 3, Foreign whites 3." Soldiers, dependents, and convicts totaled 121.

Morehead City had increased in population with: "633 Native Whites, 533 Colored, and 2 Foreign Whites." A school teacher, a doctor, craftsmen and railroad personnel, and many fishermen and farmers were included. Newport listed 597 White and 371 Colored inhabitants. The other sound-side communities were similar: increased population with the familiar mix of fishermen and farmers, laborers and boat builders, mariners, and lighthouse keepers. By 1870 most of the river ports had regained those people who had fled from the Union invaders. Even Winton and Washington, the most severely damaged towns, were rebuilding as best they could as their citizens returned. Some of the Sand Banks lost population as newly freed Negroes moved to Roanoke Island or to the mainland. There was one last big change in the northern part of the Sand Banks and the main, and it was not a result of the war. Neither was the change geographical or caused by storms, but rather political. Change was wrought by the state. Large chunks of Currituck, Hyde, and Tyrrell Counties were removed and combined into Dare County. The settlement formerly called "Upper End" or "Dough's Creek" was erected as county seat. It was named Manteo and was officially christened as such by the U.S. Post Office Department in 1873.[65]

A part of the Bodie Island beach remained in Currituck County, from near Caffrey's Inlet to the Virginia line, and including the Currituck Beach lighthouse. It was also called Nags Head in the census, and encompassed 320 people. Their occupations were mariners, carpenters, teachers, two lighthouse keepers, and many fishermen. The other Currituck County townships listed the occupations of the other coastal communities as before, but with increases in steam engineers and steam millwrights, though Poplar Branch township still possessed one wind millwright.

The other Nags Head, the Dare County one, listed as Nags Head township, had a population of one thousand. This is misleading, because the township included Roanoke Island, previously listed separately. Probably nearly half of the one thousand people lived on the island, not on the beach. The many farmers listed were not beach dwellers, though most of the fishermen were. The census listed 316 "Colored", the remainder of the wartime Roanoke Island population, still living on their small plots.

The former slaves had as hard a time as most of their white neighbors. Many historians have written about the hard lot of the former Confederates during those years. Later historians have taken exception to that view and claimed that the Blacks had to endure the worst of it. Both schools were right. It was a miserable time for everyone except a few Carpetbaggers and their Scallywag colleagues.

Most of the former slaves were unprepared for freedom, as Horace James had learned at Roanoke Island, but they were joyful in the possession of it. The Federal Government created the Freedmen's Bureau to oversee the Negro's welfare and help them make the transition to freedom and the management of their own affairs. The northern Missionary Societies continued to send teachers to help. The Bureau was understaffed and underfunded for the task, but did what it could. Unscrupulous carpetbaggers, with a fine display of non-discrimination, preyed alike on the ignorant of all races. Such people were probably responsible for the widely believed rumor that each Freedman would be given "forty acres and a mule." Land was what the Freedmen wanted, but no program existed to help them get it. Many of the former contrabands settled on Roanoke Island and in James City wanted to buy their little plots, but had no money. Although some of the Radicals in Congress urged that the land of former Confederates be confiscated and divided among the Blacks, such an unconstitutional action was resisted by more sensible congressmen. Other land became available legally through tax sales after the war, but Congress passed no act to buy it and finance the resale to Freedmen. Instead, the former owners saw their farms gobbled up by carpetbaggers and their ilk. It was, indeed, a miserable time for Tar Heels of whatever color.

Some relief came to the Freedmen with the creation of a new North Carolina state constitution in 1868. The new constitution prohibited slavery and secession, of course, and repudiated Confederate debts. It ordained universal manhood suffrage and abolished property qualifications for voting and holding office. It established a uniform system of public schools for all, with special education for the handicapped. The constitution abolished debtor prison, established a uniform system of justice, addressed the method of electing county officers, and secured the rights of married women. It was a great step forward for both races.[66] However, the state was still ruled by a military government which overturned state and local elections at will. The nation's capitol was involved in a new war between the executive branch and the Radicals in the Congress over Reconstruction measures. This new war held back recovery. More positive help for the Blacks came from the northern Missionary Societies, which continued to send teachers and money and to sponsor schools. The Reverend Horace James, Eliphalet Whittlesley, and Winthrop Tappan began an experiment to prove that the Freedmen could perform well under proper supervision. The threesome leased two plantations, Avon and Yankee Hall, about seventeen hundred acres, on the Tar River. Their purposes were to make a profit and to demonstrate farming with free labor. By the summer of 1866 they employed 150 workers whom they paid monthly. James, the manager, built a church and school for the hands. The first year's cotton was not of the best quality, but it sold well and the partners made a profit. They made labor contracts for 1867.[67]

The partners, along with the Freedmen's Bureau, became involved in the imbroglio between the Radical Republicans and the President. A number of officials of the Bureau, including Colonel Whittlesley, were tried for peculation. James was charged with complicity in the death of a Negro prisoner who was shot while attempting to escape. Both James and Whittlesley were exonerated, though two Bureau men were convicted.[68]

Reverend James and his partners learned in 1867 that farmers must be gamblers. Luck and the weather turned against their plantations and the cotton crop was a failure. James paid the hands, returned the land to the lessor, and returned themselves to New England.[69]

Horace James yet suffered another disappointment. He had organized a Congregational Church for both races in New Bern. The church flourished while James attended, but withered after he left, the members returning to their old denominations. Many of the Negroes were attracted to a church organized especially for Blacks that had been first chartered in Pennsylvania in 1793. It was named the African Methodist Episcopal Zion Church, and it spread rapidly in the state. An AME Zion Church was founded by the Blacks in Washington in 1865.[70] The Reverend Andrew Cartwright, a former slave living on Roanoke Island, established the Good Hope AME Zion Church in Currituck County in 1866.[71] Other AME Zion Churches filled in the Black communities around the sounds in subsequent years.

Many of the Freedmen farmed for their former masters on a share-cropping arrangement, as few landowners had enough cash to pay wages. The Freedmen's Bureau helped by advising and writing contracts, but the Bureau's life was short. By 1870 a combination of Democrats and a few remaining Whigs again controlled the North Carolina government. Although the Military Government was still operative, voter registration for Blacks declined.

As the years rolled past and the decade of the 1880s arrived, the southern Sand Banks began to develop as the Nags Head area had done earlier. The 1880s finally proved the truth of Jonathan Price's statement made in 1795. Writing of his survey of Ocracoke Inlet and the islands he noted: "This healthy spot is … the resort of many of the inhabitants of the main."[72] Ocracoke was the resort of people from Washington and New Bern and land around Pamlico Sound, just as Nags Head's visitors came from the plantations and towns around Albemarle Sound. Two Ocracokers advertised under the heading "Ocracoke Summer Resort Bragg Brothers have now open for the reception of Visitors two First Class Houses and First Class Fare. Open to the Sea and Sound. ($4.00) Four Dollars per week."[73] Mainlanders again began to build private summer houses on the Outer Banks. Two young soldiers, for example (and not quite selected at random), served in the Washington Grays on Portsmouth Island and liked what they saw of the two islands. On July 20, 1885, W.C. Mallison bought one acre of land from W.S. Bragg and others. The land cost sixty-five dollars.[74] The other soldier, Seth Bridgeman, had bought his lot a few years before and built a house that stands today. Bridgeman's house was particularly well ventilated, with a window arrangement copied from a house he saw in the West Indies.[75]

Also attracted to Ocracoke was the former Federal naval officer turned lumber magnate. Edward D. Springer bought three hundred acres of land near "Teache's Hole" from Henry W. Wahab for seven hundred dollars.[76] The land is still called Springer's Point.

Ocracoke was attracting new residents and planning new sources of income, while Portsmouth's population continued to dwindle. Comparative population figures for all of the Sand Banks show the trend to the end of the century.

Townships	1870	1880	1890	1900
Portsmouth	341	222	204	150
Ocracoke	368	400	466	548
Hatteras	673	821	906	987
Kinnakeet	599	631	793	842
Nags Head	1000	1104	1296	1884
Atlantic	320	332	504	393
Total	3301	3510	4169	4804[77]

The full development of Ocracoke as a resort began in 1885 when the Ocracoke Hotel was built, near the recently closed Coast Guard Station. A group of businessmen from the area erected the hotel with Moses Fowler as the first hotelkeeper. An old photograph shows an extensive, two-story building topped with a tower on a many-gabled roof. The entire building was wrapped around with a two-level veranda. The hotel's first year was so successful that the owners added twenty rooms the second year.

The Ocracoke Hotel survived the devastating hurricane of 1899 with the loss of some roof and veranda, but its "goose was cooked" in 1900. Mr. Credle, one of the owners, with a boat captain as guest, were cooking a goose on top of a Wilson heater. The two men left the stove unattended while they rushed off to fetch some pepper. They returned to find the hotel in flames.[78]

No nineteenth century newspaper advertisements for hotels on Hatteras were

Top: The steamer *Ocracoke* at dock in Ocracoke, circa 1890 (author's collection). *Above:* Steamer *R.L. Myers*, which plied the Pamlico Sound and the Tar and Roanoke rivers, in 1900. The 18-ton ship was built in Washington in 1885, and owned until 1905 by the Old Dominion Steam Ship Co. (author's collection, courtesy of Mrs. T. Harvey Myers).

found. Residents of the island have stated that there were several large boarding houses and a private hunting club, but no hotel until the 1920s.

When, in 1872, the Myers family decided to sell its steam ships, the Old Dominion Steamship Company stood ready to buy them. John Myers and Sons returned to its old trade of shipbuilding, while continuing as Old Dominion's Washington agent. The

Old Dominion Steamship Company organized a Carolina Sounds Division and dispatched the almost new steamer *Olive*, built in 1869, to run from Norfolk to Washington and New Bern. The traffic proved profitable, so other ships were added, with the *Pamlico*, the *New Bern*, and the *Vesper* joining the Sounds Division. With more hotels, cottages, and people seeking passage, Old Dominion added two more vessels. They were the fine, big steamer *Ocracoke* and the new steamer *New Bern*, which made regularly scheduled voyages between Washington, New Bern, and Ocracoke.[79] Elizabeth City and Manteo were added to the schedule. One passenger on the *Ocracoke* at the turn of the century later related a strange sight near Manteo. The ship slowed while the captain pointed out a group of people with a peculiar apparatus atop a sand dune. The captain said they were two crazy young men from Ohio who were trying to build a flying machine!

As the Gilded Age drew to a close, other changes portended. The twentieth century, with paved roads, highway bridges, state ferries, and flying machines was not yet visible, but certain previews were given by increased travel and prosperity all along the Sand Banks and around the sounds.

The Civil War enacted many changes in the entire Banks area from Nags Head to Bogue Inlet as the people, the state and the newly reunited country raced on into the future.

Epilogue

Those who cannot remember the
past are condemned to repeat it.

—George Santayana

IF WE MAKE THE EFFORT, there are useful lessons to be learned from the history of the Outer Banks. It is important to those who love the islands that we remember what has happened along the coast and take heed of what coastal geologists advise us in preserving the barrier islands.

In this account of the Sand Banks, we saw in Chapter Two that inlets close, inlets move, and new inlets open, all according to the laws of nature. We saw in Chapter Four Admiral Goldsborough's futile attempts to block the channel of an inlet, as well as his irritation when he was advised his plan would not work. A comparison of maps made during the state's history shows alterations in the shape of the coastline, wrought by nature, not by man. A useful book by two eminent geologists, *The Beaches Are Moving*, explains why these things happen. The book warns us against reliance on the engineering genius to fight the forces of nature: "The barrier islands, as their name implies, have barred the sea from the mainland. We have become so confident in our technology that engineers now propose their own barriers to bar the ocean from the islands."

We owe thanks to the wise heads and capable hands in Washington who created the National Park service, which in turn developed the wonderful National Seashore Parks. The state of North Carolina, likewise, merits our appreciation for the state parks along the coast. The time has come for government, both State and Federal, to realize that they lack both the authority and the power to ordain the shape of the coastline, or to keep static the beaches, berms, and dunes.

If the environmentalists and preservationists on the one hand and the developers on the other continue their dialogue, one hopes they will prevent over-development and manage to welcome the maximum number of visitors to North Carolina beaches, with "men rejoicing on the shore."

Author's Note

BEFORE LEAVING THE SAND BANKS, we must consider the special case of Portsmouth. Called the metropolis of the Banks by one historian, it was the business center of the area in North Carolina's early history. John Gray Blount and John Wallace ran an extensive merchandising, shipping, and warehousing center on Shell Castle Island from 1790 until after the War of 1812. But then the ship channels near Portsmouth began to fill with sand in the 1820s. Shipping moved across the Sound to Ocracoke and Portsmouth's decline began.

After the Civil War the population of Portsmouth declined even more sharply, until the last resident left in 1971. The island is included in the Cape Lookout National Seashore Park today, and is probably the least-visited of all the coastal islands. It is unique among the larger islands in that visitors cannot drive to it. Portsmouth may be visited by flying machine or by boat, but not by wheels.

From Ocracoke across the inlet, Portsmouth appears much as it did a century ago. Houses are visible among the trees, and the church steeple may be picked out with glasses. No water towers nor tall radio masts intrude upon the scene. There is a small airstrip on the island, or visitors may take ship at Ocracoke to land on Portsmouth. The vessel is commanded by a pilot, but not by Charon. Portsmouth is not a city of the dead, but rather a village sleeping, with life suspended.

The National Park Service has restored many of the old houses, the church, and the Coast Guard Station. The Dixon/Salter house has been restored and furnished as a visitor's center. Some of the old houses shelter Park Service personnel and the Coast Guard Station houses Park Service headquarters. Other houses are restored and leased to private citizens. The church, staunch, neat, and well maintained, is still used at times. Occasionally descendants of Portsmouthers return to the altar of their forefathers to be married. A visitor today will have no trouble imagining the old church piano rejoicing with wedding music as a happy wedding party marches in and out.

The Marine Hospital is long gone, but its site is plainly marked by the large brick cistern of the hospital's water system. A visitor with enough imagination can hear something here, too. By the timeless acoustics of such places, much like the sound of the sea heard in a conch shell, an intent listener may hear, faintly, faintly, Jesse Babb playing fiddle for the square dance.

A trip to Portsmouth is well worthwhile.

Appendix: Soldiers from the Outer Banks

SOLDIERS FROM OCRACOKE

List compiled by Ms. Ellen Fulcher Cloud, who combined her knowledge of Ocracoke's history and people with the rosters in *North Carolina Troops, 1861-1865*.

Company H, Thirty-third Regiment

BALLANCE, HOLLOWAY, PRIVATE.
Enlisted Oct. 17, 1861. AWOL after March 14, 1862. Re-enlisted Sept. 20, 1863. Captured in Virginia July, 1864. Died of pneumonia at Elmira, N.Y. on Nov. 7, 1864.

BALLANCE, WILLIAM R., PRIVATE.
Enlisted Oct. 17, 1861. Captured at New Bern on March 14, 1862. Exchanged and returned to duty. Wounded in right arm at Gettysburg on July 3, 1863. Returned to duty, promoted to corporal on March 1, 1864, reduced to private Dec. 1864. Deserted February 24, 1865.

BRAGG, WILLIAM B., PRIVATE.
Enlisted Oct. 17, 1861. AWOL after March 14, 1862.

FARROW, ISAAC LITTLETON, 1ST LIEUTENANT.
Enlisted Oct. 17, 1861. Mustered in as 1st Sergeant. Promoted 3rd Lieut. Dec. 1862, 1st Lieut. Aug. 1863. KIA May 5, 1864 in Wilderness. "...a brave and gallant soldier..."

FARROW, WILSON TILMON, 1ST LIEUTENANT.
Commissioned Oct. 16, 1861. Resigned March 14, 1862.

FULCHER, JOSEPHUS, CORPORAL.
Enlisted Oct. 17, 1861. AWOL after March 14, 1862.

GARRISH, BENJAMIN J., PRIVATE.
Enlisted at age 17 on Oct. 17, 1861. Wounded at Grimes Mill, Va. June 1862. AWOL after Dec. 1862.

GASKILL, ROBERT W., PRIVATE.
Enlisted Oct. 17, 1861. Reported absent, wounded Jan. 1863. Returned to duty prior to Sept. 1863. Deserted Feb. 1865.

GASKILL, WILLIAM, SERGEANT.
Enlisted Oct. 17, 1861. KIA Cedar Mountain, Va. Aug. 1862.

GASKINS, EDMOND D., SERGEANT.
Enlisted Oct. 17, 1861. Captured at New Bern March 14, 1862. Exchanged Aug. 1862. Returned to duty prior to Nov. 1862. Died in hospital of "laryngitis" and/or "pneumonia" Dec. 1862.

GASKINS, GEORGE, PRIVATE.
  Enlisted Oct. 17, 1861. AWOL after Jan. 1862.

HOWARD, AMBROSE J., PRIVATE.
  Enlisted Oct. 17, 1861. AWOL after March 14, 1862.

HOWARD, ROBERT, PRIVATE.
  Enlisted Oct. 17, 1861. AWOL after March 14, 1862. [Family history reports additional service with
  Co. F of this regiment, until wounded at Chantilly, Va.]

JACKSON, GEORGE W., 1ST SERGEANT.
  Enlisted Oct. 17, 1861. Wounded and captured at Chancellorsville, Va. May, 1863. Exchanged,
  returned to duty Oct. 1863. Killed at Wilderness, Va. May, 1864.

JACKSON, HENDERSON F., PRIVATE.
  Enlisted Oct. 17, 1861. AWOL after Jan. 22, 1862.

O'NEAL, BENJAMINE, PRIVATE.
  Enlisted Oct. 17, 1861. Captured near Greenville Nov. 1863. Exchanged April 1864, returned to
  duty.

O'NEAL, CHRISTOPHER, JR., PRIVATE.
  Enlisted at age 44 on Oct. 17, 1861. AWOL after March 14, 1862. Returned to duty March 1863.
  Transferred to Confederate Navy April 1864.

O'NEAL, FRANCIS W., PRIVATE.
  Enlisted Oct. 17, 1861. AWOL after March 14, 1862. Returned to duty in Sept. 1863. Deserted Feb.
  24, 1865.

SPENCER, ANDREW S., PRIVATE.
  Enlisted Dec. 8, 1861. AWOL after April 1862.

SPENCER, DAVID H., PRIVATE.
  Enlisted Oct. 17, 1861. Died Jan. 1, 1862.

STYRON, ELIJAH, PRIVATE.
  Enlisted Oct. 17, 1861. AWOL after March 14, 1862.

WILLIAMS, TILMOND FARROW, PRIVATE.
  Enlisted at age 16 on Oct. 17, 1861. Captured at New Bern, March 14, 1862. Exchanged, returned to
  duty Dec. 1862 after hospitalization. Wounded in thigh and hip at Chancellorsville, May 3, 1863.
  Returned to duty, promoted sergeant and first sergeant. Reduced to private Dec. 1864. Captured
  Feb. 24, 1865. Pension records show he also suffered a fractured skull and loss of his left eye.

Company F, Thirty-third Regiment

O'NEAL, JOHN, PRIVATE.
  Enlisted Sept. 9, 1861. Died of pneumonia at Gordonsville, Va. May 1862.

O'NEAL, JOHN M., PRIVATE.
  Enlisted Sept. 1861. Wounded in right thumb and thigh at Fredericksburg, Va. Dec. 1862. Thumb
  amputated. Reported absent, sick and deserted. Returned to duty Dec. 1864.

O'NEAL, WILLIAM W., PRIVATE.
  Enlisted Sept. 1861. Died at Winchester, Va. Oct. 1862.

More information on these soldiers is in North Carolina Regiments.

Additional Ocracokers listed in *Hyde County History.*

GASKILL, WILLIAM B., PRIVATE.
  Enlisted May 1861. Never reported for duty.

HOWARD, ALONZO.
  Enlisted Oct. 1861 in Co. H, 33rd Regt. Deserted Jan. 1862.

JACKSON, JAMES G.
Enlisted Sept. 9, 1861. Discharged Jan. 1862.

O'NEAL, CHRISTOPHER, PRIVATE.
Enlisted at age 17 in Co. B 17th Regt. on May 1, 1862. Served through 1864.

Ocracokers in the First North Carolina Union Regiment

This roster was compiled from a comparison of an index of the North Carolina First Union Regiment with the Ocracoke census of 1860. The list is probably correct, but not certain. Census data are noted first, followed by regimental data.

FULCHER, JOSEPH, AGE 22, PILOT.
Fulcher, Joseph, Private, Co. F, age 22. Joined Sept. 12, 1862 at Beaufort. Promoted Corporal October 1, 1862, reduced to ranks June 1864.

GASKINS, GEORGE, AGE 24, MARINER
Gaskins, George, Private. Joined March 1, 1864 at Hatteras Bank. Sailor.

JACKSON, GEORGE, AGE 38, CARPENTER.
George W. Jackson, Private, Co. I & H, age 41, fisherman. Joined August 13, 1863, at Ocracoke.

O'NEAL, GEORGE, AGE 30, MARINER.
O'Neal George J., Private. Enlisted in Co. H at Hatteras Bank. On guard duty at Ocracoke lighthouse in 1863 and special guard duty at Portsmouth and Ocracoke in 1864–1865.

O'NEAL JESSIE, AGE 23, MARINER.
O'Neal, Jessie J., Private, Co. H, Hatteras Bank.

O'NEAL, JOSEPH, AGE 24, PILOT.
O'Neal, Joseph, Private, Co. H, Hatteras Bank. Special guard duty at Ocracoke in 1864.

O'NEAL, THOMAS, AGE 42, PILOT.
O'Neal Thomas, Private, Co. H Hatteras Bank. Detached for special guard duty at Ocracoke and Portsmouth in 1865.

O'NEAL, WARREN, AGE 27, MARINER.
O'Neal, Warren, Private, Co. H, Hatteras Bank. Detached for special guard duty at Ocracoke and Portsmouth in 1865.

O'NEAL, WILLIAM, AGE 22, MARINER.
O'Neal, William P., Private, in both Companies H and I at Hatteras Bank. (There was also an O'Neal, William B., who served as sergeant in Co. H and was promoted to lieutenant in 1863.)

PRICE, NOAH, AGE 27, MARINER.
Price, Noah, Corporal, Company I, age 30. Joined June 14, 1863 at Hatteras Bank.

SCARBOROUGH, BATEMAN, AGE 38, MARINER.
Scarborough, Bateman, Private, Co. H. Joined Feb. 27, 1863 at Hatteras Bank.

SIMPSON, A.W., AGE 21, PILOT.
Simpson, Alpheus W., Sgt., Co. I, age 19 (?). Joined June 20, 1863 at Hatteras Bank. Paid $100 bounty.

STYRON, JAMES, AGE 41, MARINER.
Styron, James E., Private and Sgt. Enlisted in Co. I, Hatteras Bank in July 1863.

SOLDIERS FROM PORTSMOUTH

This list was compiled by Carolyn Burke of the BHM Regional Library by collating the males of military age listed in the Portsmouth census of 1860 with the names listed in *N.C. Troops* of the regiments recruited along the coast. As the regimental rosters list counties of origin, but neither townships nor age, the matches are uncertain. Unusual names or occupations make identification more certain. Little Portsmouth family history survives to help.

The census data are first, followed by regimental data.

SINGLETON, SPYERS, AGE 40, M.C. HOSPITAL SUPV.
Singleton, Dr. Spiers. Appointed surgeon Nov. 16, 1861 of the 36th Regiment. North Carolina Troops (2nd Regt. N.C. Artillery) Served at Fort Fisher throughout the war, captured Jan. 15, 1865.

BURGESS, ZEPHINIAH, AGE 19, MARINER.
Burgess, Zephiniah, Corp. Enlisted in Carteret Co. Oct. 18, 1861 for 12 months. Transferred to Co. H, 40th Regt. North Carolina Troops (3rd Regt. N.C. Artillery) in April 1862.

ROBERSON, WILLIAM, AGE 21, MARINER.
Roberson, William M., Private. Enlisted in Carteret Co. Jan. 27, 1862 for 12 months. Roll for Oct. 31, 1861–March 31,1862 marked "absent within the enemies lines."

ROBERTS, DAVID W., AGE 23, MARINER.
Roberts, David W., Private. Enlisted May 1861 for the war in Co. H. 10th Regt. North Carolina Troops (Topsail Rifles). Captured at Fort Macon April 26, 1862. Deserted Oct. 1862.

ROBERTS, JOHN, AGE 19, MARINER.
Roberts, John S., Corp. Enlisted in Carteret Co. Oct. 1861 in Co. G, 36th Regt. North Carolina Troops. Died at Harkers Island Jan. 1862.

ROBERTS, SAMUEL, AGE 22, MARINER.
Roberts, Samuel C., Private. Enlisted in Carteret Co. Dec. 1861 for 12 months in Co. G 36th Regt. North Carolina Troops. Roll for Oct. 1861–March 1862 marked "absent within the enemies lines."

ROSE, JOSEPH, AGE 45, FISHERMAN.
Enlisted in Carteret Co. Nov. 1861 for 12 months in Co. G, 36th Regt. North Carolina Troops. Roll for Oct. 31, 1861–March 31, 1862 marked "Absent on furlough near New Bern when it was taken."

STYRON, AMBROSE, AGE 21, MARINER.
Styron, Ambrose J., Sergeant. Enlisted in Carteret Co. Oct. 12, 1861 for 12 months in Co. G 36th Regt. North Carolina Troops. Transferred to Co. H 40th Regt. North Carolina Troops in April 1862.

STYRON, W., AGE 30, FISHERMAN.
Styron, William S., Sergeant. Enlisted in Carteret Co. in Co. G 36th Regt. North Carolina Troops. Transferred to Co. H 40th Regt. North Carolina Troops.

STYRON, JAMES, AGE 19, FISHERMAN.
Styron, James N., Private. Enlisted at age 20 in Co. H 10th Artillery, North Carolina Troops. Died at Fort Macon Dec. 1861 of pneumonia.

Portsmouthers in the First North Carolina Union Regiment

A comparison of the 1860 census data with the roster of the North Carolina First Union Regiment yields only a few names, and is probably incomplete. Census data appear on the first line, followed by military data.

DANIELS, THOMAS, AGE 23, FISHERMAN.
Daniels, Thomas, Private. Enlisted in Co. B (organized in Washington, North Carolina). Detached 1864.

LUPTON, JOSEPH, AGE 36, FISHERMAN.
Lupton, Joseph, Private. Enlisted in Co. F. (organized in Beaufort, North Carolina). Promoted to Corporal. Transferred to navy in 1864.

MASON, JAMES, AGE 35, FISHERMAN.
Mason, James, Private. Enlisted at Beaufort, North Carolina and assigned to Co. H, Hatteras Bank.

ROBERSON, JAMES, AGE 21, MARINER.
  Roberson, James E., Private. Enlisted at Beaufort in Co. F.

STYRON, JAMES, AGE 19, FISHERMAN.
  Styron, James E., Private. Enlisted June 1863 in Co. I at Hatteras Bank. Promoted to Sergeant.

SOLDIERS FROM HATTERAS

Hatteras Island, the first part of North Carolina to be occupied by Federal forces, was garrisoned by the Union army during the entire war. Hatteras Inlet was the chief port of entry for both the Federal army and navy for most of the war, which led to a continuing naval presence. Some young men joined the Confederate regiments in the early weeks.

Hatterasers in the Confederate Service

Census data are listed first, followed by troop rosters.

BASNIGHT, WILLOUGHBY, AGE ? [NOT LEGIBLE], RACE B*.
  Basnight, Willoughby, Private, Co. B, 17th North Carolina. Captured and exchanged. Transferred to Co. B, 32nd North Carolina, served until the company was disbanded April 1, 1862.

CLARK, BENJAMIN, AGE 22, MARINER.
  Clark, Benjamin F., Private Co. B, 17th North Carolina. Joined at Fort Hatteras July 1861. Captured and exchanged, transferred to Co. B, 32nd North Carolina. Present until company was disbanded April 1, 1862.

CLARK, SAMUEL, AGE 19, MARINER.
  Clark, Samuel, age 19, born in Hyde County. Private, joined at Fort Hatteras August 10, 1861. Captured and exchanged and transferred to Co. B, 32nd North Carolina. Transferred to Co. C, 56th North Carolina. Died of disease in Franklin, VA. December 19, 1862.

DAILEY, BENJAMIN, AGE 17, MARINER.
  Dailey, Benjamin B., Private. Born in Hyde County, seaman. Age 19, enlisted in Hyde County May 1, 1862. Deserted October 23, 1862, released October 1864.

DAILEY, FABIUS, AGE 21, MARINER.
  Dailey, Fabius F., Private. Born in Hyde County, age 22, seaman. Joined Co. A, 17th North Carolina at Fort Hatteras on August 10, 1861. Captured, exchanged, and transferred to Co. B, 32nd North Carolina. AWOL when company was disbanded.

FARROW, JOSEPH, AGE 34, MARINER.
  Farrow, Joseph H., Private. Joined Co. A, 17th North Carolina at Fort Hatteras on August 10, 1861. Captured, exchanged, and transferred to Co. B, 32nd North Carolina. Accounted for until company was disbanded April 1, 1862.

FOSTER, STANFORD, AGE 21, MARINER.
  Foster, Stanford L., Private. Joined Co. A, 17th North Carolina at Fort Hatteras July 29, 1861. Captured, exchanged, and transferred to Co. B, 32nd North Carolina. Accounted for until company was disbanded April 1, 1862.

GASKILL, WILLIAM, AGE 40, PILOT.
  Gaskill, William B., Private. Joined Co. B, 17th North Carolina. Enlisted May 1, 1862, never reported for duty.

O'NEAL, CHRISTOPHER, JR., PRIVATE, AGE 41.
  O'Neal, Christopher, age 34, pilot. Joined Co. H, 33rd North Carolina October 17, 1861. AWOL after March 14, 1862, returned to duty March–August 1863. Transferred to CS Navy, April 13, 1864.

---

*The B signifies Negro, which is evidently an error as the rest of his family is labeled White as is the 1850 census. This is not the first mistake discovered in the 1860 census of Hyde County.

O'NEAL, JOHN, AGE 21, MARINER.
    Two listings of O'Neal, John of Hyde County serving in the 33rd North Carolina Regiment. One
    died in Virginia in September, 1861. The other was wounded and served until paroled in April
    1865. [??]

TOLESON, GEORGE W., AGE 16, MARINER.
    Tolston, George, Private. Joined Co. A, 17th North Carolina at Fort Hatteras July, 20, 1861. Cap-
    tured, exchanged, and transferred to Co. B, 32nd North Carolina. Served until company was dis-
    banded.

WHIDBEE, JOHN B., AGE 22, MARINER.
    Whidbee, John B., Private. Joined Company at Fort Hatteras July 29, 1861. Captured, exchanged,
    and transferred to Co. B, 32nd North Carolina. Present until company was disbanded April 1,
    1862.

WILLIAMS, WILLIAM D., AGE 24, MARINER.
    Williams, William D., Private. Joined at Fort Hatteras August 10, 1861. Captured, exchanged, and
    transferred to Co. B, 32nd North Carolina. Present until company was disbanded April 1, 1862.

Hatterasers in the First Union Regiment

AUSTIN, CHRISTOPHER, AGE 16, MARINER.
    Austin, Christopher T., age 20, Private Co. I. Joined June 20, 1863 at Hatteras Bank.

AUSTIN, WILLIAM, AGE 35, MARINER.
    Austin, William D., Private, Co. I, age 37, carpenter. Joined June 19, 1863 at Hatteras Bank.

BALLANCE, WILLIAM, AGE 17, MARINER.
    Ballance, William A., Private Co. I, age 18. Joined June 18, 1863 at Hatteras Bank.

BARNET, HOWARD, AGE 22, MARINER.
    Barnett, Howard N., Private Co. I, age 25, sailor. Joined June 16, 1863 at Hatteras Bank. Dis-
    charged March 25, 1864 for chronic diarrhea.

BARNET, OLIVER, AGE 30, MARINER.
    Barnett, Oliver N., Private & Corporal Co. I, age 34, laborer. Joined June 20, 1863 at Hatteras
    Bank.

BASNIGHT, DAVID, AGE 25.
    Basnight, David, Private & Corporal Co. I, age 27, fisherman. Joined June 20, 1863 at Hatteras
    Bank.

BASNIGHT, ROBERT, AGE 28.
    Basnight, Robert B., Private Co. I, age 32, fisherman. Joined June 20, 1863 at Hatteras Bank.

BASNIGHT, WILLOUGHBY, [AGE LISTED 10 IN 1850 CENSUS], B.
    ***Basnight, Willoughby, Private Co. I, age 23. Joined June 18, 1863 at Hatteras Bank. *** Previ-
    ous CS service.

BASNIGHT, ZECH, AGE 26.
    Basnight, Zachariah, Private & Corporal Co. I, age 30, fisherman. Joined June 17, 1863 at Hatteras
    Bank.

BEST, WILLIAM, AGE 17, MARINER.
    Best, William D., Private Co. I, age 24, sailor. Joined June 27, 1863 at Hatteras Bank.

CASY, RICHARD, AGE 14. [THERE WERE TWO LISTINGS OF THIS NAME AND AGE.]
    Casey, Richard G. Private Co. H, age not given. Joined January 21, 1863 at Hatteras Bank.
    Drowned in sound January 17, 1864.

CLARK, BENJAMIN, AGE 22, MARINER.
    ***Clark, Benjamin, Private Co. H, age 24, laborer. Joined January 21, 1863 at Hatteras Bank. On
    detached duty at Ocracoke and Portsmouth.*** Previous CS service.

FARROW, CHRISTOPHER, AGE 36.
  Farrow, Christopher, Private, Co. H, age 38. Joined June 16, 1863 at Hatteras Bank. Quartered at Hatteras lighthouse January–February 1865.

FARROW, DAVID W., AGE 33.
  Farrow, David W., Private Co. I, age 37. Joined June 15, 1863 at Hatteras Bank. Drowned in Hatteras Inlet on January 17, 1864.

FARROW, JOSEPH, AGE 34, MARINER.
  Farrow, Joseph, Private, Co. I, age 35. Joined June 20, 1863 at Hatteras Bank. Previous CS service.

FARROW, JOSIAH, AGE 26, MARINER.
  Farrow, Josiah, Private, Co. I, age 28. Joined May 6, 1863 at Hatteras Bank. Drowned in Hatteras Inlet on January 17, 1864.

FARROW, LANCASTER, AGE 24, MARINER.
  Farrow, Lancaster, Corporal, Co. H, age 24. Joined January 21, 1863 at Hatteras Bank.

FARROW, R. G., AGE 30, MARINER.
  Farrow, Richard G., Private, Co. H, age 34. Joined June 19, 1863 at Hatteras Bank.

GRAY, ABNER, AGE 28, MARINER.
  Gray, Abner H., Private, Co. H, age 26. Joined January 21, 1863 at Hatteras Bank.

GRAY, ALLEN, AGE 23, MARINER.
  Gray, Allen W., Private, Co. H, age 23. Joined February 14, 1863 at Hatteras Bank.

GRAY, ANDERSON, AGE 27, MARINER.
  Gray, Anderson, Private, Co. H, age 31. Joined June 21, 1863 at Hatteras Bank.

GRAY, BANNISTER, AGE 18, MARINER.
  Gray, Bannister B., Private, Co. H, age 22. Joined January 21, 1863 at Hatteras Bank.

GRAY, BANNISTER, AGE 27, MARINER.
  Gray, Bannister M., Private, Co. I, age 30. Joined June 17, 1863 at Hatteras Bank.

GRAY, DAVID P., AGE 17, MARINER.
  Gray, David P., Private, Co. H, age 22. Joined January 21, 1863 at Hatteras Bank.

GRAY, ROBERT, AGE 23, MARINER.
  Gray, Robert W., Private, Co. H, age 24. Joined January 21, 1863 at Hatteras Bank.

GRAY, SANDERS, AGE 21, MARINER.
  Gray, Sanders P., Private, Co. H, age 21, fisherman. Joined January 21, 1863 at Hatteras Bank.

GRAY, WALLACE, AGE 38, MARINER.
  Gray, Wallace D. Private, Co. I, age 33. Joined June 17, 1863 at Hatteras Bank.

HOOPER, ABRAHAM, AGE 25, MARINER.
  Hooper, Abram F., Private, Co. I, age 29, fisherman. Joined June 17, 1863 at Hatteras Bank. Prisoner April 1865.

HOOPER, CYRUS, AGE 29, MARINER.
  Hooper, Cyrus R., Private and Sergeant, Co. H, age 32. Joined June 14, 1863 at Hatteras Bank. Promoted Sergeant July, 1863.

HOOPER, EDWARD, AGE 22, MARINER.
  Hooper, Edward O., Private, Co. H, age 22, fisherman. Joined April 9, 1863 at Hatteras Bank. Rated cook.

HOOPER, EZEKIEL, AGE 37, MARINER.
  Hooper, Ezekiel, Private, Co. H, age 38. Joined January 21, 1863 at Hatteras Bank.

HOOPER, ISAAC, AGE 24, MARINER.
  Hooper, Isaac, Private, Co. I, age 28. Joined June 14, 1863 at Hatteras Bank. Prisoner awaiting trial in 1865.

JENNETT, BENJAMIN C., AGE 14.[?]
Jennett, Benjamin, Private and Sergeant, Co. I and B, age 18, sailor. Joined June 20, 1863 at Hatteras Bank. Promoted to Sergeant, reduced to ranks.

JENNETT, JOSEPH E., AGE 18, MARINER.
Jennett, Joseph E., Private, Co. I, age 21. Joined June 16, 1863 at Hatteras Bank.

JENNETT, NACY F., AGE 22, PILOT.
Jennett, Nasa [Nacy?] F., Private, Co. I, age 25, pilot. Joined June 16, 1863 at Hatteras Bank. Drowned in Hatteras Inlet January 15 or 17, 1864.

JOHNSON, JOHN, AGE 21, MARINER.
Johnson, John B., Private, Co. I, age 22, fisherman. Joined June 20, 1863 at Hatteras Bank.

MEKIN, JAMES, AGE 15.
Meekins, James, Private, Co. H, age 18. Joined February 7, 1863 at Hatteras Bank.

MEKIN, JEREMIAH, AGE 19, MARINER.
Meekins, Jeremiah, Private, Co. H, age 23. Joined February 12, 1863 at Hatteras Bank.

MEKIN, JOHN, AGE 17, MARINER.
Meekins, John B., Private, Co. H, age 20. Joined January 21, 1863 at Hatteras Bank.

MEKINS, SELBY. AGE 21, MARINER.
Meekins, Sylvia S., Private, Co. H, age 24. Joined January 21, 1863 at Hatteras Bank.

MIDYETE, DAVID, AGE 27, MARINER.
Midgett, David O., Corporal, Co. I, age 31. Joined June 17, 1863 at Hatteras Bank. Guard at Cape Hatteras lighthouse January 1865.

MIDYETE, EDWARD, AGE 17, OYSTERMAN.
Midgett, Edward, Private, Co. I, age 19, fisherman. Joined June 17, 1863 at Hatteras Bank.

MIDYETE, EZEKIEL, AGE 23, FISHERMAN.
Midgett, Ezekiel, Private, Co. I, age 26, fisherman. Joined June 17, 1863 at Hatteras Bank.

MIDYETE, GEORGE, AGE 17, MARINER.
Midgett, George W., Corporal & Sergeant, Co. H, age 23. Joined February 2, 1863 at Hatteras Bank. Promoted Sergeant March 1865.

MIDYETE, IRA, AGE 21, MARINER.
Midgett, Ira, Private, Co. I, age 24, fisherman. Joined June 17, 1863 at Hatteras Bank.

MIDYETE, JOHN, AGE 35, MARINER.
Midgett, John H., Private, Co. H, age 39. Joined June 14, 1863 at Hatteras Bank.

MIDYETE, NATHAN, AGE 15.
Midgett, Nathan O., Private, Co. H, age 18. Joined February 4, 1863 at Hatteras Bank.

MIDYETE, RICHARD, AGE 30, MARINER.
Midgett, Richard, Private & Corporal, Co. I, age 34, fisherman. Joined June 16, 1863 at Hatteras Bank. On detached duty.

MIDYETE, RICHARD, AGE 15.
Midgett, Richard W., Private, Co. I, age 18. Joined June 17, 1863 at Hatteras Bank.

MIDYETE, WATSON L. AGE 39.
Midgett, Watson S.[?], Private, Co. H, age 40. Joined January 21, 1863 at Hatteras Bank.

MILLER, BATEMAN P., AGE 19, MARINER.
Miller, Bateman P., Sergeant, Co. A, age 23. Joined March 17, 1863 at Hatteras Bank.

MILLER, CHRISTOPHER, AGE 15.
Miller, Christopher C., Private & Sergeant, Co. I, age given as 19, 20, & 22 in records. Joined January 21, 1863 at Hatteras Bank.

MILLER, TILMAN, AGE 14.
Miller, Tilman D., Private, Co. H, age 18. Joined January 21, 1863 at Hatteras Bank.

O'NEAL, EDMUND, AGE 22, MARINER.
  O'Neal Edmund, Corporal & Sergeant, Co. H, age 25. Joined January 21, 1863 at Hatteras Bank. Reduced to Private January 1, 1864.

PANE, SANDERSON, AGE 16, MARINER.
  Payne, Sanderson, Private, Co. I, age 18, fisherman. Joined June 17, 1863 at Hatteras Bank.

PRICE, ISAAC, AGE 17, MARINER.
  Price, Isaac F., Private, Co. H, age 22, fisherman. Joined January 27, 1863 at Hatteras Bank.

PRICE, THOMAS, AGE 15, MARINER.
  Price, Thomas G., Private, Co. H, age 20. Joined January 21, 1863 at Hatteras Bank.

PUGH, TILMAN, AGE 20, MARINER.
  Pugh, Tilman F., Private, Co. I & H, age 22. Joined January 21, 1863 at Hatteras Bank. Paid $100 bounty.

QUIDBY, REDDING B., AGE 20, PILOT.
  Quidley, Redding B., Private, Co. H & I, age 22. Joined January 21, 1863 at Hatteras Bank.

QUIDLEY, JAMES, AGE 16.
  Quidley, James J., Private, Co. H, age 20. Joined January 21, 1863 at Hatteras Bank.

SCARBOROUGH, ARNOLD, AGE 20, MARINER
  Scarborough, Arnold H.[or K.], Corporal & Sergeant, Co. H, age 33?, sailor. Joined January 21, 1863 at Hatteras Bank. Promoted Sergeant January 1864, served as guard at lighthouse.

SCARBOROUGH, EZIKIEL, AGE 33, MARINER.
  Scarborough, Ezekiel, Private, Co. H, age 38. Joined June 14, 1863 at Hatteras Bank. Paid $100 bounty.

SCARBOROUGH, JOHN, AGE 29, MARINER.
  Scarborough, John H., Private, Co. H, age 30. Joined June 21, 1863 at Hatteras Bank.

SCARBOROUGH, RICHARD, AGE 24, MARINER.
  Scarborough, Richard, Private, Co. A, age 30. Joined January 21, 1863 at Hatteras Bank. Paid $100. bounty.

SCARBOROUGH, ZIAN B., AGE 31, MARINER.
  Scarborough, Zion F., Private & First Sergeant, Co. I, age 26[?]. Joined June 14, 1863 at Hatteras Bank. Paid $100 bounty.

SIMPSON, ALPHUS, AGE 16, MARINER.
  Simpson, Alpheus W., Sergeant, Co. I, age 19. Joined June 20, 1863 at Hatteras Bank. Paid $100 bounty. [An Ocracoker of the same name is listed and may be the same man, or a cousin.]

STOW, CALEB, AGE 15, MARINER.
  Stowe, Caleb B., Private, Co. I, age 17. Joined June 20, 1863 at Hatteras Bank. Paid $100. bounty.

STOW, DAVID, AGE 33, PILOT.
  Stowe, David B., Private, Co. I, age 35. Joined June 20, 1863 at Hatteras Bank. Paid $100 bounty.

THOMAS, CHARLES, AGE 30, MARINER.
  Thomas, Charles F., Private, Co. I, age 33, fisherman. Joined June 17, 1863 at Hatteras Bank. Born in New Jersey, paid $100 bounty.

TOLESON, GEORGE W., AGE 16, MARINER.
  Tolson, George W., Private, Co. H, age 24. Joined June 23, 1863 at Hatteras Bank. Paid $100 bounty.

WHIDBEE, JOHN B., AGE 22, MARINER.
  Whidbee, John, B., Private, Co. H, age 24. Joined April 29, 1863 at Hatteras Bank. Previous CS service.

WHIDBEE, JOHN, AGE 22, MARINER.
  Whidbee, John N., Private, Co. I, age 24, fisherman. Joined June 18, 1863 at Hatteras Bank.

WHIDBEE, WILLOUGHBY, AGE 25, MARINER.
  Whidbee, Wiloby, Private, Co. I, age 34. Joined June 17, 1863 at Hatteras Bank. Died in hospital at Hatteras August 18, 1863.

Williams, David W., age 30.
    Williams, David W., Private, Co. I, age 33. Joined June 20, 1863 at Hatteras Bank.

Williams, Isaac, age 24, mariner.
    Williams Isaac, Private, Co. H, age 25, sailor. Joined January 21, 1863 at Hatteras Bank.

Williams, Merchant, age 16, mariner.
    Williams, Merchant, Private, Co. H, age 21, fisherman. Joined January 21, 1863 at Hatteras Bank.

Williams, William D., age 24, mariner.
    ***Williams, William D., Private, Co. I, age 27, fisherman. Joined June 18, 1863 at Hatteras Bank.
    *** Previous CS service.

Dr. Donald Collins of the East Carolina University History Department has generously allowed me to use the rosters of the First and Second North Carolina Union Volunteer Regiments that he has compiled. Dr. Collins is writing the history of these regiments.

As the soldier lists show, more Hatterasmen joined the First Union Regiment than did men from Portsmouth and Ocracoke. Whether this was because of the length and density of Federal occupation or stronger Union sentiment is unknown. Probably by 1863 the only ways for the Hatterasers to make a living were to sell fish to each other or to work for the Union forces as fiscal or military Buffaloes.

Notes

Chapter One

1. Lawrence C. Wroth, *The Voyage of Giovanni de Verrazzano, 1524–1528* (New Haven, Conn.: Yale University Press, 1970), 134.
2. Richard Hakluyt, "Voyages, Vol. III," reprinted in Francis L. Hawks, *History of North Carolina,* Vol. I (Fayetteville, N.C.: E.J. Hale and Son, 1857), 70.
3. Thomas J. Schoenbaum, *Islands, Capes, and Sounds* (Winston-Salem, N.C.: John F. Blair, Publisher, 1982), 12.
4. Schoenbaum, *Islands*, 12.
5. John Lawson, *Lawson's History of North Carolina* (London: W. Taylor and F. Baker, 1714), reprinted (Richmond, Virginia: Garrett and Massie, 1937), 63, 64, 65. Lawson's latitude may have been exact in 1709, for Schoenbaum states that Ocracoke Inlet is slowly migrating southward. Loran currently gives the latitude as 35°6'10" north.
6. Gary S. Dunbar, *Historical Geography of the North Carolina Outer Banks* (Baton Rouge: Louisiana State University Press, 1958), 1.
7. Walter Clark, Ed., *State Records of North Carolina*, Volume XXIII, *Laws* (Raleigh: State of North Carolina, 1907), 40, 41.
8. Jean Bruyere Kell, Ed., *North Carolina's Coastal Carteret County During the American Revolution 1765–1785* (Greenville, N.C.: Carteret County Bicentennial Commission and Era Press, 1976), 1, 2.
9. Clark, *State Records*, 252, 254.
10. Samuel W. Newell, "A Maritime History of Ocracoke Inlet, 1584–1783" (unpublished M.A. thesis, East Carolina University, 1987), 12.
11. *Ibid.*, 102 and 90–102 *passim*.
12. Sarah M. Lemmon, *Frustrated Patriots: North Carolina and the War of 1812* (Chapel Hill: The University of North Carolina Press, 1973), 130.
13. *Ibid.*, 130–133 *passim*.

Chapter Two

1. William S. Powell, *North Carolina Through Four Centuries*, (Chapel Hill: The University of North Carolina Press, 1989), 246.
2. *Ibid.*, 245–267, *passim*.
3. Dunbar, *Historical Geography*, 25.
4. *Ibid.*, 25.
5. David Stick, *North Carolina Lighthouses* (Raleigh: Division of Archives and History North Carolina Department of Cultural Resources, 1980), 12.
6. *Ibid.*, 14.

7. Stick, *Lighthouses*, 17.

8. *Ibid.*, 19, 20.

9. *Ibid.*, 21–24.

10. Richard S. Barry, "Fort Macon: Its History," *North Carolina Historical Review,* Vol. XXVII (June 1959), 163–177.

11. *Ibid.*, 165.

12. Dunbar, *Historical Geography*, 27, 28.

13. Marvin P. Rozear, M.D., "North Carolina's First Hospital," *North Carolina Medical Journal*, Vol. 52, Number 6 (June 1991).

14. James M. Cox, "The Pamlico-Tar River and its Role in the Development of Eastern North Carolina" (unpublished M.A. thesis, East Carolina University, Greenville, N.C., 1989), 2.

15. *Ibid.*

16. David Stick, *The Outer Banks of North Carolina 1584–1958* (Chapel Hill: The University of North Carolina Press, 1958), 87, 88.

17. Stick, *Outer Banks*, 88.

18. Rozear, "First Hospital," 273.

19. Dunbar, *Historical Geography*, 28.

20. *Ibid.*, note, 139.

21. Alexander Crosby Brown, *Juniper Waterway, A History of the Albemarle and Chesapeake Canal* (Charlottesville: University Press of Virginia, 1981), 3.

22. Edmund Ruffin, *Agricultural, Geological and Descriptive Sketches of Lower North Carolina and the Similar Adjacent Lands* (Raleigh: Institution for the Deaf, Dumb and the Blind, 1861), 144, 145.

23. Brown, *Juniper Waterway*, 119.

24. Robert C. Black, *The Railroads of the Confederacy* (Chapel Hill: The University of North Carolina Press, 1952), 45 (attached map). Also, Powell, *Four Centuries*, 289.

25. Dunbar, *Historical Geography*, 29, 142.

26. Ann M. Merriman, "North Carolina Schooners, 1815–1901, and the S.R. Fowle and Son Company of Washington, North Carolina" (M.A. thesis, East Carolina University, 1996), *passim*. Ms. Merriman generously shared the data she had collected and used in her charts and graphs.

27. Hugh Talmage Lefler and Albert Roy Newsome, *North Carolina: The History of a Southern State* (Chapel Hill: The University of North Carolina Press, 1939), 448.

28. *Ibid.*, 449.

29. Joseph Carlyle Sitterson, *The Secession Movement in North Carolina* (Chapel Hill: The University of North Carolina Press, 1939), 228.

30. John G. Barrett, *The Civil War in North Carolina* (Chapel Hill: The University of North Carolina Press, 1963) 6–11 *passim*. Hereinafter cited as *C.W. in N.C.*

31. *Ibid.*

32. *Ibid.*, 12.

33. Richard Bush and others, eds., *Official Records of the Union and Confederate Navies in the War of the Rebellion*, Series I, Vol. 4 (Washington, D.C.: Government Printing Office, 1894–1924), 156, 340. Hereinafter cited as ORN.

34. *Wilmington Journal*, Thursday May 2, 1861.

35. Barrett, *CW in N.C.*, 14.

Chapter Three

1. C. H. Beale, "First Confederate Flag on the Atlantic," *Confederate Veteran*, Vol. XV, No. 5 (1889), 227.

2. *Ibid.*, 227, 228.

3. Horatio Williams, Jr., interview, "Ocracoke Skipper Sank His Own Ship," *The [Raleigh] News and Observer*, February 13, 1949.

4. Calvin J. O'Neal, Alice K. Rondthaler and Anita Fletcher, "The Story of Ocracoke Island," in *Hyde County History*, ed. Marjorie T. Selby, R.S. Spencer, Jr. and Rebecca Swindell (Charlotte, N.C.: Herbe Eaton, Inc., 1976), 12, 13.

5. Adam Treadwell, "North Carolina and Navy," in *Histories of the Several Regiments and Battalions from North Carolina in the Great War 1861–1865*, Vol. 5, ed. Walter Clark (Goldsboro, N.C.: State of North Carolina, 1901), 299. Treadwell was acting paymaster of the North Carolina Navy, later assistant paymaster of the Confederate States Navy.

6. Treadwell, "N.C. Navy," 299, and Brown, *Juniper*, 66.

7. Treadwell, "N.C. Navy," 300.

8. *Ibid.*, 300.

9. Barrett, 10.

10. Louis H. Manarin and Weymouth T. Jordan, Jr., Eds., *North Carolina Troops 1861–1865: A Roster*, Vol. I (Raleigh: Division of Archives and History, 1966), 113.

11. Richard S. Barry, "Fort Macon: Its History," in *The North Carolina Historical Review*, Vol. XXVII (North Carolina Department of Archives and History, April 1950), 168.

12. Barry, "Fort Macon," 169.

13. C. Wingate Reed, *Beaufort County: Two Centuries of Its History* (Raleigh: Edwards & Broughton Co., 1962), 176.

14. William Henry von Eberstein Memoir, "William Henry von Eberstein Papers," East Carolina Manuscript Collection, East Carolina University, Greenville, N.C., 123.

15. *Ibid.*

16. Manarin, *N.C. Troops*, Vol. II, 120, 121.

17. *Newbern Daily Progress*, Tuesday, May 21, 1861.

18. William Morrison Robinson, *The Confederate Privateers* (New Haven: Yale University Press, 1928), 102.

19. R.N. Scott and others, eds., *Official Records of the Union and Confederate Armies in the War of the Rebellion*, Series I, Vol. LI (Washington: Government Printing Office, 1889–1924), 113. Hereinafter cited as ORA.

20. *Ibid.*, 116–121, *passim.*

21. Robinson, *Privateers*, 104.

22. ORA, Vol. LI, 115.

23. Manarin, *N.C. Troops*, Vol. VI, 140, 133, 173.

24. *The Windsor Story 1768–1968* (Windsor: Windsor Bicentennial Commission, 1968), 53. Manarin's *N.C. Troops* confirms Wheeler's service and death, but gives no cause. A note appended to the letter states that it was typhoid fever. Typhoid was usually thought to be caused by "bad" seafood in the nineteenth century, but it is hard to understand how anything but fresh seafood would be served on the Outer Banks. Legions of army veterans may say "army cooks."

25. Robinson, *Privateers*, 102, 103.

26. *Ibid.*

27. *Newbern Daily Progress*, August 26, 1861.

28. Robinson, *Privateers*, 102.

29. ORN, Series I, Vol. 6, 780.

30. ORN, Series I, Vol. 6, 79.

31. ORN, Series I, Vol. 1, 28.

32. *Ibid.*, 29.

33. Treadwell, "N.C. Navy," 300.

34. Robinson, *Privateers*, 107.

35. Manarin, *N.C. Troops*, Vol. VI, 118–192 *passim*.

36. Manarin, *N.C. Troops*, Vol. I, Artillery.

37. ORN, Series I, Vol. 6, 794, 795.

38. Martha Matilda Fowle, "Journal," Fowle Family Collection, Brown Library, Washington, N.C. Miss Fowle's papers comprise a diary and family newsletter to her sisters, but she names them her Journal. I have followed her lead.

39. ORN, Series I, Vol. 6, 795.

40. J. Thomas Scharf, *History of the Confederate States Navy* (New York: Rogers & Sherwood, 1887), 370.

41. ORN, Series, Vol. 1, 60.

42. *Ibid.*, 71.

43. *North Carolina Times* (Washington, N.C.), August 7, 1861.

44. Fowle, "Journal," 3, 4.

45. ORN, Series I, Vol. 6, 781.

46. Robinson, *Privateers*, 112.

47. Von Eberstein, "Papers," 128.

48. *Ibid.*, 126.

49. Fowle, "Journal," 4, 5.

50. W.A. Parvin, "The Only Story that Ever has Been Wrote of the Escape of W B Willis and W A Parvin Privates Company K 10 Regt. NC State Troops Major Thos. Sparrow Nov. 1861 Escaped from Fort Warren Boston Harbor to Washington N.C.," William Augustus Parvin Papers, East Carolina Manuscript Collection, East Carolina University, Greenville, N.C., 8, 9.

51. Robinson, *Privateers*, 112.

52. ORN, Series I, Vol. 6, 781.

53. David D. Porter, *The Naval History of the Civil War* (New York: The Sherman Publishing Company, 1886), 18, 36.

54. ORN, Series I, Vol. 6, 24.

55. *Ibid.*, 78, 79, 80.

56. *Ibid.*, 106–112, *passim*.

57. Virgil Carrington Jones, *The Civil War at Sea*, Vol. I (New York: Holt-Rinehart-Winston, 1960), 198, 199.

58. ORN, Series I, Vol. 6, 119.

59. *Ibid.*, 120, 121.

60. *Ibid.*, 121, 122, 123.

61. ORA, Series I, Vol. IV, 581–586.

62. Benjamin F. Butler, *Butler's Book* (Boston: A.M. Thayer & Co. Book Publishers, 1891), 286, 287.

63. ORA, Series I, Vol. IV, 589.

64. Barrett, *C.W. in N.C.*, 41.

65. *Ibid.*, 589, 590.

66. ORN, Series I, Vol. 6, 140.

67. *Ibid.*, 141.

68. James M. Merrill, "The Hatteras Expedition, August, 1861," *The North Carolina Historical Review*, Vol. XXIX (April 1952): 212.

69. ORN, Series I, Vol. 6, 139.

70. Thomas Sparrow, "The Fall of Hatteras," in *Histories of the Several Regiments and Battalions from North Carolina in the Great War 1861–1865*, Vol. 5, 3d. Walter Clark (Goldsboro, N.C.: Published by the State, 1901) 35, 36.

71. *Ibid.*

72. Thomas Sparrow, Portsmouth, to John D. Whitford, New Bern, 12 August 1861 with enclosure, "John D. Whitford Papers, 1861–1863," North Carolina Division of Archives and History, Raleigh.

73. *Ibid.*

74. *Ibid.*, 45, 46, 47, *passim*. Sparrow's claim of a record breaking bombardment was made long before the artillery bombardments of World War I. Fort Fisher probably equaled or exceeded Fort Hatteras in volume of shelling. Even so, it was hot and heavy.

75. *Ibid.* Captain Sparrow observed that in the midst of the shellfire, "a feeling of perfect security, not to say indifference" came over him. This saving feeling in times of stress has been described by other soldiers in ruder language than the captain used, as not giving a damn.

76. *Ibid.* 52, 53. Captain Sparrow's opinion of General Butler was that generally held by all the southern soldiers. As the war progressed Butler could have easily won an unpopularity contest in the Confederacy, even against General Sherman. He might have won in the North, too.

77. ORN, Series I, Vol. 6, 124, 129.

78. ORA, Series I, Vol. IV, 58.

79. von Eberstein, *Papers*, 128.

80. *Ibid.*

81. *Ibid.*, 129.

82. Fowle, "Journal," 4.

83. Kenneth E. Burke, "The History of Portsmouth, North Carolina" (thesis, University of Richmond, 1974), 63.

84. Daniel Harvey Hill, *Bethel to Sharpsburg*, Vol. I (Raleigh: Edwards and Broughton, 1929), 172, 173.

85. *Ibid.*

86. Barrett, *C.W. in N.C.*, 47.

87. Merrill, "Hatteras Expedition," 218.

88. ORN, Series I, Vol. 6, 137, 138.

89. Ben Dixon MacNeill, *The Hatterasman* (Winston-Salem: John F. Blair, Publisher, 1958), 160. Author MacNeill disclaims being an historian, but his book is the most available source of family and oral history of the island. He lived on Hatteras for many years, exploring and collecting history.

90. Fowle, *Journal*.

Chapter Four

1. Rush C. Hawkins, "Early Coast Operations in North Carolina," in *Battles and Leaders in the Civil War*, Vol. I, Eds. R.U. Johnson and C.C. Buel (New York: Century Co., 1887), 634, 635. Hereinafter cited as *B and L.*

2. ORA, Series I, Vol. IV, 607.

3. ORA, Series I, Vol. IV, 607–611 *passim* and Vol. II, 61, 62.

4. ORA, Series I, Vol. IV, 613.

5. William H. Parker, *Recollections of a Naval Officer 1841–1865* (New York: Charles Scribner's Sons, 1883), 211.

6. W.R. Roberts to John D. Whitford, September 14, 1861, "Whitford Papers," North Carolina Division of Archives and History, Raleigh.

7. ORN Series I, Vol. 6, 220, 221.

8. *Ibid.*, 223.

9. ORA, Series I, Vol. IV, 242, 243.

10. D.H. Hill, *Bethel...*, 185–192 *passim*.

11. Manarin, *Regiments*, Vol. IV, 515.

12. Hawkins, "Early Coast Operations," in *B and L*, 637.

13. Scharf, *C.S. Navy*, 278, 279 and ORN, Series I, Vol. 6, 276, 277.

14. Scharf, *C.S. Navy*, 379.

15. Scharf, *C.S. Navy*, 381.

16. *Ibid.*

17. ORA, Series I, Vol. IV, 622–624.

18. ORN, Series I, Vol. 6, 291, 292.

19. Charles F. Johnson, *The Long Roll: Impressions of a Civil War Soldier* (reprint, Sheperdstown, W.V.: Carabelle, 1986), 56, 59.

20. *Ibid.*, 79.

21. *Ibid.*, 110.

22. ORN, Series I, Vol. 6, 412, 397.

23. *Ibid.*, 403.

24. Georges Kling, *Le Commandant Jean Joseph De Brun et Le "Prony"* [Commodore Jean Joseph De Brun and the "Prony"] (Société d'Études Historiques de la Nouvelle Caledonie, 1985). The *Prony* was a ship of some note in the French navy, having carried the French expeditions exploring and charting the French colonies in the south Pacific. The material on the *Prony* was translated by Thomas Conlon of Washington, NC. The French journal is from the library of Gordon Watts.

25. ORN, Series I, Vol. 6, 398.

26. *Ibid.*, 785.

27. *Ibid.*

28. *Ibid.*, 399.

29. *Newbern Daily Progress*, Jan. 15, 1862.

30. ORN, Series I, Vol. 6, 234.

31. *Ibid.*, 260–268.

32. *Ibid.*, 345.

33. *Ibid.*, 410.

34. *Ibid.*, 429.

35. Tom Parramore, "When Hatteras Was the Capital," *The News and Observer*, June 29, 1969.

36. ORA, Series III, Vol. I, 631.

37. D.H. Hill, *Bethel to Sharpsburg*, 180.

38. ORN, Series I, Vol. 6, 173.

39. Norman C. Delaney, "Charles Henry Foster and the Unionists of Eastern North Carolina," *North Carolina Historical Review*, Vol. XXXVII, 355.

40. Powell, *N.C. Biographies*, Vol. 4, 227.

41. Delaney, *Foster and the Unionists*, note on p. 348.

42. *Ibid.*, 355.

43. *Ibid.*, 356, 357.

44. ORA, Series III, Vol. I, 630, 631.

45. Delaney, *Foster & Unionists*, 358.

46. J.G. de Roulhac Hamilton, Ph.D., *Reconstruction in North Carolina* (Gloucester, MA: Peter Smith, 1964), note on p. 86.

47. Delaney, *Foster and Unionists*, 358–360, *passim*.

48. Ellen Fulcher Cloud, Ocracoke, to Fred Mallison, January 18, 1992, listing Ocracokers in the Confederate service, cross-checked with Louis H. Manarin, Ed., *North Carolina Troops 1861–1865*, Vol. X (Raleigh: Division of Archives and History, 1983), *passim*.

49. Manarin, *N.C. Troops*, Vol. I, 173.

Chapter Five

1. ORA, Series I, Vol. IX, 352.

2. ORA, Series, Vol. IX, 711, 712.

3. D.H. Hill, *Bethel to Sharpsburg*, 191, 192.

4. Manarin, *NC Troops*, Vol. IV, 424 *passim*, and Clark, *NC Regiments*, "Eighth Regiment," 388, 389.

5. *Ibid*., Manarin, 424 *passim*, and Clark, "The Fall of Roanoke Island," Vol. V, 62 *passim*.

6. ORA, Series I, Vol. IX, 127. A legion was a brigade-sized unit containing all arms, infantry, cavalry, and artillery. There were but ten legions in the Provisional Army of the Confederate States, and only one, Wise's, from Virginia. See Lee A. Wallace, *A Guide to Virginia Military Organizations, 1861–1865* (Lynchburg, Va.: H.B. Howard, Inc., 1986), 150.

7. ORA, Series I, Vol. IX, 116.

8. *Ibid*., 130–140 *passim*.

9. *Ibid*., 129.

10. Ambrose E. Burnside, "The Burnside Expedition," in *Battles and Leaders of the Civil War*, R.U. Johnson and C.C. Buell, eds., (reprint edition, Book Sales, Inc., Secaucus, N.J.), 660.

11. *Ibid*., 661.

12. *Ibid*., 663, 664.

13. *Ibid*., 664, 665, and ORN, Series I, Vol. 6, 582, 583.

14. Alfred S. Roe, *The Twenty-Fourth Regiment Massachusetts Volunteers 1861–1866* (Worcester, Mass.: Twenty-Fourth Veteran Association, 1907), 44–48 *passim*.

15. John K. Burlingame, *History of the Fifth Regiment of Rhode Island Heavy Artillery* (Providence: Snow & Farnham, 1892), 14–17.

16. W.P. Derby, *Bearing Arms in the Twenty-Seventh Massachusetts Regiment of Volunteer Infantry During the Civil War 1861–1865* (Boston: Wright & Potter Printing Company, 1883), 50, 51.

17. *Newbern Daily Progress* (New Bern, N.C.), January 18, 25, 27 (1862).

18. ORN Series I, Vol. 6, 583, and Augustus Woodbury, *Major–General Ambrose E. Burnside and the Ninth Army Corps* (Providence: Sidney S. Rider & Brother, 1867), 32, 33.

19. George Driver, Hatteras, to Edward Driver, Salem, MA., January 17, 1862, William Howard Hooker Collection, East Carolina Manuscript Collection, East Carolina University, Greenville, N.C.

20. MacNeil, *Hatterasman*, 170, 171. MacNeil believed the firewood was needed to fuel the ship's boilers, but the vessels used coal and brought colliers with them. They could use green wood in an emergency, as the Mosquito Fleet did after Chicamacomico, but coal was far more efficient.

21. ORA Series I, Vol. IX, 156, and Wallace, *Guide*, 127, 137. According to Wallace there was considerable confusion about which companies belonged to which regiment.

22. ORA, Series I, Vol. IX, 133–145, *passim*.

23. Parker, *Recollections*, 225, 226.

24. ORN, Series I, Vol. 6, 586 and ORN Series II, Vol. 1, 27–246 *passim*.

25. ORN, Series I, Vol. 6, 472.

26. *Ibid*., 6, 586.

27. Johnson, *Longroll*, 88.

28. ORA, Series I, Vol. IX, 357, 358.

29. ORN, Series I, Vol. 6, 586, 587, 588.

30. ORN, Series I, Vol. 6, 588, 589 and Parker, *Recollections*, 229–232.

31. Burlingame, *Fifth Regiment*, 21, 22.

32. ORA, Series I, Vol. IX, 76, 85, 86.

33. ORA, Series I, Vol. IX, *Foster's Report*, 86.

34. *Ibid.*

35. *Ibid.*, 78.

36. *Ibid.*, 87.

37. *Ibid.*, 87, 88, 98, 99, 178.

38. *Ibid.*, 79.

39. *Ibid.*, 85, 173.

40. *Ibid.*, 84.

41. Burlingame, *Fifth Rhode Island*, 24.

42. ORA, Series I, Vol. IX, 191.

43. Parker, *Recollections*, 237–239, and Clark, *N.C. Troops*, Vol. V, "N.C. Navy," 307–309, 311.

44. ORA, Series I, Vol. IX, 192.

45. ORA, Series I, Vol. IX, 192, 193.

46. Parker, *Recollections*, 242–243.

47. Roe, *Twenty-Fourth Regiment*, 62, 63.

48. Derby, *Bearing Arms*, 69.

49. Barrett, *C.W. in N.C.*, 91, note.

50. William Marvel, *Burnside* (Chapel Hill & London: University of North Carolina Press, 1981), 61.

51. ORN, Series I, Vol. 6, 637, 638.

52. Burlingame, *Fifth Regiment*, 26, 27.

53. ORN, Series I, Vol. 6, 654, and Hawkins, "Early Coast Operations," 646, 647.

54. *Ibid.*

55. ORA, Series I, Vol. IX, 196, 197.

56. Thomas C. Parramore, "The Burning of Winton in 1862," *North Carolina Historical Review*, Vol. XXXIX (Winter 1962): 18–31, *passim*.

57. Barrett, *C.W. in N.C.* 95.

58. *Ibid.*, 91.

59. Vincent Colyer, *Report of the Services Rendered by the Freed People to the United States Army in North Carolina in the Spring of 1862, After the Battle of Newbern* (New York: Vincent Colyer, 1864), 6, 9.

60. ORN, Series I, Vol. 6, 632.

61. ORA, Series I, Vol. IX, 159.

62. *Twenty-Fourth Regiment*, 70, 71, 412.

63. Barrett, *C.W. in N.C.*, 90.

64. *Ibid.*, 89, 90.

65. Letter, Thomas Capehart, Chowan County, to Lucy Good Capehart, South Gaston, N.C., April 23, 1885, Capehart family papers held by A.A. Capehart, Jr., Washington, N.C.

66. ORA, Series I, Vol. IX, 183–191.

67. Woodbury, *Burnside*, 50.

68. ORA, Series I, Vol. IX, 360, 362.

Chapter Six

1. George Driver, Schooner *Highlander* in Pamlico Sound, to Brother Sam, Salem, Massachusetts, January 31, 1862, William Howard Hooker Collection, Manuscript Collection, East Carolina University Library, Greenville, N.C.

2. Rush C. Hawkins, "Early Coast Operations," 647.

3. ORN, Series I, Vol. 7, 110.

4. Clement A. Evans, ed., *Confederate Military History* (Atlanta, Ga.: Confederate Publishing Co., 1899), Vol. IV, *North Carolina* by D.H. Hill, Jr., 298, 299.

5. ORA, Series I, Vol. IX, 424.

6. *Ibid.*, 442.

7. Von Eberstein, "Memoir," 130.

8. Manarin, *N.C. Troops*, Vol. I, *Artillery, passim*, and Reed, *Beaufort County*, 177, 178.

9. ORA, Series I, Vol. IX, "Branch's Report" of March 26, 1862, 241–247 *passim*.

10. *Ibid.*, 242.

11. Manarin, Vols., I, II, IV, VII, VIII, IX, *passim*.

12. ORA, Series I, Vol. IX, Reports, 241–263, *passim*.

13. Roe, *Twenty-Four Massachusetts*, 80–82.

14. ORN, Series I, Vol. 7, 109, 112.

15. ORA, Series I, Vol. IX, 212.

16. *Ibid.*, 218.

17. *Ibid.*

18. ORN, Series I, Vol. 7, 117. Rowan evidently did not know that a sure way to kill the spirit of attacking infantry is to kill the men with friendly fire. Perhaps some of Burnside's tough infantry colonels called on the commander and reasoned with him about this.

19. ORA, Series I, Vol. IX, 225, 226.

20. *Ibid., Clark's Report*, 267, 268.

21. *Ibid., Rodman's Report*, 237, 238.

22. *Ibid.*, "Sinclair's Report," 262, 263, and "Campbell's Report," 250, 251.

23. *Ibid.*, 245.

24. *Ibid.*, 264, 265.

25. *Ibid.*, 255, 256, 260, 261.

26. Lida Tunstall Rodman, "William Blount Rodman: A Brief Sketch of His Service in the Confederacy," *Carolina and the Southern Cross*, Vol. 1, No. 8, (October 1913), 5.

27. ORN, Series I, Vol. 7, 111, 112.

28. Barrett, *C.W. in N.C.*, 105, 106.

29. von Eberstein, *Memoir*, 131 and *passim*.

30. Barrett, *C.W. in N.C.*, 106.

31. ORA, Series I, Vol. IX, 246, 247.

32. Manarin, *N.C. Troops*, Vol. IV, 358. Lieutenant–Colonel Craton resigned sometime during the battle. Craton managed to get himself appointed colonel of the 50th N.C. in April 1862, according to Vol. V, 149. He resigned his post in November by reason of "fistula in ano, the sequence of chronic diarrhoea and dyspepsia...." He seemed to be that kind of officer.

33. *Ibid.*, 450, 455.

34. *Ibid.*, 211.

35. *Ibid.*, 207.

36. Scharf, *C.S. Navy*, 795.

37. ORN, Series I, Vol. 7, 138, 139.

38. ORA, Series I, Vol. IX, 281, 282.

39. William N. Still, Jr., *Iron Afloat* (New York: Vanderbilt University Press, 1971), 150.

40. ORN, Series II, Vol. II, 174.

41. Robert G. Elliott, *Ironclad of the Roanoke: Gilbert Elliott's Albemarle* (Shippensburg, Pa.: White Mane Publishing Co., Inc., 1994), 55, 63.

42. Leslie S. Bright, William H. Rowland, and James C. Bardon, *CSS Neuse: A Question of Iron and Time* (Raleigh, N.C.: Division of Archives and History, 1981), 6.

43. ORN, Series I, Vol. 7, 170.

44. ORA, Series I, Vol. IX, 305.

45. Rush C. Hawkins, "Early Coast Operations," 655. Hawkins stated the man had been sent by the enemy to purposely lead them astray. Then again, he may have been just stupid.

46. ORA, Series I, Vol. IX, 327.

47. *Ibid.*, 327, 330.

48. *Ibid.*, *Reports*, 306–311 *passim.*

49. *Ibid.*, 316, 317.

50. *Ibid.*, 277, 278, 282.

51. *Ibid.*, 273.

52. *Ibid.*, 278–280.

53. Paul Branch, Jr., *The Siege of Fort Macon* (Morehead City, N.C.: Herald Printing Company, 1994), 16. Paul Branch, of Carteret County, a graduate of UNC and a historian, has served on the staff of Fort Macon State Park. He has written a comprehensive, well researched book that is also very readable.

54. *Ibid.*, 18, 19.

55. ORA, Series I, Vol. IX, 283, and Branch, *Fort Macon*, 44.

56. *Ibid.*, 283.

57. Burlingame, *Fifth Regiment*, 60, 61.

58. Branch, *Fort Macon*, 39, 40, and ORA, Series I, Vol. IX, 458.

59. Branch, *Fort Macon*, 37, 38, 39.

60. *Ibid.*, 48, 49, 50.

61. *Ibid.*, 52, 53.

62. *Ibid.*, 54, 55.

63. ORA, Series I, Vol. IX, 289, 290, and Paul Branch, 60, 61.

64. ORN, Series I, Vol. 7, 278–281 *passim*, and Paul Branch, 66–68.

65. ORA, Series I, Vol. IX, 292.

66. ORA, Series I, Vol. IX, 288–294, and Paul Branch 80, 89.

67. Paul Branch, 84, 85.

68. Burlingame, *Fifth Regiment*, 66, 67.

69. ORA, Series I, Vol. IX, 285, 291, 293, 294.

70. James A. Emmerton, *A Record of the Twenty-Third Massachusetts Volunteer Infantry in the War of the Rebellion 1861–1865* (Boston: William Ware & Co., 1886), 98.

Chapter Seven

1. Vincent Colyer, *Report of the Services Rendered by the Freed People to the United States Army in North Carolina* (New York: Vincent Colyer, 1864), 6.

2. *Newbern Daily Progress*, March 22, 1862.

3. Norman D. Brown, *Edward Stanly: Whiggery's Tarheel "Conqueror"* (University: The University of Alabama Press, 1974), 203–206, *passim.*

4. *Ibid.*, 206–210 *passim.*

5. *Ibid.*, 235, 236.

6. *Ibid.*, 238.

7. L.S. John Hedrick, New Bern, N.C., to Benjamin Hedrick, Georgetown, D.C., June 10, 1862, Benjamin Sherwood Hedrick Papers, Manuscript Department, William R. Perkins Library, Duke University, Durham, NC. Hereafter cited as *Hedrick Papers*. John Hedrick's letters have been quoted extensively for their personal insights on the civilians' and the soldiers' lives. Hedrick's letters not only relate the work of the customs office, but describe events and people all through the Union held territory.

8. ORA, Series I, Vol. IX, 404.

9. *Ibid.*, 404, 405, 407, 409, and 414.

10. Stephen Driver, New Bern, to George Driver, Salem, Mass., July 26, 1862. George Driver had been sent home sick, but his brother Sam kept him abreast of the regiment's actions.

11. Norman C. Delaney, "Charles Henry Foster and the Unionists of Eastern North Carolina," *North Carolina Historical Review*, XXXVII (July 1960): 362.

12. ORA, Series I, Vol. IX, 385.

13. Brown, *Stanly*, 231.

14. ORA, Series I, Vol. IX, 414.

15. ORA, Series III, Vol. IV, 965.

16. *Hedrick Papers*, L.S. John Hedrick to Benjamin Hedrick, September 25, 1862.

17. Mrs. Elizabeth O'Neal Howard of Ocracoke; interviewed by Fred Mallison, July 1993. Notes taken at Mrs. Howard's home at Ocracoke. Robert Howard was her husband's grandfather. Also, Manarin, *N.C. Troops*, Vol. IX, 214.

18. ORN, Series I, Vol. 8, 101.

19. *Hedrick Papers*, L.S. John Hedrick to Benjamin Hedrick, October 13, 1862.

20. *Ibid.*, October 16, 1862.

21. Augustus Dudley, letters constituting claims against the United States Government (circa 1895). Collection of Ellen Fulcher Cloud, Ocracoke, N.C. The date of the letters indicates some doubt about the validity of the claims in the official government mind. Part of the letters are dated 1908 and marked "Up date."

22. Brown, *Edward Stanly*, 243–247, *passim.* Brown's book provides a very good explanation of the complicated politics in occupied North Carolina.

23. *Ibid.*, 248.

24. MacNeil, *The Hatterasman*, 178, 179.

25. Jean Day, *Cedar Island Fisher Folk* (Newport, N.C.: privately printed, 1993), 47, 48.

26. *Ibid.*, 50–52.

27. Still, William, *Iron Afloat.*

28. Brown, *Edward Stanly*, 249, 250.

29. "Treasury Agents Records," Myers House Papers. Collection of documents, Brown Library, Washington, N.C.

30. *Hedrick Papers*, L.S. John Hedrick to Benjamin Hedrick, November 29, 1863, and March 13, 1864.

31. National Archives, "Compiled Service Records of Volunteer Union Soldiers Who Served in Organizations from North Carolina," MICF 381, Micro Copy 401, Reels 1–9.

32. *Ibid.*

33. Mrs. Elizabeth O'Neal Howard of Ocracoke, interview by author, July 1993, notes by author. Mrs. Howard is the granddaughter of Horatio Williams.

34. Treasury Agents documents, "Myers House Papers," Brown Library, Washington, N.C.

35. Barrett, *C.W. in N.C.*, 172, 173.

36. Burlingame, *Fifth Regiment*, 92.

37. ORA, Series I, Vol. XVIII, 475.

38. Barrett, *C.W. in N.C.* 164, 165, and ORA, Series I, part II, Vol. XXVII, 965.

39. Annie Blackwell Sparrow (Mrs. R.H. Lewis), "Recollections of the Civil War" in *Washington and the Pamlico*, 63, 64.

40. Headquarters District of Beaufort to John Rumley, July 23, 1863, Private Collections of Henry Rumley, Esq. of Washington, N.C.

41. Levi Woodbury Piggott, unpublished and untitled manuscript which could fairly be titled "Memorial of Emmeline Piggott" (date unknown), from the collection of Mrs. Stella Jean Day of Newport, NC. Levi Piggott was Emmeline Piggott's first cousin.

42. National Archives, Record Group, 416.

43. Calvin J. O'Neal, Alice K. Rondthaler and Anita Fletcher, "The Story of Ocracoke Island," in *Hyde County History*, ed., Marjorie T. Selby, R.S. Spencer, Jr., and Rebecca Swindell (Charlotte, N.C.: Herb Eaton, Inc. 1976), 47.

44. *Carteret County Heritage*, "Churches," 300–327, *passim*.

45. *Ibid.*

46. Edward R. Outlaw, Jr., *Old Nags Head*, (Norfolk, VA: Privately published by Louise Greenleaf Outlaw, 1952), 8.

47. B.F. Butler, *Butler's Book*, 256, 257.

48. Stephen Edward Reilly, "Reconstruction Through Regeneration: Horace James' Work with the Blacks for Social Reform in North Carolina, 1862–1867" (Ph.D. diss., Duke University, 1983), 3. The author credits John Hope Franklin with the definition.

49. Rev. Horace James, *Annual Report of the Superintendent of Negro Affairs in North Carolina, 1864*. (Boston: W.F. Brown & Co., Printers, 1864), 3.

50. James, *Report*, 30.

51. James, *Report*, 7, 8.

52. James, *Report*, 6.

53. Reilly, *Reconstruction*, 58, 59.

54. William S. Powell, Ed., *Dictionary of North Carolina Biography*, Vol. 3 (Chapel Hill: University of North Carolina Press, 1986), 95.

55. Still, "Shipbuilding...", 36.

56. Barrett, *C.W. in N.C.*, 175.

57. ORN, Series I, Vol. 8, 95.

58. Barrett, *C.W. in N.C.*, 176.

59. Clark, *N.C. Regiments*, Vol. II, "Forty-Second Regiment," 794, 795.

60. ORA, Series I, Vol. XXIX, 911.

61. J.V. Witt, Col. USA, Ret'd, *Wild in North Carolina* (Springfield, Va.: Privately printed, 1993), 1–3. Examples of Wild's strange behavior were ordering a search of his officer's personal belongings looking for a stolen can of meat, and ordering any man caught relieving himself within the camp thrown into the latrine.

62. Barrett, *C.W. in N.C.*, 178, and Witt, *Wild in N.C.*, 55.

63. ORA, Series I, Vol. XXIX, 912, 913.

64. *Ibid.*

65. Witt, *Wild in N.C.*, 32, 33.

66. ORA, Series I, Vol. XXIX, part II, 597.

67. Witt, *Wild in N.C.*, 59.

Chapter Eight

1. ORA, Series I, Vol. XXXIII, 1061.

2. ORA, Series I, Vol. XXXIII, 1002, 1003.

3. ORA, Series I, Vol. XXXIII, 93.

4. ORN, Series I, Vol. 9, 440–454, *passim*.

5. ORA, Series I, Vol. XXXIII, 95, 96.

6. *Ibid.*, 97, 98, 99.

7. *Ibid.*, 87, 88, 89.

8. *Ibid.*

9. *Ibid.*, 867, 868. The trial and execution created much correspondence between opposing generals, and much fuming by opposing newspaper editors. Those most affected were the men in the First and Second North Carolina Union regiments.

10. *Hedrick Papers*, John Hedrick, Beaufort, N.C., to Benjamin Sherwood Hedrick, Georgetown, February 6, 1864.

11. ORA, Series I, Vol. XXXIII, 590.

12. John W. Graham, "The Capture of Plymouth," in Clark, *Regiments*, Vol. V, 176, 177.

13. ORA, Series I, Vol. XXXIII, 297.

14. ORA, Series I, Vol. XXXIII, 1273, 1278.

15. *Ibid.*, 1307.

16. Elliott, *Ironclad*, 166.

17. Graham, "Capture of Plymouth," Clark, *Regiments*, Vol. V, 175, and Manarin, *N.C. Troops*, Vol. I, *Troops*, 51.

18. *Ibid.*, 179, 180.

19. Robert G. Elliott, *Ironclad of the Roanoke* (Shippensburg, Pa.: White Mane Publishing Co., Inc., 1994), 159–163 *passim*, 176.

20. *Ibid.*, 175, 177.

21. *Ibid.*, 178.

22. *Ibid.*, 178–184 *passim*.

23. Graham, "Capture of Plymouth," in Clark, *Regiments*, 182, 183 and ORA, Series I, Vol. XXXIII, 299.

24. *Ibid.*

25. ORA, Series I, Vol. XXXIII, 299.

26. Barrett, *C.W. in N.C.*, 220.

27. ORA, Series I, Vol. XXXIII, 300.

28. ORN, Series I, Vol. 9, 665, 668.

29. *Ibid.*, 667.

30. ORA, Series I, Vol. XXXIII, 946.

31. *Ibid.*, 990, 991.

32. *Ibid.*, 310.

33. Josephus Daniels, *Tar Heel Editor* (Chapel Hill: University of North Carolina Press, 1939), 11–16 *passim*.

34. ORN, Series I, Vol. 9, 583, 592.

35. ORA, Series I, Vol. XXXIII, 1010.

36. Roster of Company B, First North Carolina Union Volunteers, June 6, 1863, "William Blount Rodman papers," East Carolina University Manuscript Collection, Joyner Library, Greenville, N.C.

37. ORA, Series I, Vol. XXXVI, Part II, 433.

38. *Hedrick Papers*, John Hedrick, Beaufort, NC, to Benjamin Hedrick, Georgetown, April 28, 1864, and May 2, 1864. Ritch's office was in a house belonging to John Myers of Washington. After the war, Myers reclaimed his house and it remained in his family until the 1970s. The Myers heir found the lost box of the Treasury agent's papers in the attic and presented them to the Brown Library.

39. Bright and others, *CSS Neuse*, 14, 15.

40. ORN, Series I, Vol. 9, 753, 755.

41. *Ibid.*, 770.

42. ORN, Series II, Vol. I, *passim*.

43. ORN, Series I, Vol. 9, 683.

44. Francis Trevelyan Miller, Ed., *The Photographic History of the Civil War*, Vol. 6, *The Navies* (New York: Thomas Yoseloff, reprint edition, 1957), 177.

45. Elliott, *Ironclad*, 196–210 *passim*. Elliot's book contains a good shot by shot and turn by turn account of the battle. It is both readable and accurate.

46. *Ibid.*

47. ORA, Series I, Vol. XXXVI, Part II, 942.

48. *Ibid.*, 369.

49. Burlingame, *Fifth Rhode Island*, 202.

50. Manarin, *N.C. Troops*, Vol. XIII, Graham, "56th Regiment," 569.

51. Burlingame, 207, 208.

52. ORA, Series I, Vol. XXVI, Part II, 972.

53. *Ibid.*, 809

54. ORN, Series I, Vol. 10, 122.

55. Letter, John Hedrick to Benjamin Hedrick, May 30, 1864.

56. ORA, Series I, Vol. XXXVI, Part III, 424, 425.

57. ORN, Series I, Vol. 10, 152, 213.

58. *Ibid.*, 324.

59. Elliott, *Ironclad*, 233. The stories spread about the ram are too numerous to list. Had someone only thought of it, he could have told of the invention of high-octane bacon for fuel.

60. *Ibid.*, 238.

61. ORN, Series I, Vol. 10, 214, 154.

62. *Ibid.*, 129, 130.

63. *Ibid.*, 595.

64. ORA, Series I, Vol. XXXVI, Part III, 892, 893.

65. ORA, Series I, Vol. 10, 457, 737.

66. *Ibid.*, 529, 530.

67. Barrett, *C.W. in N.C.*, 227.

68. *Hedrick Papers*, John Hedrick to Benjamin Hedrick, September 1, 12, 26.

69. *Ibid.*, October 18, 22.

70. ORN, Series I, Vol. 10, 571, 611.

71. Rod Gragg, *Confederate Goliath: The Battle of Fort Fisher* (New York: HarperCollins Publishers, 1991), 100.

Chapter Nine

1. ORN, Series I, Vol. 12, 19.

2. *Ibid.*, 55.

3. Elliott, *Ironclad*, 242.

4. ORA, Series I, Vol. XLVII, Part II, 621.

5. National Archives, "Soldiers' Records," Reels 1–9.

6. ORN, Series I, Vol. 12, 20.

7. Augustus Dudley, "Claims."

8. MHP, Permit, W.P. Ketcham to Bryan D. Pede, November 21, 1863, and W.P. Ketcham to James Longman, January 28, 1864. Both permits specify canoes with substantial loads of produce or naval stores.

9. Levi Woodbury Piggott, "Memorial."

10. Barrett, *C.W. in N.C.*, 285–300 *passim*.

11. *Ibid.* and Bright, *Neuse*, 17.

12. ORA, Series I, Vol. XLVII, 443. The *Stonewall* was a unique vessel. Clad in 4½-inch steel armor, she was armed with one 12-inch rifle and two 6-inch rifles. She arrived in Cuba in May to learn that the war was over. She was later sold to the Japanese government and crossed the Pacific Ocean.

13. ORA, Series I, Vol. XLVII, 318.

14. Burlingame, *Fifth Rhode Island*, 257, 258.

15. Louis H. Manarin, Ed., *A Guide to Military Organizations and Installations of North Carolina 1861–1865* (Raleigh: The North Carolina Confederated Centennial Commission, 1961), Volume III, *passim*.

16. Douglass Southall Freeman, *R.E. Lee: A Biography*, Vol. IV (New York: Charles Scribner's Sons, 1935), 155.

17. Ralph W. Donnelly, *Service Records of Confederate Enlisted Marines* (Washington, N.C.: Published by the author, 1979), 8.

18. Oral family history related by Mrs. Elisabeth Bishop Schirmer to her grandchildren, and retold by one of them, Miss Mary Elisabeth Mallison, to the author. Account reinforced by notations in the family bible and other family papers.

19. ORN, Series I, Vol. 12, 135.

20. Jamer B. Gardner and others, eds., *Record of the Service of the Forty-Fourth Massachusetts Volunteer Militia in North Carolina* (Boston: privately printed, 1887), 226, 231.

21. W.P. Derby, *Bearing Arms in the Twenty-Seventh Massachusetts Regiment of Volunteer Infantry During the Civil War* (Boston: Wright & Potter Printing Company, 1883), 530.

22. Powell, *N.C. Biography*, Vol. III, 95.

23. *Hedrick Papers*, July 10, 19, 20, August 11, 27.

24. *Ibid.*, John Hedrick to Benjamin Hedrick, September 22, 1867.

25. U.S. House of Representatives, *Report of the Department of Commerce and Navigation*, Serial Set 1301 (unnumbered).

26. David Stick, "Lighthouse Chronology" in Outer Banks History Center, 6, 7.

27. Ellen F. Cloud, *Ocracoke Lighthouse* (Ocracoke, N.C.: Live Oak Publications, 1993), 10, 11.

28. David Stick, *North Carolina Lighthouses* (Raleigh: Division of Archives and History, 1980), 48, 49.

29. *Ibid.*, 43, 55.

30. Stick, *N.C. Lighthouses*, 52.

31. Stapleton, Harriet Lawrence, "Lighthouse Keepers," in *Carteret County Heritage*, 420, 421.

32. *Newbern Daily Progress* of Raleigh, N.C., November 25, 1862. This was a paper that editor J.L. Pennington published for a few months after he left New Bern just ahead of Burnside's troops.

33. ORN, Series I, Vol. 12, 139–164, *passim*.

34. *Ibid.*, 163.

35. ORA, Series I, Vol. II, *Report of Surgeon D.W. Hand, U.S. Volunteers, Medical Director in North Carolina*, 241.

36. Ben B. Salter, *Portsmouth Island Short Stories and History* (Atlantic, N.C.: privately published, 1972), 20.

37. National Archives, Microfilm Publications, "Returns from U.S. Military Posts 1800–1916."

38. *Ibid.*

39. *Ibid.*

Chapter Ten

1. Mattie E. Edwards Parker, Ed., *Colonial Records: Higher Court Minutes* (Raleigh: Division of Archives and History, 1981), 77.

2. Dunbar, *Historical Geography*, 29, and Stick, *Outer Banks*, 212.

3. Stick, *Outer Banks*, 212, 213.

4. Dunbar, *Historical Geography*, 78.

5. *Ibid.*

6. George Brown Goode, Report to Congress by the United States Department of Commerce, *Report of the United States Commission of Fish and Fisheries for 1879*, "The Natural and Economical History of the American Menhaden, Part V," Serial Sets of reports.

7. Stick, *Outer Banks*, 213, 214.

8. *Ibid.*, 214–218 *passim*.

9. *Ibid.*

10. Dunbar, *Historical Geography*, 32, 33 and notes.

11. Dunbar, *Historical Geography*, 76.

12. Rufus McGowan of North Creek, interview of Fred Mallison while hauling seine, written notes, circa September 1952.

13. Dunbar, *Historical Geography*, 74.

14. *Ibid.*, 75.

15. Dunbar, *Historical Geography*, 83.

16. *Ibid.*, 85.

17. Stick, *Outer Banks*, 224, 115.

18. Dunbar, *Historical Geography*, 69, 70.

19. Elizabeth Baum Hanbury, ed., *Currituck Legacy: Baum Family of North Carolina*, "Market Hunting and Hunt Clubs" (Manteo: published by author, 1985), 153–159.

20. *Ibid.*, 154.

21. Dunbar, *Historical Geography*, 70.

22. David Stick, *Graveyard of the Atlantic* (Chapel Hill: The University of North Carolina Press, 1952), 50, 248.

23. Stick, *Outer Banks*, 168.

24. MacNeil, *Hattersman*, 188, 189.

25. David Stick, *North Carolina Lighthouses* (Raleigh: Division of Archives and History, 1980), 63–66.

26. *Ibid.*, 68, 69.

27. Stick, *Outer Banks*, 170–173.

28. *Ibid.*, 174.

29. Sara Roberts Styron, interview by Jim and Nancy Godwin and Rebecca Harriett, August 19, 1979, CaLo Oral History Project, Outer Banks History Center, Manteo, N.C., transcript p. 6.

30. Marion Gray Babb, CaLo Oral History, 9.

31. Catherine W. Bishir, *The "Unpainted Aristocracy": The Beach Cottages of Old Nags Head* (Raleigh: Division of Archives and History, 1983), 6.

32. *Ibid.*, 7.

33. *Ibid.*, 10.

34. Edward R. Outlaw, Jr., *Old Nags Head* (Norfolk, Va.: privately printed, 1952), 21.

35. *Elizabeth City Weekly Transcript*, July 6, 1867.

36. Outlaw, *Old Nags Head*, 16.

37. *Edenton Clarion*, July 10, 1880.

38. Outlaw, 16, and Stick, *Graveyard*, 250.

39. U.S. House of Representatives, *Report of the Department of Commerce and Navigation*, 40th Congress, 1868. Serial Set 1384 (unnumbered), Microprint Collection, Joyner Library, East Carolina University.

40. James M. Cox, "The Pamlico-Tar River and Its Role in the Development of Eastern North Carolina" (thesis, East Carolina University, 1989), 101, 102. Abstracted from the 1870 report to the 41st Congress, Serial Set 1458.

41. W.B. Rodman, Raleigh, letter to Camilla Rodman, Washington, February 16, 1868, "Rodman Papers," East Carolina Manuscript Collection, East Carolina University, Greenville, N.C.

42. *Eastern Intelligencer* (Washington, N.C.), September 14, 1869.

43. Louis G. May, "The Story of Beaufort County's Lumber Industry," in Ursula Loy and Pauline Worthy, eds., *Washington and the Pamlico* (Washington, N.C.: Washington-Beaufort County Bicentennial Commission, 1976), 331.

44. Louis May of Washington, N.C., interview by author, July 31, 1996; notes by author. Also information from Mr. May's extensive collection of published material on mills in the state was examined.

45. *Ibid.*, 338, 339.

46. "A Trip Through the Varied and Extensive Operations of the John L. Roper Lumber Co. in Eastern North Carolina and Virginia," *American Lumberman*, April 27, 1907, *passim.*

47. Dudley, *"Claims."*

48. S.R. Fowle and Company Records, ledger dated 1860–1869, East Carolina Manuscript Collection, East Carolina University, Greenville, N.C. The Fowle firm, founded in 1819, figured prominently in Washington's history. The company was unique in that it meticulously kept and preserved its records, most of which are held by East Carolina University.

49. Selby and others, *Hyde County History*, "Story of Ocracoke," 14.

50. S.R. Fowle Company, ledger 1860–1869.

51. "Ship Arrivals," *Washington Index* (Washington, N.C.), June 25, 1867.

52. S.R. Fowle Company, ledger 1860–1869.

53. *The Daily Herald* (New Bern, N.C.), January 26, 1868.

54. *Washington Weekly Index* (Washington, N.C.), July 2, 1867. Such a pleasant and enduring relationship was established between the firms of Jos. Potts and Zophar Mills that at least one male child in each generation has been named Zophar Potts up to the present day. The name has been shortened to Zoph.

55. *Washington Index*, June 1, 1869.

56. *The Republic-Courier* (New Bern, N.C.), November 1, 1873.

57. *North Carolinian* (Elizabeth City, N.C.), May 11, 1871.

58. *Albemarle Register* (Elizabeth City, N.C.), August 25, 1874.

59. *Edenton Clarion*, July 10, 1880.

60. *Albemarle Enquirer* (Edenton, N.C.), July 15, 1886.

61. Loy and Worthy, *Washington and Pamlico*, 238.

62. S.R. Fowle Company, ledger, 174, 68.

63. Robert H. Burgess, *Chesapeake Bay* (Centerville, Md.: Tidewater Publishers, 1963), 112, 113.

64. National Archives, Microfilm records of the Ninth Census for Carteret, Hyde, and Dare counties, N.C.

65. Stick, *Outer Banks*, 316, 317, and Hanbury, *Currituck Legacy*.

66. William S. Powell, *North Carolina Through Four Centuries* (Chapel Hill and London: University of North Carolina Press, 1989), 393.

67. Stephen Edward Reilly, "Reconstruction Through Regeneration: Horace James' Work with the Blacks for Social Reform in North Carolina, 1862–1867" (Ph.D. diss., Duke University, 1983), 174–179.

68. *Ibid.*

69. *Ibid.*

70. David Lewis Moore, "History of Metropolitan African Methodist Episcopal Zion Church" (S.T.M. degree thesis, Yale University, 1987), 1, 5, 6.

71. *Currituck County Heritage*, 89. Andrew Cartwright emigrated to Liberia a few years later. Further information on him and his church would be interesting.

72. Dunbar, *Historical Geography*, 38.

73. *Washington Gazette* (Washington, N.C.), June 12, 1884.

74. Hyde County Register of Deeds, Courthouse in Swan Quarter, N.C., Book 17, p. 270.

75. Martha Ellen Nunnelee Kugler, interview by Fred M. Mallison, July 1970; notes taken by author. Mrs. Kugler was owner of the house. Hyde County Deed Book 38, 131.

76. Hyde County Deed Book 16, 413, 414.

77. Dunbar, *Historical Geography*, 93.

78. Selby and others, *Hyde County History*, "Story of Ocracoke," 28.

79. Loy and Worthy, *Washington and Pamlico*, 238.

Bibliography

PRIMARY SOURCES

Manuscripts

Driver, George, letters. William Howard Hooker Collection. East Carolina Manuscript Collection, East Carolina University, Greenville, N.C.

Eberstein, William Henry von, Papers. East Carolina Manuscript Collection, East Carolina University, Greenville, N.C.

Fowle, Martha Matilda. "Journal." East Carolina Manuscript Collection, East Carolina University, Greenville, N.C.

Hedrick, John Addison. "Letters to His Brother." Benjamin Sherwood Hedrick Papers. Manuscript Department, William R. Perkins Library, Duke University, Durham, N.C. Copies of the letters are also in the Carteret County Library, Beaufort, N.C.

Parvin, William Augustus, Papers. "…Escape from Fort Warren…" Manuscript Collection, East Carolina University, Greenville, N.C.

Rodman, William Blount, Papers. East Carolina Manuscript Collection, East Carolina University, Greenville, N.C.

S.R. Fowle and Company Records. East Carolina Manuscript Collection, East Carolina University, Greenville, N.C.

Treasury Agent's Records. "Myers House Papers." Document Collection, Brown Library. Washington, N.C.

Whitford, John D., Papers. North Carolina Division of Archives and History, Raleigh, N.C.

Private Collections

Capehart, Thomas. "Letter to Lucy Good Capehart." Capehart family papers held by A.A. Capehart, Jr. of Washington, N.C.

Dudley, Augustus. Letters constituting claims against the United States Government (Circa 1895). Collection of Ellen Fulcher Cloud of Ocracoke, N.C.

Piggott, Levi Woodbury. Untitled manuscript which could fairly be called "Memorial of Emmeline Piggott," date unknown. Collection of Mrs. Stella Jean Day of Newport, N.C.

Rumley, John. Letter from the U.S. Provost-Marshal dated July 23, 1863. Collection of Henry Rumley, Esq., of Washington, N.C.

S.R. Fowle and Son Company. Documents and ledgers in the collection of Miss Elizabeth (Bea) Morton of Washington, N.C.

Published Document Collections

Bache, A.D., Superintendent. *United States Coast Survey, 1865.* Contains many charts of North Carolina. The United States Geological Survey Archive in the National Archives Cartographic Section, Alexandria, Virginia.

Clark, Walter, Ed. *The State Records of North Carolina.* 16 vols. Raleigh: State of North Carolina, 1895–1905.

Davis, George B., Leslie J. Perry, Joseph W. Kirkley. *Atlas to Accompany the Official Records of the Union and Confederate Armies.* Washington, D.C.: Government Printing Office, 1891–1895. Reprint Edition. New York: Arno Press, Crown Publishers, Inc., 1978.

Goode, George Brown. "The Natural and Economical History of the American Menhaden." United States Commission of Fish and Fisheries, Part V. *Report of the Commissioner for 1877, 1879.*

Parker, Mattie E. Edwards, Ed. *Colonial Records: Higher Court Minutes.* Raleigh: Division of Archives and History, 1981.

Rush, Richard, and others, Eds. *Official Records of the Union and Confederate Navies in the War of the Rebellion,* 31 Vols. Washington, D.C.: Government Printing Office, 1894-1924.

Saunders, William L., Ed. *The Colonial Records of North Carolina,* 10 Vols. Raleigh: State of North Carolina, 1886–1890.

Scott, R.N., and others, Eds. *The War of the Rebellion: A Compilation of the Official Records of the Union and Confederate Armies.* 80+ Vols. Washington, D.C.: Government Printing Office, 1894–1901.

United States National Archives. *Compiled Service Records of Volunteer Union Soldiers Who Served in Organizations from North Carolina.* MICR 813.

United States Census Records for North Carolina on microfilm

Seventh Census, 1850, for Carteret, Hyde, and Currituck counties; Eighth Census, 1860, for Carteret, Hyde, and Currituck counties; Ninth Census, 1870, for Carteret, Hyde, Dare, and Currituck counties.

Contemporary Books, Collections

Avery, William B. *The Marine Artillery with the Burnside Expedition and the Battle of Camden, N.C.* Soldiers and Sailors Historical Society of Rhode Island. Providence: N. Bangs Williams & Co.,1880.

Bates, Jo Anna Heath, Ed. *Heritage of Currituck County, North Carolina.* Winston-Salem: Albemarle Genealogical Society, Currituck Historical Society, and Hunter Publishing Company, 1985.

Burlingame, John K. *History of the Fifth Regiment of Rhode Island Heavy Artillery.* Providence: Snow and Farnham Printers and Publishers, 1892.

Butler, Benjamin F. *Butler's Book.* Boston: A.M. Thayer & Co. Book Publishers, 1892.

Clark, Walter. *Histories of the Several Regiments and Battalions from North Carolina in the Great War, 1861–1865.* 5 Vols. Goldsboro, N.C.: State of North Carolina, 1901. Includes

Treadwell, Adam, "North Carolina Navy" (Vol. V); Sparrow Thomas, "The Fall of Hatteras" (Vol. V); Graham, J.W., "The Capture of Plymouth" (Vol. V).

Colyer, Vincent. *Report of the Services Rendered by the Freed People to the United States Army, in North Carolina in the Spring of 1862 , After the Battle of Newbern*. New York: Privately printed by Vincent Colyer, 1864.

Davis, Pat, Kathleen Hamilton, and Kay Slaughter Hewitt. *Heritage of Carteret County, North Carolina*. Winston-Salem: Carteret County Historical Research Association of Beaufort, North Carolina and Hunter Publishing Company, 1982.

Derby, W.P. *Bearing Arms in the Twenty-Seventh Massachusetts Regiment of Volunteer Infantry During the Civil War*. Boston: Wright & Potter Printing Company, 1883.

Duyckinck, Evert A. *History of the War for the Union*. 2 Vols. New York: Johnson, Fry and Company, 1862.

Emmerton, James A. *A Record of the Twenty-Third Massachusetts Volunteer Infantry in the War of the Rebellion 1861–1865*. Boston: William Ware & Co., 1886.

Hakluyt, Richard. "Voyages Vol. III." In Hawks, Francis L., *History of North Carolina*, Vol. I. Fayetteville, N.C.: E.J. Haleand Son, 1857.

Jacksman, Lyman and Amos Hadley. *History of the Sixth New Hampshire Regiment in the War for the Union*. Concord, N.H.: Republican Press Association, 1891.

James, Horace. *Annual Report of the Superintendent of Negro Affairs in North Carolina. 1864*. Boston: W.F. Brown & Co., Printers, 1865.

Johnson, Charles F. *The Long Roll: Impressions of a Civil War Soldier*. Reprint, Shepherdstown, W.V.: Carabelle, 1986.

Johnson, Robert Underwood, and Clarence Clough Buell, Eds. *Battles and Leaders of the Civil War*. New York: Century Magazine, 1887, reprint Secaucus, N.J.: Castle, 1991.

Lawson, John. *Lawson's History of North Carolina*, 2nd ed. London: W. Taylor and F. Baker, 1714. Reprint, Richmond, Va.: Garrett and Massie, Publishers, 1937.

Mann, Albert W., Ed. *History of the Forty-Fifth Regiment Massachusetts Volunteer Militia*. Boston: Wallace Spooner, 1908.

Parker, William H. *Recollections of a Naval Officer 1841–1865*. New York: Charles Scribner's Sons, 1883.

Porter, David D., Admiral. *The Naval History of the Civil War*. New York: The Sherman Publishing Company and Hartford, Conn.: Charles P. Hatch, 1886.

Roe, Alfred S. *The Twenty-Fourth Regiment Massachusetts Volunteers 1861–1865*. Worcester, Mass.: Twenty-Fourth Veteran Association, 1907.

Ruffin, Edmond. *Agricultural, Geological and Descriptive Sketches of Lower North Carolina and Similar Adjacent Lands*. Raleigh: Institution for the Deaf, Dumb and the Blind, 1861.

Scharf, J. Thomas. *History of the Confederate Navy*. New York: Rogers & Sherwood, 1887.

Woodbury, Augustus. *Major-General Ambrose E. Burnside and the Ninth Army Corps*. Providence: Sidney S. Rider & Brother, 1867.

Newspapers

The following were found in the microfilm collections of Joyner Library, East Carolina University, and the Brown Library of Washington, N.C.

Albemarle Enquirer (Edenton, N.C.), 1886.

Albemarle Register (Elizabeth City, N.C.), 1874.

New Bern Daily Herald (New Bern, N.C.), 1868.

Newbern Daily Progress (New Bern, N.C.), 1861, 1862 (CSA).

Newbern Progress (New Bern, N.C.), 1862–1864, (USA).

Eastern Intelligencer (Washington, N.C.), 1869.

Edenton Clarion (Edenton, N.C.), 1880.

New Berne Journal of Commerce, 1866.

Washington Index (Washington, N.C.), 1869.

Washington Weekly Index (Washington, N.C.), 1867.

North Carolina Times (Washington, N.C.), 1861 (CSA).

North State Press (Washington, N.C.), 1868.

Republic Courier (New Bern, N.C.), 1868.

Union Advance Picket (Washington, N.C.), 1862 (USA).

Wilmington Journal (Wilmington, N.C.), 1861–1864 (CSA).

Interviews

Austin, Junius, pilot of Ocracoke. Interview by author 16 July, 1992. Interview conducted while cruising the inlet and visiting Beacon Island, Shell Castle, and Portsmouth. Notes in possession of author.

Babb, Marion Gray, last resident of Portsmouth. Interviewed by Jim and Nancy Godwin and Rebecca Harriett, July, 1979. Recorded by the" CaLo Oral History Project." Outer Banks History Center, Manteo, N.C.

Cloud, Ellen Fulcher, Ocracoke historian. Interview by author, July, 1992. Notes in possession of author.

Fulcher, Fannie Pearl, Ocracoke resident and teacher. Interview by author, July 1992 and again in 1993. Notes in possession of author.

Howard, Elizabeth O'Neal, Ocracoke resident, entrepreneur, and former postmistress. Interview by author July 1992, and again in 1993. Notes in possession of author.

Kugler, Martha Ellen Nunally, owner and frequent resident in the Seth Bridgeman house at Ocracoke. Interview by author July 1981. Notes in possession of author.

McGowan, Rufus, fisherman of North Creek. Interview while fishing net with author, September 1955. Notes in possession of author.

Morgan, John Irvin, of Washington and Hatteras, and Charles Stowe of Hatteras. Interview by author September 1996. Notes in possession of author.

Styron, Sara Roberts of Portsmouth. Interviewed by Jim and Nancy Godwin and Rebecca Harriett, August 19, 1979. CaLo Oral History Project. Outer Banks History Center, Manteo, N.C.

Unpublished Works

Beaufort County Indexes and Deed Books. Register of Deeds Office, Washington, N.C.

Cloud, Ellen Fulcher. Rosters of Confederate soldiers from Ocracoke.

Holland, F. Ross Jr. "A Survey History of Cape Lookout National Seashore." Washington, D.C.: U.S. Department of the Interior, National Park Service, 1968.

Hyde County Indexes and Deed Books. Register of Deeds Office, Swan Quarter, N.C.

Stick, David. Collected Papers. "History of Portsmouth Post Office" and "History of Ocracoke Post Office," from U.S. Post Office Department Historical Library, File No. 173. Manteo, N.C.: Outer Banks History Center.

SECONDARY SOURCES

Books

Barrett, John G. *The Civil War in North Carolina*. Chapel Hill: The University of North Carolina Press, 1963. The best book on the subject.

Bishir, Catherine W. *The "Unpainted Aristocracy."* Raleigh: Division of Archives and History, Third Printing, 1983.

Black, Robert C. III. *The Railroads of the Confederacy*. Chapel Hill: The University of North Carolina Press, 1952.

Branch, Paul, Jr. *The Siege of Fort Macon*. Morehead City, N.C.: Herald Printing Company, 6th Printing, 1994.

Brown, Alexander Crosby. *Juniper Waterway: A History of the Albemarle and Chesapeake Canal.* Charlottesville: University Press of Virginia, 1981.

Brown, Norman D. *Edward Stanley Whiggery's Tarheel "Conqueror."* University: The University of Alabama Press, 1914.

Burgess, Robert. *Chesapeake Bay*. Centerville, Md.: Tidewater Publishers, 1963.

Cloud, Ellen Fulcher. *Ocracoke Lighthouse*. Ocracoke, N.C.: Live Oak Publications, 1993.

Daniels, Josephus. *Tar Heel Editor*. Chapel Hill: The University of North Carolina Press, 1939.

Day, Stella Jean. *Cedar Island. Past and Present*. 2 vols. Newport, N.C.: Privately Printed, 1973.

_____. *Cedar Island Fisher Folk*. Newport, N.C.: Privately Printed, 1993.

Dunbar, Gary S. *Historical Geography of the Outer Banks of North Carolina*. Baton Rouge: Louisiana State University Press, 1958.

Elliott, Robert G. *Ironclad of the Roanoke: Gilbert Elliott's Albemarle*. Shippensburg, Pa.: White Mane Publishing Company, Inc., 1994.

Evans, General Clement A., Ed. *Confederate Military History*. 12 Vols. Atlanta, Ga.: Confederate Publishing Company, 1899.

Freeman, Douglas Southall. *R.E. Lee: A Biography*. 4 vols. New York: Charles Scribner's Sons, 1935.

Gragg, Rod. *Confederate Goliath: The Battle of Fort Fisher*. New York: HarperCollins Publishers, 1991.

Hanbury, Elizabeth Baum. *Currituck Legacy: Baum Family of North Carolina.* Published by author, 1985.

Hawks, Francis L. *History of North Carolina.* Fayetteville, N.C.: E.K. Hale and Son, 1858-59.

Hill, Daniel H. *Bethel to Sharpsburg*, Vol. I. Raleigh: Edwards & Broughton Company, 1926.

Jones, Virgil Carrington. *The Civil War at Sea.* 3 vols. New York: Holt-Rinehart-Winston, 1960.

Kaufman, Wallace and Orrin Pilkey. *The Beaches Are Moving.* Garden City, N.Y.: Anchor Press/Doubleday, 1979.

Kling, Georges. *Le Commandant Jean-Joseph de Brun et Le "Prony."* Société d'Études Historiques de la Novelle Caledonie, 1985. From the Library of Professor Gordon Watts. Translation by Thomas Conlon, Esq.

Lefler, Hugh Talmage, and Albert Day Newsome. *North Carolina— The History of a Southern State.* Chapel Hill: The University of North Carolina Press, 1985.

Lemmon, Sarah M. *Frustrated Patriots: North Carolina and the War of 1812.* Chapel Hill: The University of North Carolina Press, 1973.

Loy, Ursula and Pauline Worthy, Eds. *Washington and the Pamlico.* Washington, N.C.: Washington–Beaufort County Bicentennial Commission, 1976.

Manarin, Louis H., and Weymouth T. Jordan, Jr., Eds. *North Carolina Troops, 1861–1865: A Roster.* 13 vols. Raleigh: Division of Archives and History, 1966–1993. Louis H. Manarin was editor and compiler of the first four volumes and compiler of all the unit histories. Weymouth T. Jordan was editor of all volumes after Vol. IV.

Manarin, Louis H. *A Guide to Military Organizations and Installations of North Carolina 1861-1865.* Raleigh: The Confederate Centennial Commission, 1961.

Marvel, William. *Burnside.* Chapel Hill and London: University of North Carolina Press, 1985.

Miller, Francis Trevelyan, Ed. *The Photographic History of the Civil War* Vol. 6, *The Navies.* Reprint edition. New York: Thomas Yoseloff, 1957.

Outlaw, Edward R., Jr. *Old Nag's Head.* Norfolk, Va.: Privately published by Louise Greenleaf Outlaw, 1952.

Phisterer, Frederick, Ed. *New York in the War of the Rebellion 1861 to 1865.* Albany, N.Y.: Weed, Parsons and Company, 1890.

Pilkey, Orrin H., Jr., William J. Neal, Orrin H. Pilkey, Sr., and Stanly R. Riggs. *From Currituck to Calabash.* Durham: Duke University Press, 1980.

Powell, William S., Ed. *Dictionary of North Carolina Biography.* 4 vols. Chapel Hill: University of North Carolina Press, 1986.

_____. *North Carolina Through Four Centuries.* Chapel Hill: The University of North Carolina Press, 1989.

Ripley, Warren. *Artillery and Ammunition of the Civil War.* New York: Van Nostrand Reinhold Company, 1970.

Robertson, James L., Ed. *Medical and Surgical History of the War of the Rebellion.* 6 vols. Originally published 1883. Reprint edition, *The Medical and Surgical History of the Civil War*, in 15 vols. Wilmington, N.C.: Broadfoot Publishing Co., 1992.

Robinson, William Morrison. *The Confederate Privateers.* New Haven: Yale University Press, 1928.

Salter, Ben B. *Portsmouth Island Short Stories and History*. Atlantic, N.C.: Privately printed, 1972.

Schoenbaum, Thomas J. *Islands, Capes and Sounds of The North Carolina Coast*. Winston-Salem: John F. Blair, Publisher, 1982.

Selby, Marjorie T., R.S. Spencer, and Rebecca Swindell, Eds. *Hyde County History*. Swan Quarter, N.C.: Privately printed, 1976.

Shears, David. *Ocracoke: Its History and People*. Washington, D.C.: Starfish Press, 1989.

Steelman, Joseph F., Ed. *Of Tar Heel Towns, Shipbuilders, Reconstructionists and Alliancemen*. Greenville, N.C.: East Carolina University Department of History, 1981.

Sitterson, Joseph Carlyle. *The Secession Movement in North Carolina*. Chapel Hill: The University of North Carolina Press, 1939.

Stick, David. *Graveyard of the Atlantic, Shipwrecks of the North Carolina Coast*. Chapel Hill: The University of North Carolina Press, 1951.

_____. *North Carolina Lighthouses*. Raleigh: Division of Archives and History, 1980.

_____. *The Outer Banks of North Carolina 1584–1958*. Chapel Hill: The University of North Carolina Press, 1958.

Trotter, William R. *Ironclads and Columbiads: The Coast*. Winston-Salem: John F. Blair, Publisher, 1991.

Wallace, Lee A. *A Guide to Virginia Military Organizations 1861–1865*, Rev. 2nd Ed. Lynchburg, Va.: H.E. Howard, Inc., 1986.

Weiss, George. *The Lighthouse Service: Its History, Activities, and Organization*. Baltimore: The Johns Hopkins Press, 1926.

_____. *The Windsor Story 1768–1968*. Windsor, N.C.: Windsor Bicentennial Commission, 1968.

Wroth, Lawrence C. *The Voyages of Giovanni de Verrazzano 1524-1528*. New Haven: Yale University Press, 1970. Published for the Pierpont Morgan Library.

Theses, Dissertations

Burke, Kenneth E., Jr. "The History of Portsmouth, North Carolina, from Its Founding in 1753 to Its Evacuation in the Face of Federal Forces in 1861." Thesis, University of Richmond, 1976.

Cox, James M. "The Pamlico-Tar River and Its Role in the Development of Eastern North Carolina." M.A. Thesis, East Carolina University, 1989.

Logan, Byron E. "An Historical Geographic Study of North Carolina Ports." Ph.D. diss., University of North Carolina, 1956.

Merriman, Ann M. "North Carolina Schooners, and the S.R. Fowle and Son Company of Washington, North Carolina." M.A. Thesis, East Carolina University, 1996.

Moore, David Lewis. "History of Metropolitan African Methodist Episcopal Zion Church." S.T.M. Degree Thesis, Yale University, 1987.

Reilly, Stephen Edward. "Reconstruction Through Regeneration: Horace James' Work with the Blacks for Social Reform in North Carolina, 1862–1867." Ph.D. diss., Duke University, 1983.

Journal Articles

Beale, C.H. "First Confederate Flag on the Atlantic." *Confederate Veteran* Vol. XV, No. 5 (1889).

North Carolina Historical Review (numerous articles)

Barry, Richard S. "Fort Macon: Its History." *North Carolina Historical Review* Vol. XXVII (April 1950).

Delaney, Norman C. "Charles Henry Foster and the Unionists of Eastern North Carolina." *North Carolina Historical Review* Vol. XXXVII.

Merrill, James M. "The Hatteras Expedition, August, 1861." *North Carolina Historical Review* Vol. XXIX (April 1952).

Parramore, Thomas C. "The Burning of Winton in 1862." *North Carolina Historical Review* Vol. XXXIX (Winter 1962).

"A Trip Through the Varied and Extensive Operations of the John L. Roper Lumber Co. in Eastern North Carolina and Virginia." *American Lumberman* (April 27, 1907).

Index